GW00368117

Mastering Standard C

A Self-Paced Training Course in Modern C

Rex Jaeschke

McGRAW-HILL BOOK COMPANY

London • New York • St. Louis • San Franciso • Auckland
Bogotá • Guatemala • Hamburg • Lisbon • Madrid • Mexico
Montreal • New Delhi • Panama • Paris • San Juan • São Paulo
Singapore • Sydney • Tokyo • Toronto

Copyright © 1989 Professional Press, Inc.

All rights reserved. No part of this publication may be reproduced, stored in a retrieval system, or transmitted in any form or by any means whatsoever, except in the case of brief quotations embodied in critical reviews and articles.

Printed in the United States of America.

First published in 1989 by
Professional Press, Inc.
101 Witmer Road
Horsham, PA 19044

Published in the United Kingdom by
McGraw-Hill Book Company (UK) Limited
Shoppenhangers Road
Maidenhead, Berkshire, England SL6 2QL

European, Middle Eastern, and African sales and distribution rights to this book are owned by McGraw-Hill Book Company (UK) Limited.

ISBN 0-0770748-5-8

Library of Congress Cataloging-in-Publication Data

Jaeschke, Rex

    Mastering Standard C: a self-paced training course in modern C/
by Rex Jaeschke
     p. cm.
    Includes bibliographic references.
    ISBN 0-9614729-8-7
    1.C (Computer program language) I. Title.
    QA76.73.C15J337 1989
005.26—dc20   89-39403
                                 CIP

Contents

Preface

In September 1983, I proposed a series of tutorial articles on C to the Editorial staff of *DEC PROFESSIONAL*. The first installment appeared in January 1984 under the title of "Let's C Now" and columns have appeared regularly since then. During 1985, it occurred to me that publishing a set of edited reprints organized as a study workbook would be a good idea, so Volume 1 of *Let's C Now* was born. It included the first 13 columns. In late 1986, I did the same thing with the second 13 columns and Volume 2 was published.

Since the two volumes were published, a number of things have happened that have caused me to completely revise the material, resulting in this new edition. First, I have almost twice as much experience with C and with many different implementations of it. Therefore, I can provide better examples and explanations and detail more of the language and implementational idiosyncrasies. Also, in late 1984, I joined the ANSI C Standards Committee and became actively involved in that committee's deliberations in forming the first standard for the C language. When an ISO Standard's group was formed, I became involved with that as well.

The first ANSI Standard for C was voted out in September 1988 and likely will be adopted by ANSI in mid-1989. Since ANSI has added a lot of new terminology as well as new capability and clarification of existing practice, it was necessary to bring the materials up to date to reflect modern C. One problem I had to deal with in coming to this decision was, "Should I use the new ANSI capabilities, even if many readers' compilers did not yet support them?" My solution was to use only those new capabilities that already were being widely implemented (such as function prototypes). However, I also discuss many of the new additions without having the main examples rely on their being supported. In a case where there is both an old and a new way of doing something, I primarily have used the new way and mentioned the old way in passing.

Of course, any published work always can be improved with more and better examples, and numerous typographic errors go undetected. I thank all those readers who reported such problems and technical errors and I have adopted their remarks as appropriate.

Perhaps the biggest reason for wanting to revise the books is that I have been using them as course material for my five-day Introductory C seminars for the last few years, and I wanted to make them suitable as a self-paced study workbook, based on the columns written to date. I say based, because more than half of the original chapters have been completely rewritten.

This book is still aimed at the programmer new to C who has little or no access to other C programmers, but who does have access to a C compiler. The most important addition has been the large number of exercises and worked solutions. These make it possible to measure the students' progress as they go. Exercises that have solutions are indicated with an asterisk (*).

Some acknowledgements are in order. First, thanks to Dennis Ritchie (and others) of Bell Labs for creating the C Language. The two people responsible for getting implementations of the language into a vast number of environments are P. J. Plauger, founder of Whitesmiths, Ltd. and ANSI C secretary, and Ron Cain. "Bill" Plauger started the whole third-party C compiler industry and Ron Cain gave us small-C, a useful language subset compiler for the eight- and 16-bit world. Not only did small-C significantly help to popularize C, it gave us a look at the internals of a compiler that was written in itself.

To the staff at Professional Press, I say thank you. Always courteous and helpful, they make the effort all worthwhile. They have even managed to teach me something about writing, a remarkable feat in itself.

As always, I welcome reader feedback and constructive criticism. Feel free to contact me with your suggestions so they may be considered in future printings.

Rex Jaeschke

Trademark Acknowledgements

DEC, VAX, VAX/VMS, Ultrix, PDP, RSTS and RSX are trademarks of Digital
    Equipment Corporation.
MS-DOS and XENIX are trademarks of Microsoft.
PC-DOS is a trademark of IBM.
POSIX is a trademark of IEEE.
UNIX is a trademark of AT&T.

Chapter 1

Getting Started

Welcome to the wonderful world of C. Throughout this book, we will look at the statements and constructs of the C programming language. Each new construct will be introduced by example with corresponding explanations and, where possible, the examples will be error-free, complete programs or subroutines. I encouraged you to enter, run and modify these examples, because the only realistic way to master any language is to write programs in it, run them and debug them.

All program examples have been taken directly from the manuscript text file and tested using various compilers running on several DEC and/or non-DEC systems. While most material presented will be processor- and operating system-independent, implementation-defined aspects will be mentioned where applicable. Unless otherwise noted, each example has been written so that it conforms to the ANSI C Standard and can be ported (without change) to any compiler conforming to that standard.

I have assumed that you know how to use your particular text editor, C compiler, debugger and linker. Comments on the use of these utility programs will be limited to points of particular interest to the C programmer.

1.1 Putting C in Perspective

C is a mid-level or systems language. That is, it fits somewhere between assembler and high-level languages. On the one hand, it has many of the capabilities traditionally found only in assembly languages. For example, C allows the programmer to get quite close to the host machine architecture and instruction set using constructs such as register variables and bit-fields. On the other hand, it supports high-level language constructs such as `if-else`, `while`, `for` and `case` statements.

Perhaps one of the worst mistakes you can make with C is to think it is a high-level language. C looks enough like a high-level language that it can seduce you into believing it is one. If you treat C as just another language that is an alternative to PASCAL, FORTRAN, BASIC or COBOL, for example, you likely will never exploit C's full potential. You also may use the language for tasks for which it is not particularly well suited, such as financial number crunching and report generation.

Dennis Ritchie developed C around 1972 at AT&T's Bell Labs. The UNIX operating system, another Bell Labs development (designed by Ken Thompson and Ritchie), then was rewritten in C. (Previously, UNIX was written in assembler and B, a precursor to C.) UNIX and C (and DEC) have been closely associated ever since, and every UNIX and UNIX-like operating system includes a C compiler. C was designed

1

by and for professional programmers and is by no means a language for the beginner. Many of C's more powerful capabilities, particularly pointers to data and code, require advanced programming experience before they can be fully exploited.

One major reason that software developers use C is the ease with which properly designed programs may be ported across different hardware and system software environments. With rapid development of newer and faster processors, software houses somehow must design programs that will have a life beyond the current systems. The time and cost of rewriting software for new target machines is too prohibitive if the vendor is to retain a reasonable market share. Many system software houses use C as a tool to assist with program portability. The recursive nature, re-entrant code generation and ease of implementing b-trees makes C popular, particularly with vendors of file access methods and database management systems.

Using C in itself does not guarantee portability—it is very easy (and useful) to write machine-dependent C code. The decision to make a program portable must be made before the program is designed. There are many different aspects of portability that must be reviewed, and designing portable programs takes care and discipline.

C can provide power similar to assembly language yet maintain machine independence largely because the C language has no provision for any data input and output. "What? No I/O? What sort of language is this?" I hear you say. Well, these capabilities are provided with your compiler as part of a standard run-time library. Of course, you also can write replacement or supplementary routines yourself. This may seem awkward at first, but once you have written a few programs it becomes a simple extension to the structured programming approach. Note, though, that having I/O outside the language does have its drawbacks, as we shall see.

Most C compiler vendors do not provide source code to their run-time library routines. However, I will be writing complete (and sometimes partial) versions of some of these commonly supplied functions, not so you can copy and use them, but so you can learn from them. We also will be developing numerous other simple but useful subroutines. Unless a source routine is stated as being part of the standard C run-time library, you can assume it is my own invention.

For many years, the definitive reference for C was *The C Programming Language* by Brian W. Kernighan and Dennis M. Ritchie (Prentice-Hall, 1978). However, since that time, numerous additions have been made to the language, preprocessor and library in AT&T's compiler (and many others). Also, an ANSI C Standards Committee began work in 1983 and should complete the first standard by mid-1989. At that time, the Standard will become the formal definition. (Note that in April 1988, a second edition of Kernighan and Ritchie's book was published, incorporating all the new things in the draft ANSI Standard available at that time.)

Throughout these chapters, their book will be referred to as K&R, its industry-wide nickname. K&R has a tutorial format and encourages the reader to program examples and problems. It assumes prior programming experience and is primarily a user's guide, although a language reference manual is included. Many C compiler manuals refer to K&R (First Edition) for C language specifics.

C is a simple language with only about 30 keywords. Due to the power of the basic statements and constructs, and the fact that the programmer effectively can extend the language by using callable functions and still maintain portability, there is little need for language extensions. However, they do exist in some compilers and vary from one vendor to another. Programmers should be aware of any non-standard conventions in production compilers they use or evaluate.

Note that numerous aspects of C are *implementation-defined*. That is, they legitimately can vary from one implementation to another. According to ANSI C, an implementation must document how they handle such things. Another category of behavior is that which is *undefined*. That is, if the result of some action is undefined, an implementer can implement it however it wishes and it doesn't have to say how or to be able to reproduce that behavior in similar circumstances. It is a good idea to know (and absolutely necessary if you want to write portable code) when you are stepping from guaranteed to implementation-defined to undefined behavior. (Many programmers learn a language on only one machine and they don't discriminate between the things the language guarantees them and those aspects provided by that particular implementation of the language.)

Depending on their language background, programmers new to C initially may find programs hard to read because almost all code is written in lowercase. Lower- and uppercase letters are treated by the compiler as distinct. In fact, C language keywords must be written in lowercase. If you ever have wondered what all those special punctuation marks on a VT1xx, VT2xx or other ASCII keyboard are for, the answer may be, "to write C programs." C uses almost all of them for one reason or another. (Note that many older or cheaper ASCII terminals do not have the complete character set used by C. Missing characters usually include {, }, | and \, which are commonly used punctuation marks.) Keywords are reserved and the language has been designed as simple and unambiguous, which aids considerably in the writing of C compilers.

C encourages, indeed forces, a structured, modular approach to programming through the use of callable subroutines, called *functions*. Functions can be compiled separately, with external references being resolved at link-time.

Unlike PASCAL, C is weakly typed. It permits the programmer to do seemingly silly things, particularly in mixed mode arithmetic. This allows the programmer to perform powerful tricks and to make nasty errors. C code can be very tight and obscure to the point of being unreadable and, therefore, unmaintainable. But with care and discipline, a programmer can generate nicely formatted and easy-to-read code. However, like in other languages, good code doesn't happen automatically—you have to work for it.

"If C is so great, how come everybody isn't using it?" Well like all other languages, C is not all things to all people. For many applications, COBOL, FORTRAN and BASIC do just fine, as does assembler. One aspect of C that discourages commercial programmers from using it is that there is no support for group moves or compares of character strings or arrays. Such capabilities must be provided by external functions which generally are provided in the compiler vendor I/O library. Unless a programmer really needs the unique capabilities provided by C, he or she is unlikely to use it as a production language. To C or not to C? That can be a difficult question. (My apologies to William Shakespeare.)

1.2 Basic Program Structure

Let's begin by looking at the basic structure of a C program:

```
/* The smallest possible C program */

main()
{
}
```

A source program is made up of a series of tokens where a *token* is the smallest possible unit of source. C has six different categories of tokens: keywords, identifiers (variables and function names, for example), constants, string literals, operators and punctuators. For the most part, C is a free-format language. However, in some cases, some kind of separator is needed between tokens to delimit them unambiguously. *White space* performs this function. White space is one or more consecutive characters from the set: space, horizontal and vertical tab, form-feed and new-line.

Comments are delimited by /* and */ and may occur anywhere white space can occur. Comments can not be nested.

A C program consists of one or more functions that may be defined in any order in one or more source code files. A program must contain at least one function, called `main`. This specially named function indicates where the program is to begin executing (its entry point) and has the same purpose as the PROGRAM statement in FORTRAN, for example. There is no syntactic difference between `main` and any other C subprograms; they all have the same basic structure and are referred to as functions.

The parentheses following the function name surround the formal argument list. The parentheses are required, even if no arguments are expected. The function `main` can have arguments, but in this case does not. (Passing command line arguments to `main` is discussed in Chapter 7.)

The body of a function is enclosed within a matching pair of braces. All executable code must reside in this body. Statements are executed in sequential order unless control or looping statements dictate otherwise. A program terminates when it returns from `main`, either by dropping into the closing brace of that function, or via the `return` statement. (It also is possible to terminate a program by calling one of several library routines such as `exit` and `abort`.)

White space should be used liberally to improve program readability. It is ignored by the compiler unless it is part of a quoted literal string (or a character constant, as we shall see later) or when it is present to separate tokens.

In the above example, we can remove all the white space and still have the correct program:

```
main(){}
```

However, the first version is clearly superior in its readability. Since white space characters are, for the most part, ignored, you are encouraged to use them (particularly spaces, horizontal tabs and blank lines) to "open up" the code. Remember, whatever style you develop when learning a language, that is the one you will be stuck with, so you should give some thought to programming style from the outset. The style used in this book is primarily that used in K&R and, given the huge number of programmers who learned C from that text, this style is very popular.

Although both versions of the above example compile and run without error, they have no executable code and, therefore, do nothing.

Exercise 1-1: Compile and link the empty program `main(){}` and see how big a disk file the executable requires. Look at a linker map to see what goes into a seemingly "empty" program.

Exercise 1-2: Comment out a block of code that already contains comments and see what messages (if any) your compiler produces. That is, see if your compiler supports nested comments.

Exercise 1-3*: Compile and link a program that does not contain a `main` function and see what messages your linker produces.

Let's consider a program with multiple functions:

```
/* Smallest C program with two functions */

main()
{
        sub();
}

/* sub has no executable code */

sub()
{
}
```

C encourages programmers to break up large programs into a number of smaller functions. A source file may contain one or more functions which can be defined in any order. Unlike PASCAL, C function definitions can not be nested. That is, the function `sub` must be defined outside of the braces delimiting the function `main`. A function is invoked by naming it, along with a list of arguments surrounded by parentheses. Arguments are optional, but the delimiting parentheses are not, as shown by the call to `sub` above.

Each C statement must be terminated by a semicolon. In the example above, the function call is considered to be a statement. The semicolon is a statement terminator, not a statement separator as in PASCAL. When function `sub` terminates at its closing brace, control is returned to the caller; in this case, to the statement immediately following the one that invoked `sub`.

Notice how spaces, tabs and blank lines are used to make the program format more pleasing to the eye. Also, the opening and closing braces are aligned to better indicate each function's scope. K&R goes to some pains to recommend a program formatting style. Although their recommended style is widely used and seems to work well, the programmer is encouraged to experiment. Whatever style you adopt, be consistent.

Exercise 1-4: See how your compiler reacts to having a function defined inside another function.

Exercise 1-5: Create a `main` program in file `a.c` and a function `sub` in file `b.c`. Call `sub` from `main`. (You will need to find out how to link multiple object modules for this exercise.)

Exercise 1-6: Omit the semicolon from the end of a statement. Add an extra one and see what happens.

1.3   Identifiers

One category of tokens is identifiers. An *identifier* can identify a number of possible things. The most common use of identifiers is to name variables and functions; `main` and `sub` are the only identifiers in the previous example. An identifier name may be constructed from the following character set: upper- and lowercase letters, the digits 0–9 and the underscore. (Some implementations, most noticeably VAX C, also permit the dollar character.) However, an identifier may not begin with a digit. You are strongly urged not to define your own identifiers that begin with an underscore because that space of names is reserved for C implementers. (Actually, the ANSI C rules are not quite that strict, but for the sake of simplicity, this rule will stand you in good stead and it is much simpler to remember.) Of course, you can use an identifier beginning with an underscore if you are referencing something provided by your implementation that has such a name.

Originally, identifiers were significant in only the first eight characters. Excess characters were permitted but ignored. ANSI C requires that internal identifiers (those without external linkage) be significant up to at least 31 characters. The Standard permits external identifiers to be significant to as few as six characters because this seems to be a common denominator for many linkers, librarians and other system development tools.

As stated earlier, casing in names is significant such that `TOTAL`, `Total` and `total` all could be different variables. However, ANSI C permits the casing of external names to be folded, again, to accommodate linkers, etc. (Note that while UNIX, most MS-DOS and other linkers are case-sensitive, you are cautioned from utilizing this feature. It is hard enough trying to come up with meaningful names without having to worry about case differences.)

All identifiers (with the exception of preprocessor macro names which we will see later) traditionally are written using lowercase letters. A variation of this approach involves the capitalization of the first letter in each word; e.g., `Total`, `MaximumNumber` and `Days_Of_The_Week`.

Exercise 1-7*: Which of the following are valid identifiers?

```
name
Todays'date
day_of_week
TOTAL$COST
_
_Xyz_
_____ABC___
first-name
LastNameOfMyFathersGrandfatherInLaw
X32BITS
3WiseMen
Oxabcd
xabcd
```

Exercise 1-8*: Find out what the identifier significance is for your compiler, for both internal and external identifiers. See if you can confirm this by writing a program. Find out if your compiler has a switch to specify the length of identifier significance. Also, see if your compiler or linker has switches to activate or deactivate case recognition of externals. If you have an object module librarian and/or symbolic debugger, are they case-sensitive and what is the identifier significance they can handle?

1.4 Introduction to Formatted Output

C has no input or output statements as part of the language. As previously indicated, a standard set of I/O routines is provided as part of a run-time library of functions supplied by the compiler vendor. One such library function is `printf` which permits formatted output on the *standard output* device. (This device is typically the user's terminal, although by using command-line redirection as available on UNIX and MS-DOS, standard output can be redirected to some other device or even a file.)

```
/* write to standard output device */

#include <stdio.h>

main()
{
        printf("Hello.\nWelcome.\nGreetings.\n");
}
```

produces the following output:

```
Hello.
Welcome.
Greetings.
```

To make certain information about the library routine `printf` available to the compiler, the line `#include <stdio.h>` is necessary. This line is a directive aimed at the *C preprocessor*, a program that processes the source before passing it off to the compiler proper. This (and other preprocessor directives) will be discussed more formally in Chapter 6.

In this example, `printf` is called with one argument, a *string literal*. The character string to be printed is enclosed in double quotes and is printed verbatim, except for certain special character sequences such as those beginning with a backslash. The `\n` is a special single character which is C's notation for a *new-line*. (On many systems, a new-line may generate a carriage-return/line-feed pair on output, while on others it may produce just a line-feed.) A new-line is not automatically appended by `printf`, so `printf` may be invoked multiple times to print an output line a piece at a time. C does not state what the internal representation for a new-line must be, although most ASCII implementations represent it as a line-feed character. Whatever its representation, it is guaranteed to produce the same effect on all standard C implementations.

The backslash is an escape character prefix that indicates that the following character is to be interpreted as other than its usual meaning. The standard sequences are:

Standard C Escape Sequences	
Escape sequence	*Meaning*
\a	alarm (ANSI)
\b	backspace
\f	form-feed
\n	new-line (line feed)
\r	carriage return
\t	horizontal tab
\v	vertical tab (ANSI)
\\	backslash
\'	single quote
\"	double quote
\?	question mark (ANSI)
\nnn	octal bit pattern nnn
\xhh	hexadecimal bit pattern hh (ANSI)

The escape sequence mechanism allows character set independence for these special characters. Those marked "(ANSI)" are inventions of ANSI C, although \v has existed for some years in various implementations. Most are self-explanatory; however, a few need further explanation. To enclose a double quote in a string, you must use \". Single-character constants have the form 'x' in which the single quote would be represented as '\''. \? was added when trigraphs were added by the Standard. (*Trigraphs* are alternate spellings for nine punctuation characters needed in writing C source, but which are missing from the ISO-646 character set used by various European machines and terminals. A trigraph has the general form ??x where x is a punctuation character. For example, ??< and ??> are alternate ways of writing an open and close brace, respectively. Trigraphs are not discussed further in this book.)

The sequence \nnn is a one- to three-octal digit sequence such as \12 and \045. Such sequences represent a character having the corresponding bit pattern. (If a sequence contains something like \1234 and the 34 is not part of the octal representation, you will need to use \01234 instead.) Similarly, \xhh is a bit pattern represented in hexadecimal. (Most systems currently recognize two to three hex digits although ANSI C permits more.) The use of such sequences is implementation-defined because it generally requires knowledge of the host's character set.

Consider the following program which prints a string containing numerous escape sequences and "regular" characters:

```
#include <stdio.h>

main()
{
        printf("\"\\abc'\'6 Bells\7\07\007\x7\x07\a\"\n");
}
```

On an ASCII terminal, the output produced is the text:

```
"\abc''6 Bells"
```

followed by six BEL characters. (On ASCII, the BEL is CTRL/G or 7.) The sequence \a is designed to generate an alarm (bell, buzzer, etc.) on any output device—it is not character set-dependent, although it is possible an output device may not have such an "attention" capability.

The earlier program could be written as:

```
#include <stdio.h>

main()
{
        printf("Hello.\n");
        printf("Welcome.\n");
        printf("Greetings.\n");
}
```

or as:

```
#include <stdio.h>

main()
{
        printf("Hello.\n"); printf("Welcome.\n"); printf
        ("Greetings.\n");
}
```

All three examples produce the same output; however, the first one is more readable and will execute faster because it only involves one call to the printf function. The third example shows that multiple statements may exist on the same source code line, provided each is terminated by a semicolon. (We saw earlier that this is permissible because arbitrary white space can be used to separate tokens. Whereas new-lines and horizontal tabs are used to separate statements in the second case, the third case uses spaces.) This practice is discouraged because it generally makes the code less readable. It certainly can make the mechanics of editing more difficult since it is now more work to insert a statement between any two of the existing statements or to delete one of these statements.

Function printf can be used for far more than outputting text and escape sequences as the next few examples demonstrate:

```
/* define and print an integer variable */

#include <stdio.h>

main()
{
        int year;

        year = 1988;
        printf("The year %d was a leap year.\n", year);
}
```

which produces:

```
The year 1988 was a leap year.
```

The variable year is declared to be of type int, a signed integral type typically the size of a machine's native word size, for example, 16 bits on a 16-bit machine, 32 on a 32-bit, etc. Variables must be explicitly declared. This "evil" is necessary if you are to overcome the nasty errors possible with default typing as implemented in FORTRAN and BASIC. On any programming project of significant size, explicit declaration becomes more of an asset than a liability.

A *declaration* consists of a type followed by a list of identifiers that have that type, such as:

```
int start, end, inc;
int count1, count2;
```

with each declaration set being terminated with a semicolon as shown. A declaration assigns certain attributes (including type) to the identifier being declared. If a declaration causes space to be allocated to that identifier (as in `start`, `end`, `inc`, `count1` and `count2` above), that declaration is also a *definition*. All definitions also are declarations but not all declarations are definitions.

Variables are assigned values using the = symbol. The value assigned may be a constant, the value of another variable or the result of a function, or an expression involving any or all of these. If necessary, the type of the right-hand expression is converted to match that of the left-hand side expression.

This time, the `printf` function call has two arguments, a character string and the integer variable `year`. The string serves as a format or *edit mask* and contains a special sequence `%d` which causes the first argument after the string to be interpreted and printed as a decimal integer. As we can see, the `%d` is replaced by the value of the `int` argument, with no leading white space or zeros. Other edit masks exist for each data type and the masks present in the string determine the number, order and type of arguments `printf` should expect after the first one. The value of `year` will be inserted into the text string when it is printed, followed by a new-line as indicated by the `\n`.

If the number and/or type of arguments following the string do not match those specified in the edit mask, the results typically will be undefined, except that it is permitted to specify fewer masks than there are arguments, in which case, the excess arguments are ignored. (With I/O not being part of the language, the compiler can not compare the edit masks with the argument types as FORTRAN can in its FORMAT statement, for example. The responsibility for this matching is left solely to the programmer.)

The following example shows how `printf` can be used to format multiple values:

```
/* print two integer values */

#include <stdio.h>

main()
{
        int i = 10;      /* initialize i in declaration */

        printf("%d squared = %d\n", i, i * i);
}
```

which produces:

```
10 squared = 100
```

Here, the declaration of i also includes the *initializer* "= 10". If multiple variables are being declared in the same declaration, they can each be initialized as follows:

```
int i = 10, j = 20, k = 30;
```

Function printf has three arguments, the last of which is an expression with the value 100. Each of the two arguments after the edit mask string is printed in place of their corresponding %d edit masks as shown.

Exercise 1-9: If your compiler can produce a machine code listing, see if you can determine how the new-line character \n is represented.

Exercise 1-10*: If your terminal understands escape sequences such as clear screen, position cursor, go to home, etc., use printf to clear the screen and go to line 10, column 5 and print the text HELLO! If your terminal is a dot-matrix printer, perhaps you can produce condensed or italic text.

Exercise 1-11*: Print out a string containing characters of the form \x where x is not one of the special escape sequences. What is printed?

Exercise 1-12: See if you can determine the size of the printf library function from your linker's storage allocation map. (Since printf must be able to display many different types in many different ways, it is quite large.)

1.5   Arithmetic Data Types

In the examples above, all variables are declared to be of type int. The range of the values that can be stored in an int variable is implementation-defined as are all C data types. The complete set of arithmetic data types available are: the signed and unsigned varieties of char (character), short int (short integer), int, long int (long integer); the floating-point types float (single precision floating-point), double (double precision floating-point) and long double (an ANSI C invention). The only other scalar type is a pointer, which will be introduced later, as will arrays and other aggregate types.

Specific storage requirements for DEC implementations are as follows:

Arithmetic Type Sizes on Various Machines		
type/machine	*PC/PDP-11*	*VAX*
char	8 bits	8 bits
short [int]	16 bits	16 bits
int	16 bits	32 bits
long [int]	32 bits	32 bits
float	32 bits	32 bits
double	64 bits	64 bits
long double	64 bits	64 bits

The type unsigned int may be abbreviated to unsigned, short int to short, and long int to long.

By definition, the range of a short int must be less than or equal to that of an int, which must in turn be less than or equal to that of a long int. (On a PDP-11 or a 16-bit PC, short and int typically are equivalent, while on 32-bit machines such as the VAX, int and long may be equivalent. It is conceivable that all three have the same precision, on a 64-bit machine, for example.) Likewise, the precision and range of a float must be less than or equal to that of a double, which in turn must be less than or equal to that of a long double. Again, all three types may have the same representation. In the case of the VAX in the table above, long double initially was implemented the same as double. However, since the VAX supports a more precise floating-point type (type H) than that used for double, it is possible long double will be remapped in some future release of VAX C.

A char must be large enough to represent every character in the host character set. On ASCII and EBCDIC systems, char is typically eight bits.

Obviously the range and precision of these types are important to programmers writing code that is to be portable across different machine architectures. Fortunately, there are techniques available to assist in writing code for machines with different word sizes.

ANSI C added the keyword signed which can be used with any of the integral types to explicitly declare a signed value. Except when used with char, this keyword has no effect because the other three integral types are signed by default. However, the signedness of a "plain" char is implementation-defined. The unsigned keyword can be used when unsigned arithmetic is needed, or larger and nonnegative ranges are required.

Exercise 1-13: Find out the size and precision of all the arithmetic types for your implementation. Are all bits allocated to an object actually used to represent that object? Is long double supported? If so, is it different from double? Are short, int and long all different or is there some overlap?

Exercise 1-14*: What is displayed by the following program? Can you explain why? (Note that the type of 1.234 and 1.6 is double and that when a double is multiplied by an int, the int is promoted to double and the result has type double.)

```
#include <stdio.h>

main()
{
        printf("%d\n", 12345, 321);
        printf("%d %d\n", 654);
        printf("%d %d\n", 1.234, 23);
        printf("%d\n", 1.6 * 5);
}
```

Exercise 1-15*: Write a program with three int variables named cost, markup and quantity which equal $20, $2 and 123, respectively. Print the result of retail cost * quantity where retail cost equals cost + markup.

1.6 Automatic Variables

In the `printf` examples involving the variables `year` and `i`, these identifiers are defined inside the braces of `main`, an area that is reserved for executable code. The definition `int year;` can be considered as "executable," because storage for the variable `year` is allocated at run-time, not at compile time. Variables defined within a function are local to that function and are not accessible to other functions. They are created each time their parent function is invoked and they disappear when that function exits. For this reason, they are known as *automatic variables*. Apart from type, another attribute an identifier may have is *class*. One kind of class can be indicated via the keyword `auto`. For example, `year` could have been defined as `auto int year;` however, since `auto` is the default class for such identifiers and need not be specified, this keyword is seldom used.

Storage for automatic variables typically is allocated on the hardware stack. Therefore, a large number of concurrent automatic variables may cause stack overflow. The size of the stack may be determined by the compiler and/or linker used. DEC's Task Builder has a default stack size allocation of 256 (decimal) words. Use the TKB STACK option to change this as necessary. With VAX/VMS, the stack size should not be a problem because the linker allocates 20 pages to the user mode stack and VMS automatically increases the stack size as necessary at run-time. (The initial stack size allocated by the linker also can be changed using the STACK option.) Most MS-DOS linkers permit the stack size to be specified at link-time and some DOS C implementations permit the stack size to be specified on the command-line each time a C program is run.

Space for automatic variables generally is reserved by adjusting the stack pointer rather than by pushing zero or some other known value onto the stack a number of times. C makes no guarantee about the initial value of automatic variables, so you should explicitly initialize them if they need to contain a predictable value.

Let's look at a set of automatic variable declarations:

```
sub()
{
        char c1,c2;
        short s;
        int i;
        long l;
        unsigned u;
        float f;
        double d;
}
```

On the PDP-11 (or an IBM-PC), 24 bytes are reserved on the stack for the eight automatic variables, one for each `char`, two each for `short`, `int` and `unsigned`, four each for `long` and `float` and eight for `double`. On the VAX, 28 bytes are reserved, with two extra for the `long` and `unsigned` variables. When function `sub` terminates, this storage space is released by adjusting the stack pointer to its value on input.

Originally, most C compilers generated assembler source rather than object code. However, this is no longer the case, although many compilers do provide a compile-time switch (or separate utility) to permit you to inspect the machine code generated. (On VAX C, use the /LIST/MACHINE compilation switches.) While a knowledge of this generated code is not necessary to master C, it may help you to understand your particular implementation of the language.

Exercise 1-16*: What is displayed by the following program and why?

```
#include <stdio.h>

main()
{
        int i, j;

        j = 23;
        printf("%d\n", j + i);
}
```

1.7   Numeric Constants

An arithmetic constant may have either an integral or floating-point type, depending on the presence or absence of a decimal point, exponent and type suffix.

C does not support negative constants. Constants of the form *−constant* are expressions containing the unary minus operator and a positive constant expression. (ANSI C also has added the unary plus operator.)

Integral Constants

We have seen various examples of integral constants, such as 1988, 10, 20 and 30. Each such constant has a base (radix). If an integral constant has a prefix of 0x (or 0X), it is interpreted as a hexadecimal constant and is permitted to contain the characters a–f (and A–F) as well as the digits 0–9. If the prefix is just a 0 (zero), the constant is interpreted as being octal and only the digits 0–7 are permitted. All other integral constants are deemed to be decimal. There is no binary radix.

Since constants are expressions, they have a type as well as a value. However, the type of a given integral constant expression is implementation-defined because it depends on the precision of integral types on any given machine. The following table shows the steps used by a compiler to find the type of an integral constant expression:

Integral Constant Typing Rules		
type/base	*decimal*	*octal or hex*
`int`	1	1
`unsigned int`	-	2
`long int`	2	3
`unsigned long int`	3	4

If the value of a decimal constant can be represented as an `int`, that is its type. If it can not, and it fits in a `long int`, that is its type, otherwise it has type `unsigned long int`. (If it can not even be represented as `unsigned long int`, the behavior is undefined.) For octal and hexadecimal constants an extra step, `unsigned int`, is added.

An integral expression also can be made explicitly to be `long int` by adding a suffix of L. (Alternatively, the suffix l may be used; however, it may be difficult for readers to distinguish this from the digit 1 and you should use L instead.) Of course, if L is present, the int steps in the above table are skipped.

ANSI C also permits an integral constant expression to be typed explicitly as **unsigned** by using a U (or u) suffix. If U is present, the **signed int** and **long int** steps in the above table are skipped.

The unsigned and long suffixes can be combined in any of eight possible groupings UL, Ul, uL, ul, LU, Lu, lU, lu. While all these suffixes are equivalent, UL is probably the most readable. If one of these is present, the type is **unsigned long int**.

Some examples of valid integral constants are:

```
12345
012034
0x12abCD
OXFEDcba
5L
0931
0xAb2L
27u
065U
0x234UL
```

We already have seen that the **printf** mask for displaying an **int** as a decimal value is %d. To display it in octal, use %o. To get hexadecimal, use %x. The mask for **unsigned int** in decimal is %u while **unsigned int** in octal or hexadecimal requires %o and %x, respectively. To display a **signed** or **unsigned long int** in any of these ways, place an l (lowercase ell) before the d, x or o character. For example, %ld is required to display a **signed long int** in decimal.

ANSI C requires %x to use lowercase hex letters (a–f) while %X uses the uppercase letters (A–F) instead. (Prior to ANSI C, it was implementation-defined whether you got upper- or lowercase letters from %x, or whether %X was supported.)

Exercise 1-17: What is the type of each of the following integral constants on your implementation? Can you confirm your answers? (Hint: Display each using the edit mask that corresponds to your answer.)

```
35000
35000U
OL
4ul
0238765345
02345L
03456U
0x0
0xFL
OXffffFu
```

Exercise 1-18*: Define a **long int** called **value** and initialize it to 123456. Display **value** in decimal, octal and hexadecimal in three columns, each separated by a horizontal tab. (If your terminal lets you change the tab settings, do so and rerun the program.) Make sure your program is completely portable.

Floating-Point Constants

A floating-point constant must contain either a decimal point, an exponent or both. The exponent can be written using either e or E and it may be signed. Both the value and exponent parts are interpreted as decimal.

Prior to ANSI C, the only floating-point constant type was double. ANSI C added float constants which contain an F (or f) suffix. Also, since ANSI C invented the long double type, long double constants are also possible by using an L (or l) suffix.

To display floating-point values with printf, use the following masks: %f, double; and %Lf, long double. These masks display their values using six decimal places by default. The field width and precision can be specified using %10.5, for example, which requests a field width of 10 and five fractional digits. Like the integral masks, printf will use a larger field width if it needs it for these masks.

To produce output containing an exponent, use %e (or %Le). ANSI C requires that a lowercase e produce an exponent containing that letter, while %E and %LE use E instead. Like FORTRAN, the %g (and %Lg) uses the shorter of %f and %e (or %Lf and %Le). Again, %g uses a lowercase e in the exponent; %G uses E. Prior to ANSI C, it was implementation-defined whether you got upper- or lowercase letters from %e and %g, or whether %E and %G were supported.

There is no way to display a float value using printf. While ANSI C now permits you to pass a float argument to a function, you have to do something special to have it actually stay that type. In the case of printf, this is not possible and any float arguments are "widened" to double before they are passed. (Type widening and narrow types will be discussed with function prototypes in Chapter 4.)

The following are valid floating-point constants:

```
.952
1.234
000333.
3.6578e34
3.45E+34
56.78E-234
12e5
345.F
321e6L
3.456f
```

These are valid in the sense that they are well-formed. However, some of them may have too much precision or too large an exponent to be accurately represented, or to be represented at all. You also should remember that double and long double (and even float) can have exactly the same representation.

1.8 Explicit Type Conversion

Occasionally, we need to temporarily interpret an expression as having a different type. And while some languages achieve this via a family of intrinsic functions, C provides an operator for this purpose. It is called the *cast* operator and has the following general format:

(*type-T2*)   *expression-of-type-T1*

This unary prefix operator consists of a type inside parentheses and, with very few exceptions, you can cast an expression of any type into any other type. (You can not cast from or to arrays, structures and unions, however). Therefore, `(double) 25` is an expression having type `double` and value 25.0, and `(int) d`, where d has type `double`, is an expression having type `int` and the value corresponding to the integral part of d (presuming the resultant value can be represented in an `int`).

The cast operator associates right to left, so expressions such as:

```
(double)(long int) d
```

are possible and predictable.

1.9 Chapter Summary

- The C language has no I/O statements. These capabilities are provided by a run-time library that accompanies your compiler. You also may write your own I/O routines to supplement or replace those in the library.

- Numerous aspects of C are implementation-defined. That is, they legitimately can vary from one implementation to another.

- Almost all C code is written in lowercase. Note that upper- and lowercase letters in identifier names are treated as being different. In fact, C language keywords must be written in lowercase.

- C encourages, indeed forces, a structured, modular approach to programming through the use of callable subroutines called functions. Functions can be compiled separately, but they may not be nested.

- Comments are delimited by `/*` and `*/` and may occur anywhere white space can occur. (White space includes one or more consecutive characters from the set: space, horizontal and vertical tab, form-feed and new-line.) Comments can not be nested.

- Each program must contain a function called `main` which marks the program's entry point. Function `main` does not need to be the first function in any source file.

- A function is invoked by naming it, along with an optional list of arguments surrounded by parentheses (which are not optional).

- A source program is made up of a series of tokens where a token is the smallest possible unit of source. C has six different categories of tokens: keywords, identifiers (variables and function names, for example), constants, string literals, operators and punctuators.

- C is a free-format language. Spaces, horizontal tabs and blank lines should be used liberally to improve program readability.

- Each C statement must be terminated by a semicolon.

- An identifier name may be constructed from the following character set: upper- and lowercase letters, the digits 0–9 and the underscore. (Some implementations, most noticeably VAX C, also permit the dollar character.) However, an identifier may not begin with a digit.

- You are strongly urged not to define your own identifiers that begin with an underscore since that space of names is reserved for C implementers.

- ANSI C requires that internal identifiers (those without external linkage) be significant up to at least 31 characters. The Standard permits external identifiers to be significant to as few as six characters and to be case indistinct.

- To make certain information about library I/O routines available to the compiler, the line #include <stdio.h> is necessary if standard I/O routines are to be called. This line is a directive aimed at the C preprocessor, a program that processes the source before passing it off to the compiler proper.

- The backslash is an escape character prefix that indicates that the following character is to be interpreted by other than its usual meaning.

- Multiple statements may exist on the same source code line, provided each is terminated by a semicolon.

- Variables MUST be explicitly declared.

- The edit mask sequences in printf's first argument determine the number, order and type of arguments that are expected after that first one. The behavior is generally undefined if the argument list is not compatible with the edit masks describing it.

- The complete set of arithmetic data types available are: the signed and unsigned varieties of char (character), short int (short integer), int, long int (long integer) and the floating-point types float (single-precision floating point), double (double-precision floating point) and long double (an ANSI C invention).

- The range and precision of all data types is implementation-defined although ANSI C does impose some minimum limits. For example, int may be 16 bits on one system and 32 on another.

- Storage for automatic variables is allocated at run-time, not at compile time.

- C makes no guarantee about the (default) initial value of automatic variables.

- Originally, most C compilers generated assembler source rather than object code. This is no longer the case, although many compilers do provide a compile-time switch (or separate utility) to permit you to inspect the machine code generated.

- C does not support negative constants. Constants of the form *-constant* are expressions containing the unary minus operator and a positive constant expression. (ANSI C also has added the unary plus operator.)

- If an integral constant has a prefix of 0x (or 0X), it is interpreted as a hexadecimal constant and is permitted to contain the characters a–f (or A–F) as well as the digits 0–9. If the prefix is just a 0 (zero), the constant is interpreted as being octal and only the digits 0–7 are permitted. All other integral constants are deemed to be decimal. There is no binary radix.

- The type of an integral constant expression is implementation-defined because it depends on the precision of integral types on the host machine.

- An integral expression explicitly can be made to be long int by adding a suffix of L (or l). It can be typed explicitly as unsigned by using a U (or u) suffix. L (or l) and U (or u) may be specified together in any order.

- The following printf masks can be used to display integral values: %d, int as decimal; %o, int as octal; %x, int as hexadecimal and %u, int as unsigned decimal. A mask of %l*m*, where *m* is one of d, o, x or u, is used for displaying a long int.

- ANSI C requires the printf mask %x to use lowercase hex letters (a–f) while %X uses the uppercase letters (A–F).

- A floating-point constant without a suffix has type double. A suffix of F (or f) makes it type float while the suffix L (or l) indicates long double.

- The printf masks %f, %e, %E, %g and %G are used to display double values. To display a long double value, use an L before the above mask characters, as in %Le and %LG. These masks display their values using six decimal places by default. The field width and precision can be specified using something like %10.5f.

- Function printf has no edit mask for float values because such expressions are converted to double before the function is called.

- C provides the cast operator to interpret temporarily an expression as having a different type. A cast consists of a type inside parentheses. It is a unary operator and is written before its operand.

- A summary of common printf edit masks follows:

Common printf Display Masks

Display Mask	Output Format	Type Expected
%d	signed decimal	int
%o	unsigned octal	int
%u	unsigned decimal	int
%x	unsigned lowcase hex	int
%X	unsigned upcase hex	int
%ld	signed decimal	long int
%lo	unsigned octal	long int
%lu	unsigned decimal	long int
%lx	unsigned lowcase hex	long int
%lX	unsigned upcase hex	long int
%e	lowercase exponent	double
%E	uppercase exponent	double
%f	fractional (6 dec pl)	double
%g	shorter of %e or %f	double
%G	shorter of %E or %f	double
%Le	lowercase exponent	long double
%LE	uppercase exponent	long double
%Lf	fractional (6 dec pl)	long double
%Lg	shorter of %Le or %Lf	long double
%LG	shorter of %LE or %Lf	long double
%c	character	int
%s	string	char array

- A summary of common `printf` edit masks follows:

Common `printf` Display Masks

Display Mask	Output Format	Type Expected
%d	signed decimal	int
%o	unsigned octal	int
%u	unsigned decimal	int
%x	unsigned lowcase hex	int
%X	unsigned upcase hex	int
%ld	signed decimal	long int
%lo	unsigned octal	long int
%lu	unsigned decimal	long int
%lx	unsigned lowcase hex	long int
%lX	unsigned upcase hex	long int
%e	lowercase exponent	double
%E	uppercase exponent	double
%f	fractional (6 dec pl)	double
%g	shorter of %e or %f	double
%G	shorter of %E or %f	double
%Le	lowercase exponent	long double
%LE	uppercase exponent	long double
%Lf	fractional (6 dec pl)	long double
%Lg	shorter of %Le or %Lf	long double
%LG	shorter of %LE or %Lf	long double
%c	character	int
%s	string	char array

Chapter 2

Looping and Testing

Like most programming languages, C has several different methods of implementing conditional and unconditional branching and looping. In this chapter we will look at several of these methods and comment on their use.

We also will introduce some elementary character I/O capabilities using the keyboard and screen (or printer) and will look at several of the C preprocessor directives. The preprocessor is an integral part of any C development environment.

Two of the most powerful (and unusual) operators in C are those that increment and decrement their operands. These operators (++ and --) are the only ones in C that actually modify their operands. All other operators cause some operation to be performed on the value of their operands—they do not actually modify them directly. In this chapter, we will use these operators only with integral operands. Their full potential will not be realized or appreciated until we deal with pointers in Chapter 7.

2.1 The while Construct

The syntax for a while loop is:

```
while ( expression )
        statement;
```

A while loop consists of a controlling expression and a one-statement body. While the expression evaluates to true (any non-zero value), the body is executed. Note that the parentheses surrounding the expression are part of the while syntax—they are not redundant grouping parentheses. Source characters such as (,) and ; are punctuators and, since these are source tokens, they can be separated with an arbitrary amount of white space as we saw in Chapter 1.

Let's look at a simple example:

```
/* The while construct */

#include <stdio.h>

main()
{
        int counter = 1;

        printf(" i\ti*i\n----------\n");
        while (counter <= 10) {
                printf("%2d\t%3d\n", counter,
                        counter * counter);
                ++counter;
        }

        printf("----------\n");
        return;
}
```

The output produced by this program is:

```
 i        i*i
----------
 1          1
 2          4
 3          9
 4         16
 5         25
 6         36
 7         49
 8         64
 9         81
10        100
----------
```

The first `printf` call produces the table header lines. The `int` variable `counter` is used as the loop control variable and is initialized with a value of 1.

The `while` expression in parentheses, `counter <= 10`, is evaluated and, if the result tests true, the body of the loop (the statements enclosed by the inner pair of braces) is executed and the controlling expression is evaluated again. When the test becomes false (i.e., the expression evaluates to zero), in this case, when `counter > 10`, the loop ends and execution continues at the statement following the end of the loop. If no statement follows the loop, the function terminates. If the controlling expression is initially false, the loop is never executed. This means that the program will behave rationally regardless of the initial value of the controlling expression.

The body of the loop may be a simple or a compound statement. A *compound statement* (or *block*) is a group of declarations and/or statements delimited by { and } which syntactically is treated as one large single statement. A compound statement may be used anywhere a statement is permitted. Each function must contain at least one compound statement, the function's body. A compound statement may contain other simple and compound statements. One common programming error is the omission of the braces from around a compound statement.

Consider the following example:

```
while ( expression )
        statement-1;
        statement-2;
statement-3;
```

Judging by the indented format, it appears that the programmer intended both statement-1 and statement-2 to be included in the loop body. However, because no braces exist to define a compound statement, the body is considered to be the simple statement statement-1. Statement-2 (like statement-3) is executed regardless of the expression evaluation and then only after the loop has been terminated or skipped. This error typically occurs when the loop body originally had only one statement (and hence did not require delimiting braces) with another statement added later. Beware: Hasty code modifications and enhancements may be difficult to debug, particularly in this case where the code seems to "line up" and looks correct at a passing glance.

To force the loop body to include both statements, the code should read:

```
while ( expression ) {
        statement-1;
        statement-2;
}
statement-3;
```

As a matter of style, you might wish always to make the body a block even if it contains only one simple statement. That way, the braces will be there should you ever decide to add more statements. Note too, that a block even can be empty. That is, the braces need not have any tokens between them. (Such constructs are not used very often, however, since they rarely serve any useful purpose.)

The controlling expression in the example above uses the common symbol <= to mean "less than or equal to." The complete set of relational and equality operators follows:

Relational and Equality Operators	
Operator	Meaning
>	greater than
>=	greater than or equal
<	less than
<=	less than or equal to
==	equal to
!=	not equal to

These operators must be written as shown with no white space between the > and =, for example. That is, >= is a token—it is not the two tokens > and =. (When building source tokens, a C compiler must treat >= as the greater/equal operator, even though the characters > and = are valid tokens themselves. That is, the tokenizer must form the longest possible token it can. So, by putting white space between these characters, we cause a different [and invalid] token sequence to be recognized.)

Note the unusual looking operator != which means "not equal to." (Some languages use <> instead.) Equality is tested for using == which is totally different from the assignment operator =. This visual distinction is useful because equality and assignment are quite different operations and it is similar to the approach taken in PASCAL where = and := are used. However, while the use of two different tokens for these operations makes the compiler's job simpler, it can (and usually does) cause grief for the programmer, particularly if he is used to languages where = is used for both.

If we wish to have an infinite loop, we need to ensure the controlling expression always evaluates to true. And, since any non-zero value (both positive and negative) tests true, we need an expression with a non-zero value. The most common expression used is the constant one, as in while (1){...}. Clearly, we must now terminate the loop by some other means.

In the previous example, each time the body of the loop is executed, the value of counter and counter squared are printed on the same line separated by a tab. Note that expressions such as (counter * counter) may be used as function arguments. In fact, C allows any arbitrarily complex expression to be used wherever an expression is required, provided that arbitrary expression has the appropriate type.

Note that the two columns of values are printed right-justified with leading spaces. This is achieved by using a width specifier in the printf edit mask. For example, the mask %2d tells printf to display the first argument (of type int) in decimal, right-justified with leading spaces. If, however, the number of displayable digits in the value exceeds the width specified (in this case, two), all are printed. That is, the width is a minimum width specifier. It can be used with all printf edit masks.

The unary increment operator ++ is a common and succinct notation used throughout C and it may be used as either an expression prefix or suffix. The expressions ++counter and counter++ are both equivalent to counter = counter + 1 in that all three cause the value of counter to be incremented by one. However, if a and b are int variables, a = b++ and a = ++b give different values to a. In the first case, a is set to the value of b before it is incremented while, in the second case, a is assigned the value of b after b is incremented. The easy way to remember this is: The value of x++ is the value of x BEFORE it is incremented, since x is written before the ++. If x follows the ++, the value is that AFTER the increment has been done.

When the value of the incremented expression is not used (as in this program example), it is a matter of personal preference whether you use prefix or postfix notation. (I prefer prefix since it reads left-to-right as "increment x".) Note that ++ is a single token.

There is an analogous decrement operator --. It, too, can be written using prefix or postfix notation.

From this discussion, it might seem that ++ and -- are operators that simply increment and decrement by 1 (or 1.0 for floating-point operands), respectively. While this is true for arithmetic operands, these operators have a much more powerful role when used with pointers, as we shall see in future chapters.

The return statement causes control to be returned to the calling function. A return from main terminates the program. Dropping into the outermost closing brace in a function is equivalent to executing a return statement (without a return value). So, in this example, the return statement is superfluous.

Note the way that the brace pairs are lined up to make the logic flow more obvious. K&R recommends this format, which greatly improves program readability.

Exercise 2-1*: Implement a `while` loop varying the `double` variable d from 10.0 down to -10.0 in steps of 2.5. For each iteration, display the value of d and d squared. Make the columns line up properly.

Exercise 2-2*: Using a `while` statement, loop from 1.0 to 1.000001 in steps of 0.0000005. Each time through the loop display the iteration count as an integer. Is there anything special you need to consider in the controlling expression to make this program portable? Does it make a difference whether you use a `float`, `double` or `long double` variable to control the loop?

Exercise 2-3: What output does the following program produce and why?

```
#include <stdio.h>

main()
{
        int i = 105;

        while (i > 100)
                printf("value of i is %d\n", i);
                --i;

        printf("loop is done\n");
}
```

2.2 More on Incrementing and Decrementing

There are three different ways to increment the value of a variable:

```
/*1*/    i++   (or ++i )
/*2*/    i = i + 1
/*3*/    i += 1
```

Given a reasonably efficient compiler, all three expressions should generate the same code. However, the advantage of cases 2 and 3 is that they can increment by more than one at a time.

The token `+=` is an operator and is an abbreviated form of assignment. In fact, it is one of a family of compound assignment operators that have the form *op=*. An expression of the general form `exp1` *op=* `exp2` is equivalent to `exp1` = `exp1` *op* `exp2`, when *op* is one of the following operators: +, -, *, /, %, >>, <<, &, ^, and |.

Consider the following statements:

```
printf("%d %d %d\n", --i, j++, ++k + 4);

printf("%2d\t%3d\n", counter, counter * counter++);
```

Each of the argument expressions given to `printf` in the first statement use the increment or decrement operator and the results are entirely predictable (once we know the value of i, j and k, before the call). However, the result of the second statement is not. In fact, it is undefined. Specifically, the order of evaluation of arguments in a function call list is undefined. They may be evaluated left-to-right, vice versa or in some other predictable or arbitrary manner. It's up to the compiler.

If the argument list were evaluated left-to-right, the second statement could be used to replace the compound statement in our earlier example. The problem is, if the right-most expression were evaluated first, `counter` may well have been incremented before it is used in the other two places. That is, the first two references to `counter` may get its new value rather than its old one.

A similar problem occurs with the following expression:

```
table[i] = table[i++] + 6
```

Although we haven't discussed arrays yet, the expression `table[i]` designates the *ith* element of array `table`. In this case, the order of evaluation is not guaranteed to be left-to-right. Again, it is not defined by C. (Note that assignment is an operation and = is a binary operator with two operands.) Except where otherwise stated, the order of evaluation of operands to binary operators is undefined.

The result of the following expressions is undefined:

```
i + i++
i - i++
i * i++
i / i++
f(i, ++i)
f(i++, i)
f(i++, ++i)
```

In certain cases, the compound assignment operators can help avoid such undefined expressions. For example, the array assignment problem shown earlier can be rewritten as:

```
table[i++] += 6
```

Now, `i` (and `i++`) is only evaluated once and, by definition, the value of `i++` is the value of `i` before it is incremented.

2.3 Basic Character I/O

Let's look at a simple, yet powerful program that uses the `while` construct just discussed:

```
/* Elementary I/O */

#include <stdio.h>

main()
{
        int c;

        c = getchar();
        while (c != EOF) {
                putchar(c);
                c = getchar();
        }
}
```

The functions `getchar` and `putchar` are part of the standard C run-time library. (Even though they may look like intrinsic functions, as exist in BASIC and FOR-TRAN, they are not part of the language.) `getchar` gets a character from standard input and `putchar` writes a character to standard output.

This program copies characters from standard input to standard output until end-of-file is reached. As it happens, there are several different conventions used to represent the end-of-file marker (-1 being the most common), so it is unwise to test for end-of-file against a specific value if the routine is to be portable. Hence, `c` is compared to `EOF`, a symbolic constant defined in the standard preprocessor file `stdio.h` (which we have `#include`d).

Symbolic constants help document obscure constant values. Such constants also are known as preprocessor macros or simply as *macros*. A macro name is an identifier and, using K&R's convention, we will write macro names so that they don't contain lowercase letters. (There are certain exemptions to this style rule and they will be discussed as appropriate.)

Symbolic constants are recognized by the C preprocessor which replaces each of their references in the source file with some "predefined" string. Hence, the `EOF` in the `while` statement is replaced with some character string (possibly -1) before the input line is passed to the compiler. As well as referring to macros provided in `stdio.h`, a programmer can define his own macros as we shall see later.

The character read by `getchar` is stored in variable `c`, which has type `int` rather than the `char` you might have expected. This is because `getchar` returns an `int` rather than a `char`. If it returned a `char`, there would be no way to distinguish end-of-file from an actual character on systems where all bits in a `char` are significant. (This is the case on EBCDIC and ASCII systems that use an extended character set. For example, DEC's VTxxx terminals and most PCs have a compose key or alternate way of specifying character bit patterns.) Therefore, you may need more bits than exist in a `char` to represent a unique end-of-file value. For this reason, `getchar` returns an `int` so that if an actual character is being returned, the low-order byte typically contains that `char` and the remaining upper bytes contain zero bits. If end-of-file is being returned, the whole `int` contains some implementation-defined non-char representation. This is the value assigned to EOF.

As we have seen, getchar() is an expression having type int. Its value is whatever is returned from that function. Therefore, such an expression can be used whenever that type of expression is required. For example, in place of f(10), we could write f(g()) provided function g returned an int. Note that while getchar takes no arguments, the parentheses are required.

The algorithm used in the above example is very common and is often the only one possible for some languages. However, in C we can express the same thing in a different way. For example:

```
/* Alternate character I/O method */

#include <stdio.h>

main()
{
        int c;

        while ((c = getchar()) != EOF)
                putchar(c);
}
```

The difference here is that the while controlling expression contains an embedded assignment, something not possible in many languages. It is valid throughout C since assignment is defined as an operation and = is a binary operator. Therefore, exp1 = exp2 is itself an expression with a type and value. The type and value correspond to those of the left-hand expression. For example, if i is an int variable, the type of the expression i = 6 is int and its value is 6. (Now that we know that both i = 6 and i == 6 are valid expressions, but with completely different meanings, we can see the possible dangers of using = when == was meant.)

C has many operators and, consequently, operator precedence is necessary. Appendix A contains a complete precedence table; however, for this case, it is sufficient to state that the != operator has a higher precedence than =, so we need grouping parentheses to force the assignment to be done before the comparison. If they were omitted, the result from getchar would be compared to EOF and the result of that expression (either true or false) would be assigned to c. (When a compiler generates true and false values, it uses the values 1 and 0, respectively. That is, 4 == 3 has the value 0 and 4 != 3 has the value 1.)

This example may seem trivial, but UNIX, MS-DOS and other systems allow redirection of standard input and output at the command language interface level. If this is done, then the program becomes an amazingly simple general purpose file copy utility which is device-independent.

For example, on a UNIX or MS-DOS system, if this program had the name mycopy, the command:

```
mycopy <infile.dat >outfile.dat
```

would copy the file infile.dat to outfile.dat. The symbol < causes the standard input to be redirected to the file infile.dat while > redirects standard output to outfile.dat. Another symbol, >>, indicates that the output file should be appended to. (Some systems, such as DEC's RSX, do not provide a facility to redirect standard I/O. However, some compilers running on such systems generate code to do redirection from within the application program itself, by parsing the command-line arguments looking for <, > and >>. VAX/VMS supports I/O redirection via the ASSIGN/USER_MODE facility.)

Function `putchar` takes one `int` argument and returns a value that is the same as the argument passed in, except in the case of a write error when `EOF` is returned. Since it only has one simple task to perform, `purchar` can be implemented very efficiently.

However, the same result can be achieved using `printf` with a mask of `%c`. (`%lc` expects a `long int` argument.) For example:

```
printf("%c", c)
```

is equivalent to:

```
putchar(c)
```

except that the `int` value returned from `printf` does not have the same meaning as that from `putchar`. Note that we have just stated that both `printf` and `putchar` return `int` values, yet we have not used the values returned in our examples. In C, it is quite permissible to ignore the value returned from a function since some functions simply return values for convenience. However, when a function returns a value that indicates a success/failure status code, you should check it. Otherwise, you may never know you are getting an error.

Exercise 2-4*: Get characters using `getchar` until EOF, displaying each character read. Store the character read into a `char` variable rather than an `int`. If your terminal allows you to enter a character as a bit pattern, see if you can enter a character that has the same bit pattern as EOF. (Hint: Display `EOF` as an `int` to see how it is represented.)

Exercise 2-5: Implement the previous example in two ways: one with an embedded assignment and one without. If your compiler generates a machine-code listing, look at the differences in the code generated.

Exercise 2-6: Determine whether `getchar` and `putchar` are buffered on your system. That is, do you have to hit the "Enter" key to get `getchar` to pass input characters back to the program?

2.4   The `for` Construct

Another method of looping is the `for` construct. Its syntax is as follows:

```
for ( exp1 ; exp2 ; exp3 )
        statement;
```

The first expression, `exp1`, can be considered the initialization part because it is evaluated only once, before the loop is entered. `exp2` is the controlling expressions: If it tests true, the body of the loop is executed. Then `exp3` is evaluated and the controlling expression is evaluated again. The process repeats until `exp2` tests false, in which case control is transferred to the next statement beyond the body of the loop.

Any or all three of the expressions are optional, although the semicolons are not. If **exp1** is omitted, no initialization is done; if **exp2** is omitted, an infinite loop results; and if **exp3** is omitted, no extra expression is evaluated at the end of each loop iteration.

Therefore:

```
for (;;)
```

is equivalent to:

```
while (1)
```

There is no such thing as a controlling variable in **exp2**, since **exp2** can be any arbitrary expression that can have a true or false value. In fact, while C's **for** construct looks exactly like FORTRAN's DO, BASIC's FOR and PASCAL's for, it is much more capable because they are all restricted to dealing with the same controlling variable. In C's case, **exp1**, **exp2** and **exp3** are three expressions that need have nothing in common.

A **for** construct always can be rewritten using **while** (and vice versa) as follows:

```
exp1;
while ( exp2 ) {
        statement;
        exp3;
}
```

Let's look at an example:

```
/* The for construct */

#include <stdio.h>

main()
{
        long int i;

        printf("i (dec)  i (hex)    ~i (hex)\n\n");

        for (i = -3; i <= 3; ++i)
                printf("  %2ld    %08lx    %08lX\n", i, i, ~i);

        printf("\nAt the end of the loop, i is %ld.\n", i);
}
```

The output produced on a PC, PDP-11 or VAX (and any other eight-, 16- and 32-bit twos-complement system) is as follows:

i (dec)	i (hex)	~i (hex)
-3	ffffffffd	00000002
-2	fffffffe	00000001
-1	ffffffff	00000000
0	00000000	FFFFFFFF
1	00000001	FFFFFFFE
2	00000002	FFFFFFFD
3	00000003	FFFFFFFC

`At the end of the loop, i is 4.`

In this example, the body of the loop is only one statement and therefore does not need to be enclosed in braces, although it can be. Like the `while` statement, `for` does not execute the loop at all if the controlling expression is initially false. The "controlling variable" i retains its value after the loop is terminated.

Since i is a `long int`, we need the 1 prefix in the edit masks. However, we also have put a zero at the start of several masks' field width. This indicates we wish leading unused print positions to have zeros in them. (This often is done with hexadecimal values.) Also, we have used both x and X to get a hexadecimal display.

We have specified a width of eight for each hex value; however, this may be insufficient for some implementations (those with more than 32 bits in a `long int`, for example). So, while the program will run on all standard C implementations and produce the appropriate output, the output may differ in content and form from that shown because either other than twos-complement representation is used for negative integers, or more than eight hex digits are needed for the display.

The tilde symbol ˜ is the unary ones-complement operator. It may be used only with integral operands.

2.5 The `if-else` Construct

The most common way to test the value of an expression is to use the `if` statement with optional `else` clause. It has the general form:

```
if ( exp )
        statement-1;
[else
        statement-2;]
```

If the controlling expression evaluates to true, statement-1 is executed. Otherwise, if the optional `else` clause is present, statement-2 is executed. If no `else` clause is present, control transfers to the statement beyond the `if` statement.

An `else` applies to the current innermost `if`. Consider the following example:

```
if ( exp1 )
        if ( exp2 )
                statement-1;
else
        statement-2;
```

Even though the format seems to imply that statement-2 belongs to the false path of the first `if` this is not the case; it belongs to the innermost `if`.

To change this, use braces to force the innermost `if` to be complete as follows:

```
if ( exp1 ) {
        if ( exp2 )
                statement-1;
}
else
        statement-2;
```

The innermost `if` can have no `else` because the closing brace completes the innermost `if` statement, as well as the true path of the outer `if`.

The following simple example shows a nested `if/else` within a `while` loop:

```
/* The if/else construct and break statement */

#include <stdio.h>

main()
{
        int reply;

        while (1) {
                printf("\nDo you know C? (Y/N) ");
                reply = getchar();

                if (reply == 'y' || reply == 'Y') {
                        printf("\nGood.\n");
                        break;
                }
                else if (reply == 'n' || reply == 'N') {
                        printf("\nWelcome to C.\n");
                        break;
                }
                else
                        printf("\nInvalid. Try again.\n");
        }
        printf("\nThanks for your cooperation.\n");
}
```

Examples of output produced are:

```
Do you know C? (Y/N) x
Invalid. Try again.

Do you know C? (Y/N)
Invalid. Try again.

Do you know C? (Y/N) Y
Good.

Thanks for your cooperation.

Do you know C? (Y/N) n
Welcome to C.

Thanks for your cooperation.
```

Since the expression 1 is always true, the loop executes indefinitely. The loop body is a compound statement consisting of the call to printf, an assignment to reply and an if statement. Note that the else clause of the first if test contains another if test. The if construct can be nested up to some implementation-defined depth.

The symbol || represents the logical OR operator and multiple || operators (as in a || b || c) evaluate left to right. (The symbol && is used to represent the logical AND operator. This takes precedence over || if both are present. Multiple && operators also evaluate left-to-right. The ! symbol is used for the logical NOT operator and has a higher precedence than both || and &&.) Unlike most of C's binary operators, the order of evaluation of the operands to both || and && is well defined—it is guaranteed to be left-to-right. Therefore, the meaning of the expressions i || i++ and j++ && j is well defined. With ||, the second operand is evaluated only if the first tests false. With &&, the second operand is evaluated only if the first tests true.

'Y' is a character constant with type int. Its value is equal to the numerical value of Y in the machine's character set. (In ASCII, this value is 89.) 'Y' is preferred to 89 because its meaning is more obvious and the graphic representation is character set-independent.

Note that the escape sequences introduced earlier for use in string literals (particularly with printf edit masks) also can be used to represent the corresponding characters in character constants. For example, '\n' represents the new-line character as it would be returned from getchar. Likewise, '\123' represents the character with a bit representation of 0123 and '\xff' represent 0xff. As mentioned in Chapter 1, when used as a character constant, the single-quote character must be written as '\''. (Note that 'Y' is a single-character constant with type int, while "Y" is a character string consisting of one character. The two are quite different.)

The break statement causes termination of the innermost current while, for, do or switch. Control passes to the statement following the end of the construct being terminated, in this case, the while loop. You can not break out more than one level using break. For that, you will need to use goto (or some other means). A construct similar to break is continue. This statement causes control to be transferred to the end of the current innermost while, for or do construct. Then the controlling expression for that loop is re-evaluated. Simply stated, the difference between break and continue is essentially that break breaks out of a loop while continue begins the next iteration of a loop.

If you look closely at the output shown above, you will notice a problem when the letter x was input. We seem to have gotten two error messages rather than just one. Often, getchar is buffered so that you must hit the RETURN or ENTER key before the previous character is given to your program. If this is the case, the '\n' new-line character generated by the terminator key is also present in the input buffer. For this reason, getchar can not be relied on for single-key input. (Some implementations provide getche for this purpose. They also provide getch which gets one character without echoing it to the terminal. Neither of these is defined in the ANSI C library.) Likewise, putchar is often buffered so that characters are not physically output until a new-line is written or the output buffer fills.

To allow for buffered versions of getchar, we can modify the program slightly by replacing the assignment of reply with the following:

```
while ((reply = getchar()) == '\n')
        continue;
```

New-lines are ignored, although they are echoed and make the input display look a little messy.

Exercise 2-7*: Explain the output produced by the following program:

```
#include <stdio.h>

main()
{
        int i = 5;

        if (i = 10)
                printf("i equals 10\n");
        else
                printf("i equals %d\n", i);
}
```

Exercise 2-8*: Read characters using getchar and convert all uppercase to their lowercase equivalents and vice versa. Display each (possibly converted) character using putchar. Is your solution portable? If your system supports I/O redirection, test your program on its own source file.

Exercise 2-9*: For i equals -10 to +10, print the value of i and i*i. Also indicate whether i is even or odd by displaying the word EVEN or ODD at the end of each table line. Separate the columns with tabs, count the number of odd and even values and display the counts at the end of the table, after a blank line. (Hint: Integer division truncates so that 5/3 equals 1. However, 5.0/3 and 5/3.0 equals 1.666667.)

Exercise 2-10*: For each of the uppercase letters, print the letter and its internal representation value (ASCII or EBCDIC, for example). Go from Z to A. (Hint: Use a for loop and remember that 'a' is an int that has the value of the letter a in the host character set.)

2.6   The `do-while` Construct

The `for` and `while` constructs evaluate a controlling expression and, if it tests true, they execute their body. Occasionally, it is desirable to execute a statement at least once before deciding whether to repeat the process. This is where the `do-while` construct differs.

This construct has the general form:

```
do
        statement;
while ( expression );
```

The statement body is always executed once. Then the controlling expression is evaluated and, if it tests true, the statement is executed again and the process repeats. If the expression tests false, control transfers to the statement beyond the do statement.

The loop body is typically a block, although it need not be. One possible use for this construct is the reading and processing of records from a file. The first record is read and, if end-of-file is detected, an error is reported and the program terminates. If a record is returned, it is processed and another record is read. As the first read is to be handled specially, it makes sense to place it outside of the read/process loop.

The following program demonstrates this common technique:

```c
/* the do/while statement */

#include <stdio.h>
#include <stdlib.h>

main()
{
        char record[200];

        if (getrec(record) == EOF) {
                printf("Input file is empty\n");
                exit(1);
        }

        do {
                /* process input record */

        } while (getrec(record) != EOF);
}
```

The variable `record` is defined as an array of 200 characters. (Arrays will be discussed in Chapter 3.) The function `getrec` (whose source is not shown here) is called to read the next record. If end-of-file is detected, `getrec` returns the value EOF. If EOF is returned on the first read, we terminate the program by calling the library routine `exit`. This function terminates the program "normally" in that it causes output file buffers to be flushed and performs other cleanup tasks. It then takes the `int` argument passed to it and gives it to the program that started this program (either the operating system command-line processor or some other parent program)

as the program's exit code. (This can be tested using ERRORLEVEL in MS-DOS, for
example.)

An exit value of zero traditionally has meant success, however, ANSI C provides
the implementation-defined macros EXIT_SUCCESS and EXIT_FAILURE to ensure that
complete portability is possible. (VAX C uses 1 to represent a successful termination.)
These macros and the exit function itself are declared in the library header stdlib.h.

If the scope of the loop is a large number of lines, its terminating while clause may
look like a while construct having a body of only a null statement. (Null statements
are discussed in the next section.) For this reason, it is a good practice to indent all
statements in the do-while's scope and to place the closing brace of the embedded
compound statement on the same line as the while clause as shown. The trailing
semicolon terminates the do-while statement—it is not a while statement with a
null statement body.

There are several other less frequently used constructs available for implementing
looping and branching. These are switch and the inevitable goto. They are covered
in Chapter 10.

2.7   The Null Statement

In certain cases, C's syntax forces you to use a statement when you don't really have
one to use. In such cases, you can use a null statement which consists of just a
semicolon: For example:

```
/* the null statement */

#include <stdio.h>

main()
{
        int c;

        printf("Please enter you first name: ");

        /* ignore leading white space */

        while ((c = getchar()) == ' ' || c == '\t' || c == '\n'
            || c == '\f' || c == '\v')
                ;                       /* null statement */

        while (c != EOF && c != '\n') {
                putchar(c);
                c = getchar();
        }

        putchar('\n');
}
```

In the first while loop, all the work is done in evaluating the controlling expression.
However, the while construct must have a body, so we use the null statement. Since
this semicolon is important and easily could get hidden in the source, you should
write it where you normally would write the body. (In this case it's indented one

horizontal tab.) This type of loop also demonstrates the possible value of embedded assignments.

Exercise 2-11*: Given that `printf` returns an `int` value, call `printf` to display the text "Test Data" and see what value is returned. Do the same using `printf("%2d", 1234)`. Can you deduce what the return value means?

Exercise 2-12*: Show that C uses the values 0 and 1, respectively, to represent false and true.

2.8   Chapter Summary

- If the controlling expression in a `while` construct initially evaluates to false, the loop body is not executed.

- The body of a `while` loop may be a single or compound statement. A compound statement is zero or more statements surrounded by a pair of matching braces and can be used anywhere a statement is permitted.

- One common programming error is the omission of the braces from around a compound statement so that only the first statement is considered to be part of a `while`, `for` or `if` body.

- The equality and comparison operators are: `>`, greater than; `>=`, greater than or equal to; `<`, less than; `<=`, less than or equal to; `==`, equal to; and `!=`, not equal to. Note that equality uses `==` while assignment uses `=`.

- `while (1)` and `for (;;)` mean "loop forever."

- A `printf` edit mask width forces the output value to be displayed right-justified. If it contains a leading zero, leading zeros are used as filler instead of spaces.

- The increment and decrement operators `++` and `--` may be used as either a prefix or suffix. The value of `x++` is the value of `x` before it is incremented. The value of `++x` is that after the increment has been done. When applied to arithmetic expressions, `++` (and `--`) causes the expression's value to be incremented (or decremented) by 1 (or 1.0 in the case of a floating-point operand).

- The `return` statement causes control to be returned to the calling function. A `return` from function `main` terminates the program. The outermost closing brace in a function is an implied `return` statement.

- An expression of the general form `exp1` *op=* `exp2` is equivalent to `exp1 = exp1` *op* `exp2`, when *op* is one of the following operators: `+`, `-`, `*`, `/`, `%`, `>>`, `<<`, `&`, `^` and `|`.

- The order of evaluation of arguments in a function call list is undefined. They may be evaluated left-to-right, vice versa or in some other predictable or arbitrary manner—it's up to the compiler.

- Except where otherwise stated, the order of evaluation of operands to binary operators is undefined. (This applies to the following operators, among others: `=`, *op=*, `+`, `-`, `*`, `/`, `>`, `>=`, `<`, `<=`, `==` and `!=`.)

- Symbolic constants such as `EOF` are replaced by their defined values by the C preprocessor.

- The names of symbolic constants are identifiers and traditionally are written without using lowercase letters.

- The functions `getchar` and `putchar` are part of the standard C run-time library. `getchar` gets a character from standard input and `putchar` writes a character to standard output.

- Characters read by `getchar` should be stored in variables having type `int` rather than `char` so that end-of-file can be detected properly.

- In C, assignment is implemented via the assignment operator `=`. As such, an assignment expression can be part of some larger expression. The type and value of an assignment expression is that of its left-hand operand.

- Except for one special and rarely used operator (the comma operator which will be discussed in Chapter 10), `=` and the compound assignment operators have a lower operator precedence than all other operators.

- The `printf` edit mask `%c` is used to display the low byte (or character) stored in an `int` argument. (`%lc` expects a `long int` argument.)

- If the controlling expression in a `for` construct initially evaluates to false, the body is not executed.

- Any or all three expressions in a `for` are optional, although the semicolons are not. If the second is omitted, an infinite loop results.

- Since the three expressions in a `for` statement need not have anything in common, there is no such concept as a loop-controlling variable that you have in some other languages.

- A `for` construct always can be rewritten using `while` (and vice versa).

- An `else` applies to the current innermost `if`.

- The tilde symbol ˜ is the unary ones-complement operator. It can be used only with integral operands.

- The symbol `||` represents the logical OR operator. Multiple `||` operators (as in a `||` b `||` c) evaluate left to right.

- The symbol `&&` is used to represent the logical AND operator. This takes precedence over `||` if both are present. Multiple `&&` operators evaluate left-to-right.

- The `!` symbol is used for the logical NOT operator and has a higher precedence than both `||` and `&&`.

- Unlike most of C's binary operators, the order of evaluation of the operands to both `||` and `&&` is well-defined. It is guaranteed to be left-to-right.

- The `break` statement causes termination of the innermost current `while`, `for` or `do-while` loop.

- `'Y'` is a single-character constant with type `int` while `"Y"` is a character string consisting of one character. The two are quite different.

- The difference between `break` and `continue` is that `break` breaks out of a loop while `continue` begins the next iteration of a loop.

- Often, `getchar` is buffered so that you must hit the RETURN or ENTER key before the previous character is given to your program. If this is the case, the `'\n'` new-line character generated by the terminator key is also present in the input buffer.

- Unlike `for` and `while`, `do-while` executes its body before evaluating the controlling expression.

- The library routine `exit` terminates a program "normally" and passes its `int` argument to the parent environment.

- Other less-often used looping and branching constructs available include `switch` and `goto`.

- In certain cases, C's syntax forces you to use a statement when you don't really have one to use. In such cases, you can use a null statement which consists of just a semicolon.

Chapter 3

Arrays

In this chapter, we will see how to define and use arrays. While most of the examples deal with arrays of characters, the principles can be applied to arrays of any data type. Throughout this discussion, the terms *character array* and *string* will be used interchangeably because a string is implemented as an array of characters. At first glance, the handling of strings in C seems cumbersome, but with some practice, it becomes easy and the idea of calling external routines to perform string operations seems to fit in with C's "language of primitives" philosophy.

3.1   Single-Dimensional Arrays

C has no means of dealing with character strings directly. It can, however, handle single characters and arrays of characters. The need to deal with character strings (such as name and address fields) as arrays seems crude to programmers used to block-move and compare capabilities as found in BASIC, COBOL and FORTRAN-77. Because group move and compare functions are easily written in C and are generally provided by the compiler vendor anyway, the devout C disciple would exclaim, "So what?" However, the fact remains that the need to call a subroutine to implement these capabilities is foreign to most high-level language programmers and is a psychological obstacle they must overcome in using C. Let's look at a simple example in which the user's name is read from standard input and stored into a character array.

```
/* Introduce character arrays */

#include <stdio.h>

#define MAXLEN 20                  /* name can be 20 chars max */

main()
{
        char name[MAXLEN + 1];
        int c;
        int count = 0;

        printf("Please enter your name (%d chars max). ",
                MAXLEN);

        while (count < MAXLEN && (c = getchar()) != '\n')
                name[count++] = c;

        name[count] = '\0';    /* add terminating nul */

        printf("\nPleased to meet you %s.\n",name);
}
```

Some examples of input and output are as follows:

```
Please enter your name (20 chars max). George Hill<ret>

Pleased to meet you George Hill.

Please enter your name (20 chars max). <sp>abc<tab>xyz<ret>

Pleased to meet you  abc        xyz.

Please enter your name (20 chars max). 12345678901234567890ABC

Pleased to meet you 12345678901234567890.
```

The #define preprocessor directive assigns a string "value" to the identifier MAXLEN. Each occurrence of this identifier in the source file is replaced by the string assigned to by the preprocessor. MAXLEN, then, is a synonym for the compile-time constant expression 20. Its purpose is two-fold: to provide a meaningful name for a "magic" number and to permit the value to be changed in only one place if 20 no longer is an appropriate value.

The line char name[MAXLEN + 1]; declares name to be an array of 21 characters. The dimension is required to be a compile-time constant integral expression with a value greater than zero. The expression MAXLEN + 1 satisfies these criteria because MAXLEN is replaced with 20 by the preprocessor before the compiler sees it.

There are two aspects of arrays in C that are different from array definition and use in other languages. First, the [and] characters are used when declaring a dimension and specifying a particular element. Second, array elements begin at subscript zero rather than one. Therefore, the elements of name may be referenced as name[0], `name[1]` ... `name[20]`.

When referring to a particular element, the subscript can be any integral expression. C provides no subscript range-checking at run-time, nor does it allow subscripts to begin at other than zero the way FORTRAN-77 and other languages do. It is the programmer's responsibility to ensure that a subscript value is valid. Unpredictable results may occur if an array element's subscript is less than zero or greater than the largest "real" element. Variable size arrays are not permitted by the language, although they can be implemented using the dynamic memory manipulation library routines such as `malloc` and `calloc`. (Examples of using these functions appear in Chapter 9.) Space for automatic variable arrays is allocated at run-time and remains fixed throughout a program.

Since we have decided on a maximum length of 20 for `name`, why have we dimensioned `name` to 21? C allows character arrays of arbitrary length and, while it is possible to store a 20-character name in an array of 20 `char`, many of the string routines in the standard library will fail if the array is not explicitly terminated with a *null character* whose binary value is zero. The way to represent this character graphically is `'\0'`, which is a single-character constant having a value of zero (octal). (For compilers that support hexadecimal constants, `'\x0'` or `'\x00'` could be used instead. However, this practice is rare because it was not available in the early days of C and is not instantly recognizable as is `'\0'`.) Actually, the expression 0 can be used instead of `'\0'` because both have type `int` and value zero. However, when we are specifically dealing with the null character, `'\0'` is the traditional way of writing it. 0, on the other hand, is used when dealing with the number zero.

The typical approach to strings in C, then, is to allocate a fixed (maximum) amount of space for them and to place a null character immediately after the last used character. Then, when the string is being processed, its end can be detected easily. And, while the null character takes up storage space (hence, `name` has size 21), it is not considered to be part of the string. Many of the string manipulation library routines expect strings to be `'\0'`-terminated. It is quite permissible to pad the end of such an array with spaces, as COBOL does, and to not use a `'\0'` terminator. If you choose this route, you must maintain the length of the string yourself and provide your own equivalent versions of library routines such as `strcmp` and `strcpy`, which compare and copy strings, respectively.

Unless a routine knows how long a string is, it must search for the terminating `'\0'` in order to know it has processed the complete string. String lengths are not stored by the compiler and must be calculated at run-time. Note that if a trailing `'\0'` is appended, the length of a string is never the same as the length of the array in which it is stored.

The program above gets characters one at a time from standard input and stores them into the array `name` until either 20 characters (subscripts `[0]` through `[19]`) have been read or a new-line is entered. Notice how the array subscript `count` is post-incremented to ensure that the incoming characters are stored properly.

After the `while` loop terminates, a trailing null character is added to indicate the end of the character string. If `'\n'` is the first character entered, the `while` loop body is never executed and the `'\0'` is stored in `name[0]`. The string contained in `name`, therefore, consists of `'\0'` only and has a length of 0. If the name JOHN is entered, it would be stored as J O H N \0. In this case, the string is four characters long. The contents of any unused characters following the `'\0'` terminator remain intact. Leading and trailing spaces are significant. Indeed, all characters input, whether printable or not, are significant because no validation is done.

The string stored in `name` is displayed on standard output by `printf` using an edit mask of `%s`. This prints characters from the string `name` until a null character is found. If a `'\0'` is not present at the end of a character string, any program processing that string and expecting to find a `'\0'` will keep right on going until it finds one. It is the programmer's responsibility to ensure that, if appropriate, character arrays are properly terminated with a `'\0'`. When the compiler comes across a string literal (a token of the form `"..."`), it stores it as an array of `char` which is initialized with the characters contained between the quotes. An extra character is automatically appended containing `'\0'`. This is how `printf` knows it has gotten to the end of its edit mask since the first argument passed must be the address of a `'\0'`-terminated array of `char`.

As mentioned earlier, `'Y'` has quite a different meaning from `"Y"`. `'Y'` is a constant of type `int` with the value of Y in the machine's character set (89 in ASCII) while `"Y"` is a string of length one, stored as a character array of length two. `"Y"` actually is represented as the two characters Y \0.

Let's clean up the example a little by adding some elementary input validation. Specifically, all leading and trailing white space will be ignored and consecutive embedded white space will be treated as one space character. Also, the name must begin with a letter and can contain only letters, spaces, periods, hyphens and apostrophes. Any other character indicates that the name field has ended, causing input to be terminated. (This is not a foolproof validation because it permits unlikely names such as A-B-C and B.C.D.)

```
/* Validate characters stored into the array */

#include <stdio.h>
#include <ctype.h>

#define MAXLEN 20               /* name can be 20 chars max */

main()
{
        char name[MAXLEN + 1];
        int c;
        int prev_char = '\0';
        int count = 0;

        printf("Please enter your name (%d chars max). ",
                MAXLEN);

        /* ignore leading white space */

        while (isspace(c = getchar()))
                ;

        if (!isalpha(c)) {
                printf("\nMust begin with alpha character.\n");
                return;
        }
```

```
                while (count < MAXLEN && c != '\n') {
                        if (isspace(c)) {
                                if (prev_char != ' ') {
                                        name[count++] = ' ';
                                        prev_char = ' ';
                                }
                        }
                        else if (!isalpha(c) && c != '.'
                            && c != '-' && c != '\'')
                                break;
                        else {
                                name[count++] = c;
                                prev_char = c;
                        }

                        c = getchar();
                }

                if (name[count - 1] == ' ')
                        name[count - 1] = '\0';
                else
                        name[count] = '\0';

                printf("\nPleased to meet you %s.\n",name);
        }
```

Some examples of output are:

```
        Please enter your name (20 chars max). <sp>A.B.  Smith<sp>
        Pleased to meet you A.B. Smith.

        Please enter your name (20 chars max). .A. Jones
        Must begin with alpha character.
```

This program builds on much of what we already have learned. However, it does contain some new things. The `ctype.h` header inclusion is new. Like the `#include <stdio.h>` directive we have been using since Chapter 1, `#include <ctype.h>` must be used when you refer to certain library character-handling routines. This set of routines is divided into two main groups: those used to test if a character has a specific attribute (such as being alphabetic, lowercase or numeric), which have names of the form is*xxxx*, and those that convert a character to some other value (such as to upper- or lowercase), which have names of the form to*xxxx*. The complete set of routines in the ANSI C library that are handled by `ctype.h` follows:

ctype.h Library Routines	
Name	*Purpose*
`isalnum`	alphabetic or numeric
`isalpha`	alphabetic
`iscntrl`	control
`isdigit`	digit 0–9
`isgraph`	graphic (printable)
`islower`	lowercase
`isprint`	printable
`ispunct`	punctuation
`isspace`	white space
`isupper`	uppercase
`isxdigit`	hexadecimal
`tolower`	convert to lower-case
`toupper`	convert to upper-case

Each is*xxx* routine takes one argument of type `int` and returns an `int` value that is either 0 (false) or non-zero (true). Note that while each takes an `int` argument, they are meant to work on characters. In C, unless certain special things are done (by using a function prototype), when `char` arguments are passed to functions, the `char` value is converted to type `int`. So, even though `ctype` routines can be given any `int` value as an argument, their behavior is only defined if the `int` value represents a character in the host's native character set (or `EOF`). That is, `islower(10000)` produces undefined behavior. In this example, we use only two of these functions: `isspace` and `isalpha`.

Each to*xxx* routine takes one argument of type `int` and returns an `int` value, which is the (possibly) converted input argument.

Some run-time libraries also contain all or some of the following routines: `isascii`, `iscsym`, `issym`, `toascii`, `_tolower` and `_toupper`. None of these is defined by ANSI C. For more information about the functions in `ctype.h`, refer to your compiler documentation.

Throughout the program, the variable `prev_char` is used to store the previous character processed. The type of `prev_char` is `int`, not `char` as you might expect. However, you could use either type. `prev_char` is compared with the `int` expression `' '` and is initialized with the int expressions `'\0'`, `' '` and `c`. All of these `int` expressions are representable as a `char`, so if `prev_char` had type `char`, they would have been truncated (without loss of significant bits) if they were assigned to `prev_char`. Regarding comparisons, whenever a `char` meets an `int`, the `char` is converted to type `int` before the comparison is done. So, the advantage of making `prev_char` an `int` is that is can save some execution time when it is compared with `int` expressions. The actual result still should be the same as if it had type `char`.

Note the combinations of the logical NOT operator `!` and the logical AND operator `&&` used to qualify acceptable characters after the first in the name being entered. The `!` operator has higher precedence than `&&` and the `&&` operators are evaluated left-to-right. To test for the apostrophe, we need to use `'\''`.

Any basic data type supported by C can be used as the type of an array. However, the null character terminator convention only applies to arrays of `char` because there is no reserved (and portable) way of representing "special" values of any other data type.

Exercise 3-1*: Define an `int` array of one element only. Initialize it to the value 100 and display its value using `printf`.

Exercise 3-2*: Define an `int` array of 10 elements. Display the value of elements 10, 15, 100 and -5. Do you get any compilation or run-time errors? Can you explain them?

Exercise 3-3*: Define a `char` array of 20 elements and initialize it with five characters you read from standard input. Do not append a trailing `'\0'` to the string. Display the string using `printf` and explain the output. (It is possible you will not get a run-time error, since the behavior is undefined.)

Exercise 3-4*: How much storage space is taken up by the strings `"Europe"`, `""`, `"\0"` and `"\0abc\0"`?

Exercise 3-5*: Run the following program and explain the output it produces:

```
#include <stdio.h>

main()
{
        printf("%d\0%d", 10, 20);
}
```

Exercise 3-6*: Read text from the keyboard until EOF is detected. Inspect each character entered and test if it is alphabetic, a decimal digit, white space or other, incrementing one of four corresponding counters accordingly. Once the EOF has been read, display each of the four counts on a separate line. Do not include the EOF in the counts.

3.2 Multidimensional Arrays

The most obvious difference with using multidimensional arrays in C is the notation used. While many languages use the format:

```
array(i, j, ..., k)
```

C uses:

```
array[i][j][...][k]
```

This "strange" method is not there to satisfy the ego of the language's designer nor "just to be different." The format implies (perhaps) that multidimensional arrays actually are implemented as single dimensional arrays each of whose elements are another single dimensional array, etc. That is, in `int c[2][3][4]`, c is declared to be an array of two vectors, each of which is an array of three vectors, each of which is an array of four `int`s.

The following example shows a two-dimensional array being initialized at run-time. Its contents then are displayed in the form of an annotated table.

```
/* multi-dim array run-time initialization */

#include <stdio.h>

main()
{
        int iarray[4][4];
        int i, j;

        for (i = 0; i < 4; i++)
                for (j = 0; j < 4; j++)
                        iarray[i][j] = i * j;

        printf("     0   1   2   3\n\n");
        for (i = 0; i < 4; i++) {
                printf("%d ", i);
                for (j = 0; j < 4; j++)
                        printf("  %2d", iarray[i][j]);
                putchar('\n');
        }
}
```

The output produced is:

```
        0   1   2   3

0       0   0   0   0
1       0   1   2   3
2       0   2   4   6
3       0   3   6   9
```

Each element is printed individually because there is no standard way to deal with arrays as a whole. Again, this is a consequence of I/O not being part of the language. If the name of an array is passed to **printf**, it is done by address and no dimension information is passed. Therefore, **printf** has no idea of an array's dimensions or even if an array has been passed or not—it simply gets an address. It is possible, however, to write your own functions to perform formatted I/O on arrays.

The array initialization would have been much cheaper if it were done at compile-time. However, we have not yet seen how to do this. The initial values also would be much more obvious if they had appeared in a well-organized initializer list. However, if the contents of the array change and need to be restored to their original values during program execution, then run-time initialization has to be used. Array elements that need to be initialized using expressions that can not be evaluated at compile-time, must be initialized at run-time.

In C, arrays are stored in row-major order. That is, arrays are stored in memory so that an array defined as `char c[2][5][7];` occupies 70 consecutive characters and is stored as follows:

```
c[0][0][0]
c[0][0][1]
    ...
c[0][0][6]
c[0][1][0]
c[0][1][1]
    ...
c[0][1][6]
c[0][2][0]
    ...
c[0][4][6]
c[1][0][0]
c[1][0][1]
    ...
c[1][4][6]
```

C places no limit on the number of dimensions allowed with arrays. You are limited only by the amount of memory available.

3.3   Array Initializer Lists

We have seen that definitions of automatic scalars may contain an initializing expression. This idea is extended to include arrays (and, in fact, all of C's data types). However, to initialize an array, we usually have more than one initializing value.

The general format of an initializing list:

declaration = { *exp1* , *exp2* , ... , *expn* };

For scalars, the delimiting braces are optional and almost always omitted. Initializer lists for aggregates (such as arrays and structures) must include the braces even if the list contains only one expression.

Since automatic objects are initialized at run-time, their initializing expressions can be any run-time expression of the appropriate type. For example:

```
f()
{
        double values[3] = {1.2, 2.3, 3.4};
        long int count[3] = {10L, -234, 2789876};
        int i[3] = {g(), h() + 23, x() - 12};/* error */
        int k[3] = {123456, 65789, 76534};/* non-portable */
}
```

Note, though, that the initialization of i generates an error. Initializing `auto` arrays is a relatively recent addition to the language and it has a significant restriction. All expressions in the initializer list must be compile-time constant expressions, despite the fact that the `auto` array is actually initialized at run-time.

The initializer list for **k** is suspicious because the type of all three expressions may be **long int**, in which case, they will be truncated before being used to initialize **k**. (This is a common porting problem when the code originally was written for a machine where **int** and **long** had the same representation, but this is not true for one or more of the target machines.)

Initially, C did not permit automatic arrays (and other aggregates) to have initializer lists. This capability was added much later and was not universally implemented. However, ANSI C has endorsed this and all conforming implementations must provide it.

To initialize an array of more than one dimension, each dimension has its own initializer list as follows:

```
int iarray[2][3] = {
        {1, 2, 3},
        {5, 4, 3}
};
```

Here, the list contains two subinitializer lists, each having its own delimiting set of braces. Since all of the white space here is optional, we could use the following instead:

```
int iarray[2][3] = {{1, 2, 3}, {5, 4, 3}};
```

In fact, since we have specified an initializer for each element, all brace pairs except for the outermost pair can be removed leaving:

```
int iarray[2][3] = {1, 2, 3, 5, 4, 3};
```

All three methods of initializing **iarray** are correct, although they appear in decreasing order of desirability. C allows very obscure code to be written, so when you are learning a new technique, it is wise to implement it so that the code you write has some meaning beyond that required by the compiler. In the future, some poor unsuspecting maintenance programmer (possibly yourself) will have to read your code, so the easier you make it to understand, the easier it will be to modify or enhance. Writing "good-looking" code doesn't hurt your reputation either. (Remember that writing code is a small part of software engineering. The big part is being responsible for what you have written.)

If you can imply some extra meaning by organizing an initializer list in a particular way, then that is a better way. Perhaps a better example is that of initializing an identity matrix (a square matrix in which the elements of the leading diagonal contain the value 1 and all other elements contain zero).

```
/* adding meaning to the initializing list */

int sarray[6][6] = {
        {1,0,0,0,0,0},
        {0,1,0,0,0,0},
        {0,0,1,0,0,0},
        {0,0,0,1,0,0},
        {0,0,0,0,1,0},
        {0,0,0,0,0,1}
};
```

Here, the array is obviously an identity matrix. If the initializer list were written as one long line of values this information would be lost to the reader.

For example, the initializer:

```
/* alternate identity matrix */

int sarray[6][6] = {{1,0,0,0,0,0},{0,1,0,0,0,0},{0,0,1,0,0,0},
        {0,0,0,1,0,0},{0,0,0,0,1,0},{0,0,0,0,0,1}};
```

provides no obvious meaning. Although the addition of comments might explain exactly what is being done here, a picture is worth a thousand words and may not require an explanation.

Some languages, notably FORTRAN, provide a repetition count when identical consecutive initializing expressions are required. Unfortunately, C does not provide such a capability. If you wish to initialize a 100-element array with the value 1, you must specify an initializer list with 100 expressions containing 1.

It is permissible to initialize a `char` array with a string as follows:

```
char aname[5] = {'J', 'O', 'H', 'N', '\0'};
```

Each initializer actually is an `int` expression. There is no such thing as a `char` constant expression in C.

Because array initialization is done quite often in C programming, an abbreviated method is provided; for example:

```
char aname[5] = "JOHN";
```

Here, the list is replaced with a literal string containing the same characters, except that the trailing '\0' must be omitted because it is implied. The delimiting braces become optional and usually are omitted.

3.4 Default and Partial Initialization

It is permissible to initialize less than the maximum number of elements in the object being initialized. This is done simply by terminating the initializer list prematurely as follows:

```
int totals[4] = {123, 62, 76};
float f[6] = {1.2, 3.4};
int table[5];               /* no init list */
```

The elements not explicitly initialized have the same value as if zero had been assigned to them. `totals[3]`, therefore, would be set to zero and `f[2]` through `f[5]` would be set to 0.0. This is required by ANSI C since it now permits automatic aggregate initialization. There is an idiosyncrasy, however. If the list contains at least one initializer, any trailing uninitialized elements get the value zero. However, if the list is missing (as in `table` above), the initial value of all elements is undefined, the same as for automatic scalars.

Consider the following example:

```
f()
{
/*1*/    int table1[5];
/*2*/    int table2[5] = {0};
/*3*/    int table3[5] = {0, 0};
/*4*/    int table4[5] = {0, 0, 0};
/*5*/    int table5[5] = {0, 0, 0, 0};
/*6*/    int table6[5] = {0, 0, 0, 0, 0};
}
```

While cases 2–6 are equivalent, they are different from case 1 in which the initial values of all elements of `table1` are undefined.

Similarly, partial initializer lists may be used with multidimensional arrays as follows:

```
int tarray[6][6] = {
        {1},
        {0, 1},
        {0, 0, 1},
        {0, 0, 0, 1},
        {0, 0, 0, 0, 1},
        {0, 0, 0, 0, 0, 1}
};
```

Here, all elements following the 1 on each row have been omitted and default to 0. Even though this format may imply the same meaning as that used by `sarray` earlier, it doesn't hurt to explicitly initialize all elements. It only costs a few keystrokes and doesn't affect the compilation or run-time speeds.

In this example, the inner brace pairs are absolutely essential for the compiler to know which elements are to be assigned default values.

If these braces were omitted, the elements assigned would be as if the following definition were used:

```
int tarray[6][6] = {
        {1, 0, 1, 0, 0, 1},
        {0, 0, 0, 1, 0, 0},
        {0, 0, 1, 0, 0, 0},
        {0, 0, 1, 0, 0, 0},
        {0, 0, 0, 0, 0, 0},
        {0, 0, 0, 0, 0, 0}
};
```

This array definitely doesn't represent an identity matrix. In this case, even though only the first 21 of the maximum 36 initial values are specified, the compiler makes no complaints. It just appends the remaining 15 zero values.

While you can supply fewer initializer values than required, you can not provide too many. In the latter case, a compilation error will result.

The third row of the initializer list for `tarray` above contains:

```
{0, 0, 1},
```

Even though zero is the default value for each element, the leading zeros can not be omitted. You might assume that a format something like:

```
{, , 1},
```

is valid, but it is not. Only trailing values in an initializer list can be omitted. Therefore, if you have a 200-element array of which all elements except the last three are to have the value zero, you must write out the complete initializer list explicitly.

3.5 The Library String Processing Functions

The standard C library includes a family of routines capable of manipulating '\0'-terminated arrays of characters. All such functions have names of the form str*xxx*. The complete list follows:

String Routines in `string.h`	
Name	*Purpose*
`strcpy`	copy one whole string to another
`strncpy`	copy part of one string to another
`strcat`	concatenate two whole strings
`strncat`	concatenate part of one string to another
`strcmp`	compare two whole strings
`strncmp`	compare leading part of two strings
`strcoll`	locale-specific string compare
`strchr`	search for a character in a string
`strrchr`	reverse search for a character in a string
`strstr`	search a string for a substring
`strcspn`	find match with one of a set of characters
`strpbrk`	find match with one of a set of characters
`strspn`	find match with one of a set of characters
`strtok`	parse a string into specified tokens
`strlen`	find the length of a string
`strxfrm`	string transformation
String Routines in `stdlib.h`	
Name	*Purpose*
`strtod`	convert a string of digits to double
`strtol`	convert a string of digits to `long int`
`strtoul`	convert a string of digits to `unsigned long int`

The following example uses some of these functions. Refer to your compiler manual for further information on these routines. All except the last three functions are

declared in the header string.h. The last three are declared in stdlib.h. You
should #include these headers as appropriate. Note that to use some of these, you
will need to know about pointers, which will be introduced in Chapter 7.

```
/* demonstrate some library string routines */

#include <stdio.h>
#include <string.h>

main()
{
        char name[50];
        char name1[10] = "abcd";
        char name2[10] = "xyz";
        char name3[10];

        int i;

        puts("Please enter a name: ");
        gets(name);
        printf("The name >%s< is %u characters long\n",
                name, strlen(name));

        if ((i = strcmp(name, "JOHN")) == 0)
                puts("I see your name is JOHN\n");
        else if (i < 0)
                printf("%s < JOHN, alphabetically\n", name);
        else
                printf("%s > JOHN, alphabetically\n", name);

        printf("\nname1 contains >%s<\n", name1);
        strcat(name1, name2);
        printf("name1 now contains >%s<\n", name1);

        strcpy(name3, name1);
        printf("\nname3 now contains >%s<\n", name3);
}
```

An example of the output is:

```
Please enter a name:
Jack
The name >Jack< is 4 characters long
Jack > JOHN, alphabetically

name1 contains >abcd<
name1 now contains >abcdxyz<

name3 now contains >abcdxyz<
```

The functions `puts` and `gets` are library routines (declared in `stdio.h`) that put and get strings, respectively. They read and write from standard input and standard output. Function `puts` writes out its string argument until it finds a `'\0'` terminator. Then it appends a new-line. `gets` reads characters into its array argument until a new-line is detected. This new-line is not read into the array; instead, a `'\0'` is appended. Note that `gets` is not limited in how many characters it will read. To restrict the number read, you must use `fgets` instead. (This reads from a file, so to read from standard input, you specify the special file called `stdin`, defined in `stdio.h`.)

Function `strlen` returns an unsigned integer value, so we use an edit mask of `%u` with `printf`. Note that this example is not completely portable because `strlen` is permitted to return an `unsigned long`, in which case, a mask of `%lu` would be needed. (Actually, `strlen` returns type `size_t`, an implementation-defined type defined in `stddef.h`.)

Function `strcmp` (and `strncmp`) returns an `int` having a value of zero, less than zero or greater than zero depending on whether string 1 is equal to, less than or greater than string 2. In this case, we do the comparison, store the result in `i` and then test `i` against zero. The grouping parentheses are needed to get the desired operator precedence.

Notice that in our example (run on an ASCII machine) Jack is greater than JOHN because the lowercase a has a higher value than O. However, JACK would test less than JOHN on this system.

Function `strcat` appends `name2` to the end of `name1`, overwriting `name1`'s trailing `'\0'` in the process and adding a new trailing `'\0'`. It is the programmer's responsibility to ensure that `name1` has sufficient allocated space to accommodate the string being concatenated with it.

Function `strcpy` copies the whole of `name1` to `name3`. Again, `name3` must be large enough to accommodate all of `name1` including its trailing `'\0'`, which is also copied.

Take care when using the string functions; some of them require both source and destination string arguments. In such cases, the destination argument is the first one specified.

The following two calls to `strcpy` are quite different:

```
strcpy(array, "Blue");
strcpy("Blue", array);
```

The second example is a recipe for disaster because not only are we copying the arguments the wrong way around, but if string literals are stored in a read-only data area, a fatal run-time error will result. The problem is worse if strings are writable because we would not be alerted—we simply would overwrite all or part, or even beyond, the string.

To handle `strlen` in a completely portable manner, use something like this:

```
/* portable strlen usage and display */

#include <stdio.h>
#include <string.h>

main()
{
        char name[50];
        unsigned long length;

        puts("Please enter a name: ");
        gets(name);
        length = strlen(name);   /* cause conversion if needed */
        printf(">%s< is %lu characters long\n", name, length);
}
```

Since we know `strlen` returns an unsigned integral type, we assign that value to an `unsigned long int`, the largest unsigned integral type possible. Once we know for sure we have an `unsigned long int`, we can reliably display it with `printf` using `%lu`. (This may seem a bit messy, but it's trivial compared to some of the other things you need to do to get very portable code.)

3.6   Omitting the First Dimension

In certain circumstances, the first dimension can be omitted from an array definition or declaration. For example:

```
/* omitting the first dimension */

main()
{
        int vals[] = {1, 2, 3, 4, 5};
        long tab[][3] = {
                {1, 2},
                {4, 5}
        };
        char name1[] = "Jackson";
        char name2[4] = "Jack";
}
```

Provided the compiler can deduce the size of the omitted dimension, no error results. In any case, an initialization list is required. In the case of `vals`, five initializers are seen, so the dimension becomes five. In the case of `tab`, two subinitializer lists are seen, indicating there are two rows, so the first dimension becomes two. Three columns are defined even though only the first two are explicitly initialized. `name1` is dimensioned to eight, the length of the string `"Jackson"` plus the trailing `'\0'`. In the case of `name2`, there is both a dimension and an initializer. However, the number of characters in `"Jack` is five if you include the trailing `'\0'`. When written this way, the `'\0'` is ignored, resulting in the array `name2` not being a `'\0'`-terminated string.

3.7 The sizeof Operator

In some applications, the size of one array is proportional to the size of another array or variable. For example, we may have three arrays, all of which must be the same size, yet of different type. Or, perhaps, a second array must be three elements longer than the first. Another example occurs when you need to process every element in an array, yet you don't wish to hard-code the number of elements to process because that requires more changes if the array size is altered. In any case, C provides the capability to determine the amount of storage allocated to any data object. Not only that, but it calculates it at compile-time and produces a value suitable for use as a compile-time integer constant. For example:

```
/* introduce sizeof */

#include <stdio.h>

main()
{
        int values[] = {1, 23, 54, 67, 87};
        int i;

        for (i = 0; i < sizeof(values)/sizeof(values[0]); ++i)
                printf("values[%d] = %d\n", i, values[i]);
}
```

produces the output:

```
values[0] = 1
values[1] = 23
values[2] = 54
values[3] = 67
values[4] = 87
```

If the number of elements in values changes over the life of the program, you simply add or remove initializer values (or use an explicit dimension). The range of the for loop is recalculated when the program is compiled next.

The sizeof operator can be used either with an expression of any type (except void) or with any actual type declaration (again, except with void). In the above example, sizeof(i) gives the same result as sizeof(int). sizeof traffics in a byte count with sizeof(char) being one by definition. Therefore, by definition, sizeof(array)/sizeof(one element) gives us the number of elements in that array, regardless of array element type. Note that sizeof is a compile-time operator and in that respect is most unusual. First, it's an operator, yet it has a name rather than a punctuation character representation. Second, the sizeof operator is evaluated at compile-time rather than run-time. This gives rise to many interesting and useful possibilities for sizeof expressions. For example, they can be used as array dimension specifiers.

```
main()
{
        char c[] = "abcdef";
        int i[sizeof(c)];
        double d[sizeof(c) + 4 + sizeof(i)/sizeof(i[0])];
}
```

Since `sizeof(char)` is one, we do not need to use `sizeof(c) / sizeof(c[0])`. Array `d` is dimensioned to be the number of elements in `c` plus the number in `i` plus four.

The unary operator `sizeof` has very high precedence. In fact, it has higher precedence than all binary operators. For it to work, the size of an object must be able to be calculated at compile-time.

Consider the following:

```
/* non-portable usage of sizeof */

#include <stdio.h>

main()
{
        double d[10];
        int i[2][3][4];

        printf("sizeof d = %u\n", sizeof(d));
        printf("sizeof i = %u\n\n", sizeof(i));
        sub(d, i);
}

sub(d, i)
double d[10];
int i[2][3][4];
{
        printf("sizeof d = %u\n", sizeof(d));
        printf("sizeof i = %u\n", sizeof(i));
}
```

The output produced on one machine was:

```
sizeof d = 80
sizeof i = 48

sizeof d = 4
sizeof i = 4
```

Clearly, `sub` disagrees with `main` about the size of the two arrays. The program was compiled on a PC with 16-bit `int`s using the large memory model in which addresses are four bytes long. The total size of 10 eight-byte `double`s gives 80 for `d`; 24 `int`s of two bytes each gives 48.

When arrays are used as arguments to functions, their address is passed. No information about their dimension or type is passed, only the address. As such, in `sub`, the expressions `d` and `i` as used with `sizeof` represent the address of the first element in their respective arrays. Since each address takes four bytes to represent, the value 4 is displayed. Even though we have explicitly dimensioned the arrays in the formal argument list, C still treats d and i as addresses rather than arrays. Note, though, that we still can manipulate d and i as arrays in sub, simply by subscripting them as appropriate. Only the array property of the expressions d and i has been lost across the function call.

One of the most under-utilized capabilities of the C language is `sizeof`. Master it and use it as often as you can. When writing code that is to port across dissimilar environments, you may benefit greatly by using `sizeof`.

Just as `strlen`'s return type was implementation-defined, so is the type of `sizeof`. Both have the type `size_t` as declared in `stddef.h`. Because `sizeof` is an operator, a `sizeof` expression must have a type and to display a value of this type, we must know what that type is. Traditionally, C programmers dealt with `strlen` and `sizeof` as though they produced `int` values. While this works on many implementations, it will not work on all.

First, a size never needs to be signed since you can't have a size less than zero. Therefore, `sizeof` should return an unsigned integral type. The possible types, therefore, (if we are to have any useful sizes) are `unsigned int` and `unsigned long`. To display the value of a `sizeof` expression in a completely portable way, then, we must use a technique similar to that shown earlier for `strlen`. That is, assign (or cast) the `sizeof` expression to an `unsigned long int` and display that with `printf` using `%lu` as follows:

```
/* portable usage of sizeof */

#include <stdio.h>

main()
{
        double d[10];
        unsigned long size = sizeof(d);
        unsigned long numelem = sizeof(d)/sizeof(d[0]);

        printf("sizeof d = %lu\n", size);
        printf("# of elements = %lu\n", numelem);
}
```

which produced the following output:

```
sizeof d = 80
# of elements = 10
```

Strictly speaking, `sizeof` can be used without parentheses around its operand provided the operand is an expression. If it is a type declaration, the parentheses are required. Since parentheses around an expression (when used with `sizeof`) are redundant, they don't hurt. Therefore, you always should use them so you don't have to remember whether they are required or not—they are always acceptable.

Exercise 3-7*: Define a 5x30 `char` array and initialize it with the names of five people. Then loop through the array displaying the row number and name contained in that row, using `printf` and `%s`.

Exercise 3-8*: Modify the previous exercise to read the five names from the keyboard using `gets`. (Remember, a two-dimensional array is an array of arrays.)

Exercise 3-9*: An `int` array has 10 elements. Initialize each element as follows: -20, 52, 33, 0, -5, 74, -6, 1, 9, -4 and calculate the average of the values (integral average is sufficient). How can this solution be made general to handle an arbitrary size array? How can you calculate and display the floating-point average to two decimal places?

Exercise 3-10: Define an array as `int i[5, 6];` instead of `int i[5][6];` and see what error message you get. Unless your compiler is very conscientious with its messages, the result may not be particularly meaningful. (As it happens, the comma in the first case is behaving as the special comma operator and the left-hand operand of such an operator may not be a compile-time constant.) This kind of error can happen easily since other languages use a similar notation.

3.8 Chapter Summary

- C has no means of dealing with character strings directly. They are implemented as arrays of `char` having a terminating null character (with value `'\0'`). C provides a way to manipulate an array as a whole. To do this, you must call a library or user-written function.

- The `#define` preprocessor directive assigns a string "value" to an identifier. Each occurrence of this identifier in the source file is replaced by the string assigned to by the preprocessor.

- There are two aspects of arrays in C that are different from array definition and use in other languages. First, the `[` and `]` characters are used when declaring a dimension and specifying a particular element. Second, array elements begin at subscript zero rather than one.

- C provides no subscript range-checking at run-time.

- C allows character arrays of arbitrary length and, while it is possible to store a 20-character name in an array of 20 `char`, many of the string routines in the standard library will fail if the array is not explicitly terminated with a `'\0'` character whose binary value is zero. Therefore, space should be allocated for 21 characters.

- Unless a routine knows how long a string is, it must search for the terminating `'\0'` in order to know it has processed the complete string. String lengths are not stored by the compiler and must be calculated at run-time.

- A string can be displayed on standard output by `printf` using an edit mask of `%s`. This prints characters from the string until a null character is found.

- When the compiler comes across a string literal (a token of the form `"..."`), it stores it as an array of `char` which is initialized with the characters contained between the quotes. An extra character is automatically appended containing `'\0'`.

- `'Y'` is a constant of type `int` and the value of Y in the machine's character set (89 in ASCII) while `"Y"` is a string of length one, stored as a character array of length two. `"Y"` is actually represented as the two characters Y \0.

- `#include <ctype.h>` must be used when you refer to certain library character-handling routines. This set of routines is divided into two main groups: those used to test if a character has a specific attribute (such as being alphabetic, lowercase or numeric), which has names of the form is*xxxxx*; and those that convert a character to some other value (such as to upper- or lowercase), which has names of the form to*xxxxx*.

- Any basic data type supported by C can be used as the type of an array. However, the null character terminator convention only applies to arrays of `char` because there is no reserved (and portable) way of representing "special" values of any other data type.

- Multidimensional array declarations and references have the general form `array[i]` `[j] [...] [k]`. That is, in `int c[2][3][4]`, c is declared to be an array of two vectors, each of which is an array of three vectors, each of which is an array of four `int`s.

- In C, multidimensional arrays are stored in row-major order.

- Initializer lists for arrays must include the list-delimiting braces, even if the list contains only one expression.

- Prior to ANSI C, automatic arrays could not have initializer lists.

- It is permissible to initialize a `char` array with a string expression rather than a brace-delimited set of integer expressions.

- Provided an automatic array initializer list contains at least one expression, any trailing, uninitialized array elements take on the value zero. Otherwise, the initial values are undefined.

- The standard C library includes a family of routines capable of manipulating `'\0'`-terminated arrays of characters. All such function names have the general form str*xxx*. Most of them are declared in `string.h`, a few in `stdlib.h`.

- The functions `puts` and `gets` are library routines (declared in `stdio.h`) that put and get strings, respectively. They read and write from standard input and standard output.

- In certain circumstances, the first dimension can be omitted from an array definition or declaration.

- The `sizeof` operator produces the size, in bytes, of any type or expression, as a compile-time constant integer expression that is unsigned.

Chapter 4

Functions

Functions are the backbone of C programs. Each program must contain at least one function you have written yourself. You may write other functions as well and/or invoke those from the standard C run-time library or from other libraries you have written or purchased. In fact, functions permit you to extend the standard C environment to the extent that, with care, you even can replace standard run-time library routines with your own versions.

In C, the function provides the same capability that often is provided by three different constructs in other languages. Specifically, a C function can be the main program, a subroutine with zero or more arguments and no return value and a (traditional) function having zero or more arguments and a return value. And regardless of which it is being used for, each function has exactly the same structure and is invoked the same way.

4.1 Introduction

As we have seen, a function is called by naming it along with an argument list. Although the argument list can be empty, the parentheses surrounding the list must be present. There is no CALL verb to distinguish between traditional subroutines and functions, so it is the programmer's responsibility to use a function in the correct manner.

Unfortunately, the number of arguments passed is not guaranteed to be stored or made available to the called function, even though they are on some implementations (such as DEC's VAX).

The following example shows a function `slen` being called from `main`. `slen` is given a nul-terminated array of characters as an argument and computes the number of characters in the array up to but not including the terminating `'\0'`. The standard library contains such a routine, called `strlen`. However, it behaves slightly different from `slen`.

```
/* communicating between functions */

#include <stdio.h>

main()
{
        int slen(char string[]);

        printf("Length of string is %d.\n", slen("Hi there!"));
}

int slen(char string[])
{
        int i = 0;      /* string length */

        while (string[i] != '\0')
                ++i;

        return (i);
}
```

The output produced is:

```
Length of string is 9.
```

When an array is passed to a function, it is passed by address. That is, the memory address of its first element is passed. There is no way to pass the whole array to the function by value. Passing by address also is called *Call by Reference*. Since a literal string is treated by the compiler as an array of char with a terminating nul, string literals are passed to functions by address.

Function main invokes two functions—printf and slen. The formatted output function printf is contained in the standard run-time library and slen is contained in the same source code file as main. C allows functions to be in the same source file, in separate files or some combination thereof. However, a function's definition can not be inside another function's definition. That is, functions can not be nested. Each function definition is mutually exclusive of all other function definitions. If the compiler comes across a function call and it has never seen a declaration for that function, it assumes the function returns a value of type int.

In this example, we explicitly declare the type of slen as being int using the declaration:

```
int slen(char string[]);
```

The int keyword declares slen to have that type, and the parentheses indicate that slen is a function. That is, slen is a function that returns an int value. The information inside the parentheses indicates the number and type of arguments that slen expects to be passed—in this case, one argument of type "array of char." Note that we did not specify the size of the array because arrays are passed by address. slen can handle char arrays of any size. This form of declaration is known as a function prototype and is a relatively new addition to C. (It was adopted from the C++ language by the ANSI C Committee in 1984.) However, the majority of mainstream compilers currently support it. The name `string`, present in the dummy argument list, is optional—it has absolutely no affect and can be omitted. It is there to show where an identifier would go if this were an actual data declaration. If you use a name here, it does not conflict with identifiers, outside the prototype, that have the same name.

Prior to prototypes being available, the declaration would have been written as:

```
int slen();
```

indicating that the number and type of arguments expected was unknown. More likely, since the default type of a function not previously declared is `int`, `slen` would not have been declared at all. The advantage of the new style is that the compiler can detect attempts to pass the wrong number of arguments or arguments of incompatible type.

Function `slen` has only one argument, the string whose length is to be determined. The function returns an `int` value, which is the length it computes. The text `slen("Hi there!")` is used to call `slen`. This piece of text is an expression and, as such, it has a type and value. We already have said its type is `int`. Its value is whatever the function `slen` returns. Therefore, the expression `slen("Hi there!")` can be used anywhere a run-time `int` expression is permitted. (For example, it could be used to initialize an automatic variable.) In this example, the value is passed on to `printf` which interprets it (correctly) as an `int` and displays it as a decimal number.

At first glance, `printf` seems to be able to handle a variable number of arguments. It can; however, it relies completely on the contents of its first argument in determining the number and type of any other arguments following that one. Users of `printf`, therefore, must ensure that the number and type of edit masks match the remaining arguments. If you specify more arguments than are expected by `printf`, the excess arguments are ignored. If, however, the type of an argument passed does not match the type expected, or you pass insufficient arguments, the behavior is undefined.

In `slen`, the formal argument `string` must be declared appropriately so its type will be known. No storage is allocated for this dummy argument within `slen` since a copy of it was pushed on the stack. (Some implementations do not use the run-time stack for function argument lists or automatic variables. For the purposes of this book, assume they do, just for the sake of simplicity. Whether they do or not is an implementation issue and has no affect on a Standard C program.)

Function `slen` is defined beginning with the following line:

```
int slen(char string[])
```

This indicates that the function returns an `int` and expects one argument of type "array of `char`". That is, it expects to be passed the address of the first `char` in an array of `char`. No array dimension is necessary and, if one is present, it is ignored. (If present, it must be a constant integer expression with a value greater than zero.) If the function has type `int` (as in this case), the keyword `int` can be (and usually is) omitted since it is the default function return type.

The variable names `string` and `i` used by `slen` are local to `slen` and are not accessible to any other function, including `main`. `i` is incremented for each character we find before the trailing `'\0'` is detected. Therefore, an empty string (written as `""`) would have a length of zero.

The length that `slen` computes is returned to `main` by the `return` statement. The value returned is an expression whose type must be compatible with that defined for the function, in this case int. If an expression of another arithmetic type were used, it would be converted to int before actually being returned. The parentheses around the return expression are redundant grouping parentheses—they are not required to be there.

The while construct properly handles strings of any length including one containing only a '\0'. Consider the case where the string passed to slen is missing its terminating '\0'. slen will keep on incrementing i until it finds a '\0'. In doing so, the value of i may overflow; that is, i may be incremented until it exceeds its maximum possible value. On 16-bit 2's complement machines such as the PDP-11 and IBM-PC, the maximum possible size of i is 32767. Numeric overflow may result in the program aborting, or worse, it may "roll over" i to a negative number. In the latter case, incrementing 32767 by 1 gives i a value of -32768, a very strange length indeed. (Some operating systems may have the ability to detect and report integer overflow.)

It would make more sense for i to be an unsigned int because a length can never be less than zero. However, such a change would not necessarily solve the missing '\0' problem since i would still "roll over" if it reached 65535, for example. The library function strlen (declared in string.h), returns an unsigned integer type that is implementation-defined. It returns either an unsigned int or unsigned long depending on the largest string the implementation can handle. This is achieved by having strlen have a return type of size_t, an implementation-defined type.

Another (and likely) problem is that a trailing '\0' will never be found and the program will attempt to access a location outside its address space. On multiuser systems, this is prohibited and generally results in some kind of fatal memory access violation error.

ANSI C's introduction of prototypes also provided a new way of defining functions. Prior to this, functions were defined differently. For example:

```
int slen(char string[])
{
        /* ... */
}
```

would have been written as:

```
int slen(string)
char string[];
{
        /* ... */
}
```

The list of formal argument identifiers was separated from their declarations. As with the new format, the argument names must appear in the same order in which they are passed (assuming there is more than one argument). However, the order in which the type declarations occur is immaterial. Note also that the argument declarations go after the function definition and before the opening brace of the function's body.

If you look closely at the declaration and definition of slen, you will see they are identical except that the declaration has a trailing semicolon. This is no accident. In fact, this is why ANSI C permits the dummy argument names in prototypes, just so it is very easy to generate a prototype from a function definition. Note that the name string in the declaration has absolutely no relationship to the identifier of the same name within `slen`.

At the time of this writing, it is likely that 95+ percent of all existing C source is written using the pre-ANSI method of declaring and defining functions. The new style has been designed so that, with care, the old and new styles can be mixed, even in the same function. However, ANSI C has declared the old styles to be *obsolescent*. That is, it is possible that support for them will be dropped in future versions of the Standard. While this is unlikely to happen, it does indicate the importance the ANSI C Committee places on the superiority of the new style. As a member of that committee I agree with their stance, so prototype style function declarations and definitions will be used in all future examples.

4.2 Functions without Return Values

A function need not return a value when the form `return;` is used instead of `return` *exp*;. If a function does not contain a `return` statement (as is typically the case with `main`), the final closing brace is an implicit `return;`. If no expression is specified with the `return` statement or there is no `return` statement, an undefined value will be returned. Therefore, don't try to make sense out of the value returned by a function if it doesn't return one explicitly. For example:

```
/* incorrectly using a "return" value */

#include <stdio.h>

main()
{
        int f1(int);
        long f2(int);

        printf("values are %d, %ld\n", f1(10), f2(20));
}

int f1(int i)
{
        return;
}

long int f2(int j)
{
}
```

produced the following output:

```
values are 0, 927465472
```

The values 0 and 927465472 are the values found in the locations where the return values were expected. However, because no values were explicitly returned from either `f1` or `f2`, bogus values result.

If a function does not return a value, declare it explicitly by using the `void` keyword as follows:

```
main()
{
        void f(int);
        int i;

        f(10);          /* OK */
        i = f(10);      /* error */
}

void f(int i)
{
        return 10;      /* error */
}
```

If a function is declared to be `void`, it is an error to try to assign its "returned" value because there is none. Likewise, if a function is defined as `void`, it is an error to try to return a value from it. The `void` type can be applied only to functions—it is illegal to declare a data object of `void` type.

4.3   Calling by Value

In C, all scalar arguments are *passed by value*. That is, their value (rather than their address) is passed to the called function.

Called functions treat arguments passed by value as automatic variables; for example:

```
#include <stdio.h>

main()
{
        int i = 100;
        void sub(int);

        printf("i before call = %d\n", i);
        sub(i);
        printf("i after call  = %d\n", i);
}

void sub(int n)
{
        n = 5;
}
```

which produces the output:

```
i before call = 100
i after call  = 100
```

When i is used as an argument to the function **sub**, its value is passed, not its address. A copy of i is pushed onto the stack and made available to **sub** as an automatic variable. When **sub** returns, the copy is removed from the stack. Because **sub** does not know the address of the original i, it can not alter its value. It only can modify its own private, temporary copy of that variable.

It is possible to alter the value of a scalar argument, provided it is passed by address rather than by value; however, this involves the use of pointers and will be discussed in Chapter 7. Note that arrays always are passed by address and can not be passed by value.

4.4 Calling by Reference

Arrays always are passed by reference (address) and their elements can be modified directly by the called function. The function **slen** used earlier has one argument which is a **char** array. The address of this array is passed to **slen**. No information about the size or type of the array is passed with the address.

The following function, **compress**, has one argument which is a **char** array. Because the address of the array is passed, **compress** directly can modify the elements of the array by squeezing out spaces and tabs and adding a new end-of-string terminator.

```
void compress(char string[])
{
        int i, j;

        for (i = 0, j = 0; string[i] != '\0'; i++) {
                if (string[i] == ' ' || string[i] == '\t')
                        continue;

                string[j++] = string[i];
        }
        string[j] = '\0';
}
```

A word of warning with **compress**: Don't call it using a literal string argument as in **compress("ab cd")** because an implementation may store strings in read-only memory locations. Since **compress** writes back into its argument, it requires it to be stored in a read-write area of memory.

Scalars also can be passed by address by using the address-of operator. This will be covered in Chapter 7.

Exercise 4-1: If your system supports exit status codes being returned from programs when they terminate, see what value results when you return from **main** by dropping through the closing brace (no return value is supplied) and when you explicitly return with a value. What range of values can your system handle? Is the value returned the same as that used as the argument given to a call to **exit**? (It should be.)

Exercise 4-2: Does your compiler keep track of the number and size of arguments passed and can this information be accessed by the called function?

Exercise 4-3: In every call we have made to `printf`, we have never bothered to inspect its return value, assuming it has one. Check out the prototype for `printf` in `stdio.h` and see what `printf`'s return type is. What is the purpose of the return value? (Check your library documentation.)

Exercise 4-4: ANSI C requires a conforming implementation to support at least 31 arguments in function declarations and definitions. How many does your compiler support?

Exercise 4-5*: Write a function called `copy` that copies one character array to another. It expects two arguments, both `char` arrays, and it has no return value. Assume that the source array is terminated by a `'\0'` (as is the case with a string literal).

The calling sequence for `copy` is:

```
copy(destination, source);
```

This is the same sequence as for the library routine `strcpy` (declared in `string.h`).

Write a `main` program to test `copy` by calling it with various length strings, including an empty string. Use `printf` with `%s` to display the copied strings.

Exercise 4-6*: Write a function called `power` which takes two arguments, both of which have type `int`. The first one is a value and a second is a power to which the value is to be raised. For example, `power(i, j)` should return an `int` value representing i to the power j. Assume j is non-negative and that 0 to the power 0 is one (it is really undefined). Write a `main` program that loops for i = 5 to -5 and j = 0 to 3 and prints the value returned from `power` for each i and j combination. Put the output in a tabular form, one line for each value of i. (There is no exponentiation operator in C. Also, the standard header `math.h` has a function called `pow`, a `double` version of our routine `power`.)

4.5   Recursion

A function that calls itself directly or indirectly is said to be *recursive*. Like PASCAL, C allows recursive calls. Recursive code usually is easier to read and write than non-recursive code, although it doesn't necessarily increase efficiency or decrease storage requirements. As it happens, most programmers probably never will have the need to write recursive code. However, one common use for it is in implementing b-trees and binary trees in sorting and searching algorithms.

Many programmers get confused when introduced to recursion. It really does not involve any magic, so if you have a problem understanding the function `outdec` below, work through several iterations of it with pencil and paper until you are convinced that you understand it.

```
/* recursion example which prints integers using
both printf and the recursive function outdec */

#include <stdio.h>

main()
{
        int i;
        void outdec(int);

        printf("outdec\tprintf\n\n");
        for (i = -150; i <= 150; i += 50) {
                outdec(i);
                printf("\t%d\n",i);
        }
}

void outdec(int number)
{
        int val;

        if (number < 0) {
                putchar('-');
                number = -number;
        }

        if ((val = number/10) != 0)
                outdec(val);

        putchar((number % 10) + '0');
}
```

The output produced is:

```
outdec  printf

-150    -150
-100    -100
-50     -50
0       0
50      50
100     100
150     150
```

Once outdec knows it has a negative integer to print, it displays a minus sign and thereafter treats the number as positive. (This is a limitation, because on a twos-complement machine, outdec could not handle the largest negative integer. That number has no positive equivalent, so the statement number = -number; would produce an undefined result. Although outdec clearly has a limitation, it amply demonstrates the idea of recursion.)

Unfortunately, integer-to-character display conversion routines such as outdec make the low-order digits available before the high-order ones, although they must be printed in the opposite order. Therefore, the low-order digits must be stored for later use. Each time `outdec` is invoked, a different version of the automatic variable `val` is created on the stack.

The symbol `%` is the modulus binary operator. The expression (`number % 10`) produces the remainder when `number` is divided by 10. The `%` operator may be used only with integer operands.

The construct `'0'` represents the character zero in the machine's character set. In ASCII, `'0'` is represented by the number 48 and (`number % 10`) + `'0'` produces an `int` value corresponding to one of the characters `'0'` through `'9'`, depending on the value of `number`.

> **Exercise 4-7*:** Implement a recursive function `fact` which takes an `unsigned int` argument and returns an `unsigned long int` having the value of the factorial of the input argument. Test it with arguments of 0–10. What are the limitations of `fact` on your implementation? How deep can you recurse before you run out of stack space?

4.6   Some Simple Functions

In Chapter 3, we learned about a number of library routines declared in the header `ctype.h`. Below, we will look at the source code for several of these functions in order to introduce new concepts and operators.

Let's begin with `isdigit`. It takes an `int` argument that represents the character to be tested, and returns a true (non-zero) or false (zero) value depending on whether or not the input argument is a decimal digit.

A programmer new to C might program this function as follows:

```
isdigit(int c)
{
        if (c >= '0' && c <= '9')
                return (1);      /* true */
        else
                return (0);      /* false */
}
```

This version works correctly and it also will look very familiar to programmers experienced in other common languages. However, it does generate more code than is necessary by having an `if` test and two possible ways to exit. Most important, it does not take full advantage of the capabilities of C.

Consider the following version of this function:

```
isdigit(int c)
{
        return (c >= '0' && c <= '9');
}
```

The function is reduced to being trivial and is an example of the brevity possible in C. It also demonstrates the style that experienced C programmers prefer. We normally are used to seeing relational operators such as `>=` and `<=` in `if` and `while` constructs. However, they can appear in any expression in C since such expressions have `int` values. Consider the case where `c` has the value of the character `'A'`. The return expression then becomes (`'A' >= '0' && 'A' <= '9'`) which is the same as (TRUE && FALSE) which equals FALSE. This version needs only one `return` statement and no `if` test. It simply relies on the truth value of the expression being returned. Most of the other `ctype` functions can be implemented in a similar manner.

Let's look at a version of `isascii`, a function commonly supplied with ASCII-based implementations. (It is not part of ANSI C because that standard is not character-set specific.)

```
isascii(int c)
{
        return (c >= 0 && c <= 0x7F);
}
```

The value of an `int` represents an ASCII character only if its low-order seven bits are significant; that is, it has a value between zero and 127 decimal (7F hexadecimal). Why, then, do we check for `c >= 0`? Why not simply use `return (c <= 0x7F);`? Well, if we omit the zero test, we are assuming that characters are represented as unsigned values. And, while this is true for all ASCII characters, it is not true for extended characters. For example, we must make sure that `isascii` behaves correctly when we call it with the character value `'\200'`. While such a character can be stored in an eight-bit byte, it is implementation-defined as to whether or not that byte is signed. That is, the value can be represented as either +128 or -128, at the implementer's pleasure. Therefore, if we are to write portable code, we must take care of the possibility of negative characters.

To implement `tolower`, a function that returns the lowercase equivalent of its input character, we could use the following code:

```
/* This is an ASCII-specific version */

tolower(int c)
{
        if (isupper(c))
                return (c | 0x20);      /* set bit 5 */
        else
                return (c);
}
```

The algorithm here is that if the input character is an uppercase letter, we return the lowercase equivalent (without modifying the incoming argument); otherwise, we return the same value passed in. For the ASCII character set, the cheapest way to convert from one case to the other is to set or clear the sixth bit. (Setting it converts uppercase to lowercase, and clearing converts lowercase to uppercase.)

The token `|` is the bitwise inclusive OR operator. `0x20` is a hexadecimal constant whose binary value is 100000 and (`c | 0x20`) causes the sixth bit in `c` to be set to a 1. On many machines, bits are numbered from right to left starting from 0. Therefore, the sixth bit is bit number 5.

The `|` operator should not be confused with the logical OR operator `||`. The `|` operator can be used only with integer operands and results in an integer value, whereas `||` can be used with any type of scalar operand and returns an `int` value of either 0 or 1.

An even simpler version is possible using the *conditional operator*, as follows:

```
/* This is an ASCII-specific version */

tolower(int c)
{
        return (isupper(c) ? (c | 0x20) : c);
}
```

The conditional operator consists of the two characters ? and :; however, they are never written together. This operator is a ternary operator; that is, it has three operands and is the only such operator in C.

The syntax for using it is:

exp1 ? *exp2* : *exp3*

If `exp1` is true, then `exp2` is evaluated; otherwise, `exp3` is evaluated. The value of the whole expression is either `exp2` or `exp3`, which must have either the same or compatible types.

The conditional operator behaves a lot like an `if-else`; however, it has slightly different properties. The most significant difference is that the result of the conditional operator is an expression that has a type and value and so can be used anywhere an expression of that type is required. `if-else` is a language construct and, as such, has no type or value.

Consider the following piece of code:

```
if (i)
        printf("i tests TRUE\n");
else
        printf("i tests FALSE\n");
```

Here, the compiler has to set up and clean up the stack for two separate calls to `printf`, even though only one of them will be called at any time.

By using the conditional operator, we can cause less code to be generated as follows:

```
printf("i tests %s\n", (i ? "TRUE" : "FALSE"));
```

However, in using this approach, we possibly have made the code less readable.

The counterpart to `tolower` is `toupper` which uses the bitwise AND operator. For example:

```
/* This is an ASCII-specific version */

toupper(int c)
{
        return (islower(c) ? (c & ~0x20) : c);
}
```

The token `&` is the bitwise AND operator. In the discussion of `tolower` above, we saw that an ASCII alphabetic character can be converted to uppercase by setting bit 5 to a zero. The expression (c & ~0x20) achieves this. We could have used (c & 0xDF) instead; however, that assumes that the size of a character is eight bits, which isn't always the case. The term ~0x20 will produce the correct bit mask for any size character and is, therefore, machine-independent. As we learned earlier, ~ is the ones-complement (or bit-wise NOT) operator.

Like | and ||, & and && are quite different operators and should not be confused. There also is a bitwise exclusive OR operator ^, a left-shift operator << and a right-shift operator >>. There are compound assignment versions of the shift operators as well.

4.7   Terminal Escape Sequences

Many screen terminals conform to an ANSI Standard set of escape sequences which can be used to manipulate the cursor, set and change display attributes, report cursor position, clear all or parts of the screen, etc. The following functions implement a few of these sequences. However, before you go off and complete the set yourself, you should understand that there is an alternate (and possibly better) way to implement them as macros. This will be discussed further in Chapter 6.

```c
#include <stdio.h>

/* SCR_CUB - Cursor Backward */

void scr_cub(int ncolms)
{
        printf("\033[%dD", ncolms);
}


/* SCR_CUF - Cursor Forward */

void scr_cuf(int ncolms)
{
        printf("\033[%dC", ncolms);
}


/* SCR_CUU - Cursor Up */

void scr_cuu(int nlines)
{
        printf("\033[%dA", nlines);
}


/* SCR_CUD - Cursor Down */

void scr_cud(int nlines)
{
        printf("\033[%dB", nlines);
}
```

```
/* SCR_CUP - Cursor Position. (same as HVP) */

void scr_cup(int line, int colm)
{
        printf("\033[%d;%dH", line, colm);
}


/* SCR_ED - Erase in Display */

void scr_ed(int parm)
{
        printf("\033[%dJ", parm);
}


/* SCR_EL - Erase in Line */

void scr_el(int parm)
{
        printf("\033[%dK", parm);
}


/* SCR_SGR - Set Graphics Rendition */

void scr_sgr(int attrib)
{
        printf("\033[%dm", attrib);
}
```

Some of these functions are meant to handle multiple options. For example, `scr_ed` can be given three legitimate arguments, 0, 1 and 2, which indicate it is to clear to the end of the screen, to the beginning of the screen and clear the whole screen, respectively. However, since `printf` is a complex routine and must do a certain amount of work to find out exactly what it is expected to format, it is more efficient to implement `scr_ed` using `fputs` instead. Since `fputs`' job is to write its text argument out to a file, it doesn't have to decide what to do, it simply does it. (We use `fputs` instead of `puts` because `puts` appends a new-line to the output text, which we don't want. `stdin`, `stdout` and `stderr` are three special files that are always open provided you use `#include <stdio.h>`. They represent the standard input, standard output and standard error files, respectively.)

An alternate version of scr_ed then could be:

```
#include <stdio.h>

void scr_ed(int parm)
{
        static char str[] = "\033[?J";

        str[2] = '0' + parm;
        fputs(str, stdout);
}
```

Given that the int argument passed has the value 0, 1 or 2, the character '0', '1', or '2' is stored in the array str. Similarly, scr_sgr could be modified to use fputs to set the video attributes to bold, underline, blinking, etc.

Clearly, this idea can be extended to implement escape sequences for hardcopy devices. Refer to your corresponding hardware user manual for programming details.

Exercise 4-8: Write a program to determine if a "plain" char object is signed or unsigned.

Exercise 4-9*: Define an unsigned long int called word as having the value 0xF. After each of the following operations, display the value of word using hexadecimal notation. The operations are: Clear the low-order (first) and the third bits, set the fifth and seventh bits, perform an exclusive-OR with the value 060704, and find the ones-complement (in which each zero bit is made a one and vice versa). Each of the operations should modify word permanently. (Note that the operators |, & and ^ can be used as the assignment operators |=, &= and ^=, respectively.)

Exercise 4-10: Compile the two versions of tolower shown above and inspect the code generated by your compiler, assuming it has this facility. Is the version with the conditional operator appreciably smaller or more efficient? At the very least, it should not be larger or less efficient. Also check the code generated for the printf true/false example. The more arguments you give printf, the better the ?: version should be.

4.8   More on Prototypes

One reason we have been referencing stdio.h in every program in which we have used printf is so that the proper declaration for that function is seen by the compiler. That is, the header stdio.h contains a function prototype for printf (as well as all the other standard I/O functions).

If you look at your implementation's version of this header, you will find something like the following (actually, you may find something that looks different, but it will be equivalent):

```
int printf(char format[], ...);
```

Since you can call printf with a different number of arguments each time, it is impossible to state their types in a prototype except for the first, which always must

be an array of `char` that contains the edit masks (if any) and text to be displayed
(if any). To indicate that there may or may not be any more arguments following,
the ellipsis notation (three consecutive periods) is used after the comma following the
last argument of the fixed length argument length. If you call `printf` without having
such a prototype in scope, the compiler may assume `printf` has a fixed argument
list and perform certain optimizations that may prohibit `printf` from working correctly. Always `#include <stdio.h>` when using `printf` (and library I/O routines in
general).

We have used the library routines `getchar` and `putchar`. If these are implemented
as library functions (on some implementations they are implemented using macros
that expand to in-line code), their prototypes should look like the following:

```
int getchar(void);
int putchar(int c);
```

Note the use of the keyword `void` in the prototype for `getchar`. This informs the
compiler that `getchar` expects no argument and should not be called with one. This
is different from `int getchar();` which indicates no information about the expected
argument list. In the latter case, `getchar` could be called with any number and type
of arguments and the compiler would not complain. The use of `void` in this context
is not related to its use as a function return type.

To see how the compiler works with prototypes, let's look at the following program:

```
#include <math.h>

void test()
{
        double d;

/*1*/   d = sqrt(10.0);
/*2*/   d = sqrt();      /* error */
/*3*/   d = sqrt(10,10);/* error */
/*4*/   d = sqrt(10);    /* ?? */
}
```

The standard header `math.h` contains prototypes for all of the math library functions. The prototype for `sqrt` declares `sqrt` to take one `double` argument and return
a `double` value. Therefore, the first call above is compatible with the prototype.
However, calls 2 and 3 are not because one has too few arguments and the other has
too many. Both uses should produce a compilation error.

What happens with the fourth call? Clearly, the numeric literal 10 has type `int`,
yet a `double` is expected by `sqrt`. In the absence of the argument list in the function
declaration, an `int` would be passed and misinterpreted as a `double` by `sqrt`, resulting
in a bug. However, all is well in this case since the prototype causes the `int` argument
to be "widened" to `double`. That is, the value actually passed is the floating-point
equivalent of 10. It does this transparently.

In the case of a **double** argument being given when an **int** is expected, the **double** value first is converted to **int** (with appropriate truncation of the fractional part) before the converted value is passed; for example:

```
main()
{
        void f(int);

        f(10.5);        /* 10 gets passed */
}
```

The complete set of routines declared in **math.h** is as follows. Most of them are recognizable by name. For more information about these functions, consult your run-time library documentation.

math.h **Library Header**	
Name	*Purpose*
acos	Arc cosine
asin	Arc sine
atan	Arc tangent
atan2	Arc tangent of y/x
ceil	Smallest integral value not less than x
cos	Cosine
cosh	Hyperbolic cosine
exp	Exponential
fabs	Absolute value
floor	Largest integral value not greater than x
fmod	Compute a floating-point remainder
frexp	Break a fp number into integer and fraction
ldexp	Multiplies a fp number by a integral power of 2
log	Natural logarithm
log10	Base-ten logarithm
modf	Break a fp number into integer and fraction
pow	Power
sin	Sine
sinh	Hyperbolic sine
sqrt	Square root
tan	Tangent
tanh	Hyperbolic tangent

Since prototypes were invented by the ANSI Committee, most existing C code does not use them. Therefore, new-style function declarations must be able to coexist with old-style declarations if existing code is not to be broken immediately. An old-style function declaration is considered to be a prototype without an argument list. For example, **int f();** declares that function **f** has return type **int** and that no information is known about the argument list, so the compiler can not perform checking.

To indicate that a function has no arguments, and to allow the compiler to police
this, the format int f(void); should be used instead; for example:

```
void sub2(void);

test()
{
        sub2();
        sub2(10);           /* error */
}
```

Now that we have seen the new-style function definitions we can look at the way
a new-style function without arguments should be defined:

```
type sub(void) {...}
```

The keyword void goes in place of the argument list just as it does in the corresponding prototype. Actually, the void keyword can be omitted because the compiler
very quickly realizes that, since no arguments are named, there are none.

4.8.1   Prototypes and Argument Widening

Another potential benefit of prototypes is that they may be used to bypass the default-
widening rules when dealing with function arguments. (Whether or not a prototype
allows the default-widening rules to be overridden is implementation-defined.)

In the following example:

```
void f()
{
        void g();
        char c;
        short s;
        float f;

        g(c, s, f);
}
```

the char c and short int s are both widened to int and the float f is widened
to double before being passed to the function g.

In function g, the argument declarations could be:

```
void g(c, s, f)
char c;
short s;
float f;
{
        /* ... */
}
```

However, if the prototype for function g were:

```
void g(char c, short s, float f);
```

and **g** were defined this way as well, the compiler could bypass the default argument widening rules allowing the conversion overhead to be omitted. This is of particular use to programmers who use **float** instead of **double** and on systems where a subroutine call is needed for argument widening and "unwidening." They no longer need to pay the price of **float/double/float** conversions. (Note that the current **math.h** routines still require **double** arguments, though, since all existing code expects widening to occur during function calls. However, the set of math library function names with a suffix of **f** and **l** is reserved for future use by the Standard so that versions of these routines that take and return **float** and **long double** values, respectively, can be provided.)

Some compilers even may use a composite approach. That is, they might widen **char** and **short** to **int**, yet allow **float** to be passed without widening (VAX C is one such implementation).

When working with implementations that can inhibit default argument-widening, you must take care not to mix both old- and new-style function declarations and definitions when passing values of type **char**, **short** or **float**; for example:

```
/* file main.c */

main()
{
        void f(float f);

        f(1.23);
}

/* file f.c */

void f()
float f;
{
}
```

If **main** and **f** are compiled in separate modules, the call to **f** results in a **float** value being passed. However, since function **f** is defined using the old-style function definition format, it expects a wide type of **double** and, consequently, it misinterprets the value passed to it (assuming, of course, that **float** and **double** have different sizes and/or representations).

While it can be messy, by using the ellipsis specifier, it is possible to have some arguments in a list widened while others in that same list are not. The ellipsis notation causes argument type checking to cease so that any arguments that actually follow will go unchecked. These unchecked arguments are widened as if no prototype were currently in scope. An example of this is a call to **printf**.

Exercise 4-11: Find out if your compiler fully supports function prototypes and new-style function definitions. As well as writing code to use them, you should be able to tell by inspecting the contents of the standard headers. Each function declaration argument list will be empty if prototypes are not supported.

Exercise 4-12: C requires **char**, **short** and **float** arguments to be widened by default when used as function arguments. Call a function

using one of each of these three types and look at the code generated to
see what the cost of this widening is for your hardware. Also write a
function that accepts these three argument types and see what effort is
involved in narrowing them back again.

Exercise 4-13: If your implementation supports prototypes, does it permit some or all of the narrow types to be passed as narrow types without
widening?

4.9   Chapter Summary

- A function can be the main program, a subroutine with zero or more arguments
  and no return value, and a (traditional) function having zero or more arguments
  and a return value.

- A function is called by naming it along with an argument list. Although the argument list can be empty, the parentheses surrounding the list must be present.

- C does not guarantee that the number of arguments passed is stored or made
  available to the called function.

- Functions can not be nested.

- The default type of a function not previously declared is int.

- A function prototype is a function declaration that includes a return type and
  a list of comma-separated types indicating the format of the argument list expected.

- A function definition has the same format as a prototype for that function,
  except that the identifier names in the argument list are not optional as they
  are in a prototype.

- Don't try to make sense out of the value returned by a function if it doesn't
  return one explicitly.

- If a function does not return a value, declare it as void.

- If a function is declared to be void, it is an error to try to assign its "returned"
  value because there is none. Likewise, if a function is defined as void, it is an
  error to try to return a value from it.

- By default, scalar arguments are passed by value and arrays are passed by
  address.

- A function that calls itself directly or indirectly is said to be recursive. C allows
  recursive calls.

- The token % is the modulus binary operator. The expression (number % 10)
  produces the remainder when number is divided by 10, for example.

- The token | is the bitwise inclusive OR operator, & is the bitwise AND operator,
  and ^ is the bitwise exclusive OR operator. The left-shift operator is written
  using << and right-shift as >>, and >>= and <<= are their compound assignment
  counterparts.

- The conditional operator consists of the two characters ? and :; however, they are never written together. This operator is a ternary operator; i.e., it has three operands.

- In a prototype, to indicate there may or may not be any more arguments following a fixed set, the ellipsis notation (three consecutive periods) is used after the comma following the last argument of the fixed length argument length.

- A function prototype having `void` as its argument list expects no argument and should be called with none.

- The standard header `math.h` contains prototypes for all of the math library functions.

- If a function is called with an argument that is not the same type as that declared in the prototype, the value of the argument will be converted provided the two types are assignment-compatible. If not, a compilation error results.

- A prototype may be used to bypass the default-widening rules when dealing with function arguments. However, whether or not an implementation does allow the default-widening rules to be overridden is implementation-defined.

Chapter 5

Identifier Scope and Life

Mastering the type mechanism of C is straightforward. However, coming to grips with the concepts and syntax of scope and life can take some time and practice. While many languages don't provide all of the scope and life capabilities that C does, some languages provide even more. So, depending on your language background, you may be overwhelmed or frustrated.

5.1   Introduction

Apart from type, each identifier declared in a C program has at least two properties: scope and life. The *scope* of an identifier refers to the domain of the program over which that identifier can be directly referenced by name. ANSI C refers to this property as *linkage*. The *life* of an identifier is applicable only to data objects and refers to the time during which an object actually exists. ANSI C refers to an identifier's life as its *storage duration*.

There are three kinds of linkage: external, internal and none. External linkage permits an identifier to be accessed by name from any part of the program in which that identifier has been properly declared. In effect, the identifier is a global symbol that is exported to the linker for final linkage resolution.

An identifier with internal linkage can be accessed only by name from any part of the source file in which it is declared. All references to such identifiers can be resolved by the compiler and, as such, these names are not exported to the linker. Consequently, many identifiers with internal linkage and the same name may exist in a program, provided each is declared in a separate source file (or *translation unit*, as ANSI C calls it). Each such identifier designates a different entity which is accessible from its parent source file only.

An identifier that has neither external nor internal linkage has no linkage. Each declaration of such an identifier refers to a unique entity. Automatic objects are examples.

The storage duration of an identifier directly corresponds to its linkage. An object having external or internal linkage, or having no linkage but has the storage class keyword `static` in its declaration, has static storage duration. Such an object is allocated space and initialized once only before `main` begins execution. Conceptually (and typically), this space is allocated and initialized at compile-time. (C programs running on embedded systems must perform these actions at run-time because they are forever memory-resident.) Such objects retain their value across function calls. They have an initial value of zero if their declaration contains no initialization list.

Any object not having static storage duration has automatic storage duration. Specifically, this applies to all identifiers that have no linkage and do not have the `static` class keyword present in their declarations. These objects can be declared only inside of a function definition and, each time their parent block is entered, a new instance of them is created. If an initialization list is provided, the object is so initialized provided the block is entered normally (by dropping into it). Otherwise, the initial value is undefined. When the block in which the object is declared ends, the storage space is no longer guaranteed to be allocated.

Linkage and storage duration are determined by two things: the presence or absence of a class keyword in a declaration, and whether or not the declaration occurs inside or outside a function definition. For the purposes of this discussion, a declaration occurring outside a function definition will be referred to as an external declaration, while one within a function definition will be called an internal declaration.

The class keywords available in C are `auto`, `register`, `static` and `extern`. Each will be discussed in detail in the following sections. If a declaration contains a class keyword but no type specifier, the type `int` is assumed. For example, `auto i;` is equivalent to `auto int i;`. If the class keyword is omitted, the type must be explicitly stated. If both class and type keywords are present, they can be specified in any order, provided they both come before the identifier being declared. However, you always should place the class keyword first, since ANSI C has declared the placing of it anywhere else obsolescent.

5.2   The `auto` Class

This is the only class we have seen thus far. As shown below, the `auto` keyword is optional. If an internal object declaration has no class keyword, class `auto` is assumed. Since automatic objects can only be declared inside a function definition and `auto` is the default class, this keyword is rarely seen—its use always documents the default behavior.

Some examples of automatic declarations follow:

```
#include <stdio.h>

main()
{
        auto int i;
        auto unsigned long ul = 12345;
        double d;
        void f(void);

        printf("main> i = %d, ul = %lu, d = %e\n", i, ul, d);
        f();
}
```

```
void f(void)
{
        int i = -100;
        unsigned long ul;
        double d = -345.4E-3;

        printf("   f> i = %d, ul = %lu, d = %e\n", i, ul, d);
}
```

The output produced by three different compilers is as follows:

```
main> i = 5200, ul = 12345, d = 7.649152e-056
   f> i = -100, ul = 5454172, d = -3.454000e-001

main> i = 4369, ul = 12345, d = 1.801076e-226
   f> i = -100, ul = 286331153, d = -3.454000e-001

main> i = 3933, ul = 12345, d = 2.679508e-277
   f> i = -100, ul = 10355163, d = -3.454000e-001
```

Both main and f contain three automatic declarations, each occupying a different memory location. All six variables have automatic storage duration and no linkage. In main, only ul is explicitly initialized, so the initial values of i and d are undefined and the three lots of output show different values for these variables. In f, i and d are explicitly initialized, whereas ul is not; this is reflected in the output.

The three variables declared in main are allocated space when main is invoked and they continue to exist until main terminates by dropping through its closing brace (an implied return without a return value). Even though main transfers control to f, all of main's automatic variables remain in existence across the function call.

When f is invoked, space is allocated for its three automatic objects. This space is released when f returns control back to main. The scope of each function's automatic variables is their parent block; however, their life lengths differ. main's variables exist for the duration of the program while f's variables only exist while f is executing.

Because f's variables disappear when f terminates, their addresses should never be passed back to their caller or otherwise used after f has terminated. Such addresses point to where the variables used to exist. Even if these addresses are accessible (they will not be on some machines), their contents are not guaranteed to be kept intact. Returning by reference instead of by value requires some knowledge of pointers. This will be discussed in Chapter 7. Note that automatic variables may be returned by value since this involves returning a copy of them. The copy returned can exist beyond the life of the original automatic variable.

The life and scope of an automatic variable span the same amount of source code— it exists and is visible only in its parent block and any subordinate blocks. As we have seen, a block is a piece of source code, delimited by a pair of braces, occurring inside a function definition. A function contains at least one block, that delimiting its body. As the next program demonstrates, a function may have an unlimited number of blocks, some of which are subordinate to others, and all of which are subordinate to the block enclosing the whole function body:

```
#include <stdio.h>
#include <ctype.h>

main()
{
        int i;
        double d = 10.5;

        while (1) {
                printf("Enter an alphanumeric character: ");
                i = getchar();
                if (isalnum(i))
                        break;

                getchar();        /* ignore new-line terminator */
        }

        printf("B1> i = %c, d = %.2f\n", i, d);

        if (i > 'M') {
                int j = 123;
                int d = 432;

                printf("B2> i = %c, d = %d, j = %d\n", i, d, j);
        }
        else {
                long int i = 675L;
                char d = 'A';

                printf("B2> i = %ld, d = %c\n", i, d);
        }

        printf("B1> i = %c, d = %.2f\n", i, d);
}
```

Some examples of the output are as follows:

```
Enter an alphanumeric character: #
Enter an alphanumeric character: $
Enter an alphanumeric character: A
B1> i = A, d = 10.50
B2> i = 675, d = A
B1> i = A, d = 10.50

Enter an alphanumeric character: Z
B1> i = Z, d = 10.50
B2> i = Z, d = 432, j = 123
B1> i = Z, d = 10.50
```

Throughout this book, blocks will be referred to by number when we wish to reference a particular block within a hierarchy of blocks. If we consider block level 0 to be outside of all functions, then the outermost block of any function is at block level 1. The above example has three blocks at level 2: the body of the `while` loop, and the true and false bodies of the `if` construct. All three of these blocks are mutually exclusive, so only one of them can be in scope at any one time.

C permits declarations to be at the start of any block (including blocks at level 0). No declarations are present in the first level 2 block, but they are in the second and third blocks at that level.

Variables `i` and `d` at level 1 are allocated space and initialized when their parent block is entered; i.e., when `main` begins execution. If the true path of the `if` is taken, two automatic variables `j` and `d` are created and initialized. They exist until that block terminates. We now have two automatic variables called `d`, and they even have different types. While we are within the level 2 block, all expressions containing `d` refer to the inner-most declaration of that identifier, namely to the `int` version initialized to 432. That is, the inner identifier `d` hides the outer one of the same name. (Although such name hiding is possible, it generally is considered bad programming style. It provides no capability, possibly leads to confusion and prohibits access to identifiers declared in outer blocks.) In the `else` block, both of the outer variables `i` and `d` are hidden.

When execution returns to level 1, all references to `i` and `d` again pertain to the variables declared at the level, as shown by the output produced.

The reason we call `getchar` twice is that it typically is implemented using buffered I/O so that it requires a terminating new-line to be entered before the character read is given to the program. In doing so, the input buffer contains both the character entered and the terminating new-line. If the first character is not alphanumeric, the `while` loop causes the next character to be read from the buffer, so if we didn't flush the terminating new-line first, it would be read into `i` the second time, causing `isalnum` to return a value of false. To flush the new-line, we simply read it using `getchar` and throw away the character by ignoring `getchar`'s return value.

We often have seen the use of a block in place of a single statement. However, with the exception of the main body of a function, we have only used blocks to identify the body of a `while`, `for`, `do-while` or `if-else` construct.

It is possible to have a block without it being subordinate to one of these (or any other) language constructs:

```
#include <stdio.h>

main()
{
        int i;
        int j;

        /* ... */
```

```
/* insert some debugging code here -------------------- */
    {
            int temp = i * (j + 6);

            printf("i = %d, j = %d, temp = %d\n",
                    i, j, temp);
    }
/* end of debugging code ------------------------------ */

    /* ... */
}
```

For the most part, opening up an arbitrary block as done in the above example
serves little if any value, unless that block contains one or more declarations. In this
case, we have allocated space for temp and this declaration hides any identifier of the
same name in an outer block. The value of this approach is with debugging. If you
wish to create temporary variables just for local use, it is much easier to create a new
block and declare them at its start. This way, you never need to worry if something
by that name already exists. If it does, it is simply hidden from this block and all
of its subordinate blocks (if any). All of the debugging code and local declarations
are localized which makes it easier to create and remove them during debugging. By
using the appropriate code, the whole debugging block can be ignored by the compiler
without being removed. (If the debugging block contains any comments, it can not
be deactivated by enclosing it in a comment since comments may not be nested. In
such cases, use a conditional compilation directive, as described in Chapter 6.)

Earlier, a reference was made to initialization of automatic storage duration objects
by falling into their parent blocks. It is possible (though not good style) to enter a
block by other than falling into it as follows:

```
main()
{
        int i, j;

        /* ... */

        if (i > 0)
                goto label1;
        else if (i < 0)
                goto label2;

        /* ... */
```

```
            if (j <= 100) {
                    double d = 1.234;

                    /* ... */
label1:
                    /* ... */
label2:
                    /* ... */
            }
}
```

Assuming j is less than or equal to 100, if i is equal to zero, the block body of the second if is entered by dropping into it. If i is positive, the block is entered via the label label1. If i is negative, we enter through label2. Regardless of how we get to be in that block, space will be allocated for the automatic variable d. However, it is only guaranteed to be initialized if we fall into it. Otherwise, the initial value is undefined.

To implement this function, many compilers actually allocate the space for d when main is entered. That is, they allocate it at block level 1, even if the inner block is never executed. However, even if this is the case, the scope of d is still restricted to the block in which its declaration occurs. In fact, a compiler is permitted to allocate all automatic storage for a function at the time that function is entered, rather than doing it a bit at a time when each lower-level block is entered. That is, you are not guaranteed that automatic storage in blocks at the same level in a function shares the same memory locations.

In a recursive function, space is allocated for all automatic variables each time that function is called. Therefore, if a function has been called and it calls itself three times, four different sets of its automatic variables exist simultaneously, with each set only being accessible from that version of the function that created it.

5.3 The register Class

An automatic object declaration may include the register class keyword instead of auto as follows:

```
main()
{
        register long int rli;
        register char rc[10];
        register ri = 100;
        int i;
}
```

Syntactically, register is identical to auto; however, the semantics can be different. register can be applied only to internal declarations and is a hint to the compiler that the object being declared is to be used more heavily than other variables and that the compiler might wish to place that object in some fast memory location such as a machine register. The operative word here is "hint"—the compiler is under no obligation whatsoever. If a compiler can not or will not store a register variable in fast memory, that variable is treated as if it had class auto.

An implementation doesn't need to provide support for `register` other than recognizing it as a legal class keyword and replacing it with `auto`. Many compilers simply ignore the `register` keyword and implement their own register allocation scheme. On the other hand, some compilers document their register allocation algorithm so you can take advantage of it. For example, they may state that they will honor the first two `register` declarations (in lexical order) they see in the source. In the example, this would appear to honor the `register` request for `rli` and `rc`. However, `rc` is an array of 10 char. Many compilers don't have registers that size, in which case, `rc` would be treated as having class `auto` and `ri` would be implemented in a register.

Another issue has to do with the types an implementation actually can store in registers. Typically, signed and unsigned versions of `char`, `short` and `int` should fit into a register for any given implementation. And, depending on the implementation, signed and unsigned `long ints` also may fit. (If not, `rli` in the above example may get class `auto`.) An implementation may choose to use multiple registers to store one object. For example, a 16-bit system may allocate two adjacent 16-bit registers to honor a `register long` request. Machines such as the Cray have a large number of large (64-bit) registers and conceivably could accommodate quite large `register` variables.

Just as an implementation can ignore a `register` request, it also can store an `auto` object in a register. There is no way to tell whether an automatic object was stored in a register without looking at the code generated. Even if it was stored in a register, you have no control over which register actually was used unless the compiler documents otherwise. In short, the `register` class is "syntactic sugar." If it results in register storage, you have gained. If not, you haven't lost anything—it merely is treated like `auto`. In either case, the default value of a `register` class variable is undefined.

The only discernable difference between an `auto` and a `register` variable is that a `register` variable can not be used in any context where its address is required because few machines have general purpose registers which are addressable as data objects.

5.4   Class and Function Arguments

Consider the following function:

```
void f(int i, double d)
{
        int j = 100;
        char c;

        /* ... */
}
```

All four variables declared are local to function `f`. That is, the formal arguments have automatic storage duration. Space for them typically is allocated each time function `f` is called and, often, it is allocated on the run-time stack the same as for variables with `auto` and `register` class.

The formal argument list is not outside and not quite inside the function definition. Just what is the block level of the declarations of `i` and `d`? ANSI C defines them to be at block level 1, the same level as for `j` and `c`. Formal argument declarations, then, really are `auto` declarations, except they can not have initialization lists and space for them is not allocated within `f`.

What happens if an automatic variable in block level 1 has the same name as a formal argument to that function?

```
void g(int i, double d)
{
        int i = 100;
        char d;

        /* ... */
}
```

ANSI C considers the block level of the formal arguments `i` and `d` to be the same as that of any objects in block level 1, so we should get a compilation error. However, prior to ANSI C, some implementations behaved differently. They considered formal arguments to have a block level higher than 1 (somewhere between level 0 and level 1) so that the automatic declarations hid the identifiers of the same name in the argument list. This, of course, was not very helpful because it meant you could never get at the arguments passed in—they always were hidden by the inner names of the same spelling.

As we have seen, the default class of formal arguments is `auto`. However, the `auto` keyword must not actually appear.

Only one class keyword, `register`, actually can appear in a function definition's formal argument list. For example:

```
void f(double d, register int ri)
{
        /* ... */
}
```

As discussed earlier, a compiler need not pay attention to a `register` class request. However, if it cares to honor such a request when compiling this example, the value of `ri` is copied from the stack into a register each time function `f` is called. From then on, all references to `ri` in the function use the register copy rather than the version on the stack. If an argument is passed by address (that is, by reference), a copy of that address is moved to the register. The end result for both calling by value and by address is the same as if the `register` declaration were absent. Of course, a compiler always could choose to put a non-`register` class argument into a register.

Exercise 5-1: Write a `main` function that allocates automatic storage at block levels 1 and 2. Look at the code generated to see if the level 2 storage is allocated when its parent block is executed or when `main` is started up.

Exercise 5-2: Does your compiler document its register allocation scheme? Does it ignore the `register` keyword? How many registers does it have available for such use? What types can be placed in registers? Are multiple registers used for large `register` objects?

Exercise 5-3: Does your compiler always pass arguments on the stack or does it use registers? Perhaps it uses a combination of the two. It is useful to know just how the stack is used, because, on fixed memory

operating (non-virtual) systems, the amount of stack you have available
may be quite limited.

5.5   The static Class and Data Objects

Automatic objects are useful for certain kinds of things; however, sometimes it is
necessary to have a variable that retains its value across function calls. Also, for
objects whose values never change, it is expensive to keep creating and initializing
them every time their parent block is entered, especially for arrays with lengthy
initialization lists. For these situations, static class objects are more appropriate.

Objects with the keyword static in their declarations have static storage duration.
Their linkage can be internal or none depending on whether the declaration is internal
or external to a function definition. Let's begin by looking at static internals—those
static declarations inside a function and having no linkage.

```
#include <stdio.h>

main()
{
        static int si;
        static int sj = 100;

        printf("si = %d, sj = %d\n", si, sj);
}
```

The output is as follows:

```
si = 0, sj = 100
```

As you might expect from an object with static storage duration, its default initial
value is zero. Consider the following object declarations and initialization lists:

```
#include <stdio.h>

main()
{
        int g(void);

        static int sk = 123;
        int j = sk + g();

        printf("sk = %d, j = %d\n", sk, j);
}

g()
{
        return 321;
}
```

The output is:

```
sk = 123, j = 444
```

In this example, `sk` is initialized with a compile-time constant expression. This is a requirement since the initialization may be done at compile-time. However, the initialization of the automatic object `j` is done at run-time and so can involve any run-time calculable expression of compatible type. As shown, this expression involves a function call.

The following program shows the subtle difference between initializers for `static` and automatic objects:

```
void f()
{
        static int s1 = 10;     /* OK */
        int ai = s1;            /* OK */
        static int s2 = ai;     /* error */

        /* ... */
}
```

Because the value of the expression `s1` can be computed at run-time, it is permissible as an initializer for `ai`. However, `s2` must have a constant initializer and the value of the expression `ai` is not known until `f` is executed at run-time. Hence, a compilation error results.

Objects of static storage duration exist for the life of the program, so they retain their value across function calls; for example:

```
#include <stdio.h>

main()
{
        int i;
        void test(void);

        for (i = 1; i <= 5; i++)
                test();
}

void test()
{
        static double sd = 0;

        printf("sd = %.2f\n", sd++);
}
```

which produces the output:

```
sd = 0.00
sd = 1.00
sd = 2.00
sd = 3.00
sd = 4.00
```

All of the internal `static` objects defined above have no linkage— they are local to their parent and subordinate blocks. On the other hand, an external `static` object has internal linkage and can be accessed by name from anywhere in the same source file in which it is declared.

For example:

```
#include <stdio.h>

static i1 = 100;          /* int type implied */
static int i2;

main()
{
        void f(void), g(void), h(void);

        printf("main> i1 = %d, i2 = %d\n", i1, i2);
        f();
        g();
        h();
}

void f()
{
        printf("   f> i1 = %d, i2 = %d\n", i1, i2);
}

void g()
{
        int i1 = -100;

        printf("   g> i1 = %d, i2 = %d\n", i1, i2);
}

void h()
{
        static int i2 = 12345;

        printf("   h> i1 = %d, i2 = %d\n", i1, i2);
}
```

The output is:

```
main> i1 = 100, i2 = 0
   f> i1 = 100, i2 = 0
   g> i1 = -100, i2 = 0
   h> i1 = 100, i2 = 12345
```

The static externals i1 and i2 are accessible by all four functions; however, the automatic variable i1 in **g** hides the external **static** by the same name, while **g** is executing. Similarly, the **static** internal i2 in **h** hides the external **static** i2 within that function.

Since a **static** external has internal linkage, it can not be accessed from other source files; for example:

```
/* source file main.c */

#include <stdio.h>

static double d[] = {1.2, 2.3, 3.4};

main()
{
        void sub(void);

        printf("main> d = %.2f, %.2f, %.2f\n",
                d[0], d[1], d[2]);
        sub();
}
```

```
/* source file sub.c */

#include <stdio.h>

static int si = 32767;
static double d[] = {9.8, 8.7};

void sub()
{
        printf("sub> si = %d\n", si);
        printf("sub> d = %.2f, %.2f\n", d[0], d[1]);
}
```

The output produced is:

```
main> d = 1.20, 2.30, 3.40
sub> si = 32767
sub> d = 9.80, 8.70
```

The **static** array d is not seen outside of main.c. Similarly, the **static** externals defined in sub.c are local to that file. Therefore, different **static** external variables having the same name can coexist provided each is in a different source file.

All of these `static` external examples have the object being declared at the start of the source file, so its name is seen by the whole source file. However, if the object is defined after it is needed, we have to use a different approach.

The following program shows the solution:

```
#include <stdio.h>

extern int k;    /* tentative declaration */

main()
{
        void f(void);

        printf("main> k = %d\n", k);
        f();
}

static int k = 123;      /* actual declaration */

void f()
{
        printf("   f> k = %d\n", k);
}
```

The output is:

```
main> k = 123
   f> k = 123
```

Because k is defined after `main`, `main` can not access k; all variables must be declared before their use. Also, we can not declare k as `static` in two places, because that would cause the compiler to see two definitions for objects of the same name. So, we use the `extern` class keyword. This indicates to the compiler that somewhere "out there" there is a definition for an external `int` object called k. And when the compiler comes across its definition, it is able to resolve the forward reference and k has internal linkage. (Although the `extern` keyword is permissible in such situations, by placing the definition of k ahead of `main`, the forward reference becomes unnecessary. `extern` most often is used with identifiers having external linkage.)

Actually, we have been dealing with objects of static storage duration without knowing it since the early part of this book. When a literal string is seen by the compiler, it allocates space and a trailing `'\0'` for it, and initializes that space with the characters in the string. A literal string is an array of `char` having `static` class. That is, the array space is allocated and initialized prior to program execution.

As to whether or not a literal string is a `static` internal or `static` external object is irrelevant because the sharing of like literal strings is implementation-defined. For example, if the same literal string occurs multiple times within a source file, whether or not all occurences actually refer to the same `char` array or to unique arrays is implementation-defined. This is regardless of whether all occurrences are outside or inside a function definition, or both.

5.6 The extern Class and Global Definitions

The concept of global variables that can be shared among functions in separate translation units is supported in almost all languages and is well understood. However, it
can take some practice to implement this external linkage in C because there is a lack
of symmetry in the use of class keywords.

Global objects have external linkage, so, if they are used solely to resolve internal
references as shown in the next example, they are overkill. External statics should be
used instead.

```
#include <stdio.h>

int gi;           /* global definition */

main()
{
        void f(void);

        gi = 876;
        f();
}

void f()
{
        printf("gi = %d\n", gi);
}
```

If an object declaration occurs outside a function and contains no class keyword,
it is an external definition. That is, it causes the compiler to allocate space for it
and initialize it. Such objects have static storage duration. There is no implied class
keyword when one is omitted here as there is when auto is assumed for classless
internal declarations.

If these two functions resided in separate source files, a change would have to be
made to ensure that f could access gi, as follows:

```
/* source file main.c */

int gi;

main()
{
        void f(void);

        gi = 876;
        f();
}
```

```
/* source file f.c */

#include <stdio.h>

extern gi;        /* tentative definition */

void f()
{
        printf("gi = %d\n", gi);
}
```

In this case, the **extern** keyword is used to provide external linkage. (In the previous section, it was used to resolve a forward reference to a **static** external.) The compiler does not find a definition for a **static** external or a global object, so it treats the **extern** as being a reference to a global object defined in some other source file.

In the following version of function **f**, function **g** is also called. This function needs to access **gi** as well. The functions could be written as follows:

```
/* source file f1.c */

#include <stdio.h>

void f()
{
        void g(void);
        extern gi;

        printf("gi = %d\n", gi);
        g();
}

void g()
{
        extern gi;

        printf("gi = %d\n", gi);
}
```

In this example, the **extern** declaration is at block level 1 instead of level 0. These declarations do not cause storage to be allocated—they simply declare that an external object is defined elsewhere. The linkage of that identifier will be determined by the compiler based on whether or not it finds a corresponding definition in its source file. (In this case, it does not.)

By placing the **extern** declaration inside a function definition, its scope has been reduced from source file-wide to just its parent and subordinate blocks. That is why **gi** must be declared inside both functions. If 20 functions in the same source file needed access to **gi**, it would be messy to declare it in each function. The proper solution is to declare it once, at the top of the source file at block level 0. If functions in other source files also need to access **gi**, the **extern** declaration should be placed in a user-written header so it can be included as needed.

ANSI C requires that there be exactly one definition for each global object. That is, its declaration must not contain a class keyword. All other declarations of that object must contain the **extern** keyword. Note, though, that there are several global definition/reference models in existence, which differ from that defined by ANSI C. For example, VAX C permits the **extern** keyword to be omitted from all references simply because the linker does not differentiate between global definitions and references. If you use other than the ANSI C model, you should be aware of the consequences.

Also note that a data declaration that contains the **extern** keyword may not have an initialization list. Only defining instances of objects may be initialized.

5.7 Function Classes

The storage duration of all functions is, of course, `static`. Space is permanently allocated for all functions linked into a program whether or not those functions are called. However, there are two types of function linkage: internal and external. A function with external linkage causes a global symbol to be exported to the linker so that that function can be invoked from any translation unit, provided the function is properly declared.

Consider the following example:

```
extern main()
{
        extern void f(void);

        f();
}

extern void f()
{
        /* ... */
}
```

Both function definitions and the declaration of **f** contain the class keyword **extern** to indicate these functions have external linkage. Since this is the default linkage for functions, the keyword is rarely used in this context. As stated earlier, if a class is specified and a type is not, `int` is assumed. So, in this example, `main` is implicitly declared as returning an `int` value.

A function with internal linkage may be called only from functions defined in the same source file as that function's definition, as follows:

```
static int data[100];   /* private data */

extern unsigned getmem(unsigned size)
{
        extern void sub1(void), sub2(void);

        /* ... */

        sub1();
        sub2();

        /* ... */
}
static void sub1()      /* private function */
{
        /* ... */
}
static void sub2()      /* private function */
{
        /* ... */
}
```

Function `getmem` has external linkage and is the means by which the user program gains entry to this source file. It in turn uses two service routines `sub1` and `sub2` to do its job. Since `sub1` and `sub2` are designed to be called only by `getmem`, there is no reason to make their names public. Therefore, they are defined using the `static` keyword. As such, their names are not exported to the linker—all references to them are resolved by the compiler.

Note that once again in `getmem` we declare `sub1` and `sub2` using the `extern` keyword. This forward reference is resolved by the `static` function definitions later in the source file. If the function definitions did not contain the keyword `static` or they were not defined in the same file, the compiler would treat the `extern` declaration as a reference to an `extern` function.

Because a `static` function is private to its parent source file, many `static` functions having the same name can coexist, provided each is defined in a different source file. In this example, the `static` external array `data` is also private to this source file. This is the principal means of communication between `getmem` and its slave routines.

The value of private data and functions should be obvious. They permit you to use whatever names for these things you wish without worrying about name conflicts with other translation units. Therefore, they are particularly useful when writing self-contained library modules.

Some languages provide more linkage capability than C does. For example, they permit functions to be nested so that a function can be called only by its parent function. They also may permit a function to be private to functions outside of the source file in which the private function is defined. C does not support these things. It provides an "all or nothing" approach to function linkage.

5.8 Preprocessor Macro Scope

The preprocessor translates your C program into another C program by (among other things) replacing macros with their expanded definitions. As such, the preprocessor knows nothing about linkage and storage duration. Yet, such macros do have a scope in the sense that a macro is usable only after its definition, and it remains visible through the end of the source file in which it is defined. (If a header containing a macro definition is included, the included header is deemed to be part of the same file as the source that included it.)

5.9 Prototype Identifier Scope

As we learned in Chapter 4, you are permitted to optionally put identifiers in the argument list of a function prototype. For example:

```
double calc(double arg1, int arg2[]);
double calc(double, int []);
```

are equivalent. The value of using the names is to make the declarations easier to read, particularly for complex data types, and to make it easier to generate prototypes from function definitions using a text editor.

These identifiers have their own scope. They are seen only from the point of their use through the end of their parent prototype. That is, the same identifier may not appear more than once in a prototype and it never conflicts with any identifier of the same name outside the prototype. These identifiers have no linkage and, because they cause no storage to be allocated, they have no storage duration.

A prototype argument list exists only to specify the types of each argument expected. Each type declaration must contain no class keyword since linkage of function arguments is predefined and can not be changed. (However, as we saw above, the **register** keyword can be used in the formal argument list corresponding to the prototype.)

So, while you can choose these dummy identifier names at leisure, you should be aware that these names are tokens and are seen by the preprocessor when it is looking for macro calls. Therefore, you must not use a dummy identifier name that exactly matches a currently defined macro name. (A conflict is easy to avoid if you use uppercase names for macros and lowercase names for all other identifiers.)

Consider the following example:

```
#define ABC 10
#define xyz (ABC / 2)

void sub(int ABC, double xyz[]);
```

The output from the preprocessor is as follows:

```
void sub(int 10, double (10 / 2)[]);
```

which generates a compilation error because these are not valid declarations. And, while it should be easy to avoid such conflicts, don't forget that either or both of the macro definitions and prototypes can be in headers, which are included. So, unless you write your prototypes with care, you can run into trouble when you use them in the scope of other headers. And, if you purchase or otherwise obtain headers from other sources, check out the naming conventions they used for macro names and prototype argument identifiers.

5.10 Linkage and Storage Duration Attributes

The following table summarizes the scope and life of all of the object and function classes. The storage duration "block+" refers to an identifier declaration's parent block and subordinate blocks.

Storage Duration and Linkage by Class			
Class	*Linkage*	*Storage Duration*	*Default Value*
auto	none	block+	undefined
register	none	block+	undefined
static internal	none	program	0
static external	internal	program	0
external definition	external	program	0
external declaration	external	program	-
extern	internal/external	program	-
static function	internal	-	-
extern function	external	-	-

Exercise 5-4*: Prove that a static internal variable retains its value across function calls and that an automatic variable does not.

Exercise 5-5*: Prove that a static function and a static external data object can not be directly accessed from a file other than the one in which they are defined. Could such objects be indirectly accessed? Compile the source and generate a machine code listing to see what happens to the static object names.

Exercise 5-6*: Write two functions f and g which are in two separate source files named f.c and g.c, respectively. Define and initialize a global char, gc, in f.c and a global integer array gi of size 5 in g.c. Show that the functions can get at each other's globally defined data by writing a main function in main.c that calls both f and g.

5.11 Chapter Summary

- The scope of an identifier refers to that domain of the program over which that identifier can be referenced directly by name. ANSI C refers to this property as linkage.

- The life of an identifier is applicable only to data objects and it refers to the time during which an object actually exists. ANSI C refers to an identifier's life as its storage duration.

- An identifier with internal linkage can be accessed only by name from any part of the source file in which it is declared. Such names are not exported to the linker. Consequently, many identifiers with internal linkage having the same name may exist in a program, provided each is declared in a separate source file (or translation unit, as ANSI C calls it).

- An identifier that has neither external nor internal linkage has no linkage. Each declaration of such an identifier refers to a unique entity. Automatic objects are examples of this.

- The storage duration of an identifier directly corresponds to its linkage. An object that has external, internal or no linkage, but has the storage class keyword `static` in its declaration, has static storage duration. Such an object is allocated space and initialized once only before `main` begins execution. Conceptually (and typically) this space is allocated and initialized at compile-time.

- Any object not having static storage duration has automatic storage duration.

- Linkage and storage duration are determined by two things: the presence or absence of a class keyword in a declaration, and whether or not the declaration occurs inside or outside of a function definition.

- The `auto` keyword is optional and rarely used.

- C permits declarations to be at the start of any block.

- It is possible, though not good style, to enter a block by other than falling into it, by using the `goto` statement.

- Syntactically, `register` is identical to `auto`. `register` is a hint to the compiler that the object being declared should be placed in a machine register.

- Just as an implementation can ignore a `register` request, it also can store an `auto` object in a register. There is no way to tell whether or not an automatic object was stored in a register without looking at the code generated. Even if it was stored in a register, you have no control over which register actually was used unless the compiler documents otherwise.

- Formal argument declarations are really `auto` declarations, except they can not have initialization lists and space for them is not allocated within the called function.

- The default class of formal arguments is `auto`. However, the `auto` keyword may not actually appear. Only one class keyword, `register`, actually can appear in a function definition's formal argument list.

- Objects with the keyword `static` in their declarations have static storage duration. Their linkage can be internal or none depending on whether the declaration is internal or external to a function definition.

- A literal string is an array of `char` having `static` class.

- If an object declaration occurs outside a function and contains no class keyword, it is an external definition. Such objects have static storage duration.

- The `extern` keyword can be used to provide internal or external linkage depending on where and how the identifier it references is defined.

- ANSI C requires that there be exactly one definition for each global object. That is, its declaration must not contain a class keyword. All other declarations of that object must contain the **extern** keyword.

- A data declaration containing the **extern** keyword must not have an initialization list.

- There are two types of function linkage: internal and external.

- A macro is usable only after its definition and it remains visible through the end of the source file in which it is defined.

- Identifiers in prototype argument lists have their own scope. They are seen only from the point of their use through the end of their parent prototype. That is, the same identifier may not appear more than once in a prototype and it never conflicts with any identifier of the same name outside the prototype. These identifiers have no linkage and, because they cause no storage to be allocated, they have no storage duration.

Chapter 6

The C Preprocessor

In previous chapters, we have seen examples of the preprocessor directives `#define` and `#include`. So far, discussion on these directives has been limited to that necessary to explain their use in simple examples. This chapter will cover them in more detail and will introduce all the other directives.

The preprocessor is a program that scans a C source file, looking for lines beginning with a # character. (Naturally, # characters occurring within comments are ignored.) Such lines are assumed to be directives to the preprocessor indicating some action to be taken before the resulting source code lines are handed off to the compiler proper. (In many implementations, the preprocessor is the first pass of the C compiler. In others, the two are quite separate programs. The organization of, and linkage between, these tasks is implementation-defined.)

The preprocessor is, at least logically, a separate entity from the compiler and it has its own language grammar. While preprocessing tokens are almost identical to those of the C language, there are obvious and subtle differences. Perhaps the main difference is that preprocessor directives are organized by lines. Except for one or two special cases, a directive ends at the new-line, terminating the source line on which it was begun. Also, the preprocessor is not statement-based and, as such, no semicolons are needed to terminate directives. Preprocessor directives have their own defined scope—they are not subject to C's block structure or linkage mechanism.

In short, the C preprocessor is a relatively primitive string substitution facility. It can replace names with user-specified strings, it can copy in strings from other source files, it conditionally can include or exclude strings for use by the compiler and it can pass on certain information to the compiler proper.

The preprocessor often is under-utilized, but in large programming and portability projects, its use is almost mandatory. Effective use of it helps to isolate system-dependent code and data, to compile multiple versions of a product from the same base source and to assign meaningful names to "magic" numbers. Its use provides flexibility in design changes by allowing program characteristics to be based on the values of one or more symbolic constants.

Initially, preprocessor directives had to begin in the first column of a source line. However, over the years, more and more implementations have permitted white space to appear before the # character and between the # and the directive name. Both of these approaches have been sanctioned by ANSI C; however, not all implementations permit this.

As a style issue, examples in this book will not place white space between the # and directive name and, for most directives, the # will begin in column one. However, once we see how directives can be nested, leading white space will be used to indicate levels of nested as appropriate. Of course, the preprocessor should ignore all such white space.

6.1   Defining Macros

There are two types of macros. An *object-like macro* has a name and a corresponding definition. A *function-like macro* has these attributes too; however, it also has a formal list of arguments that are replaced with actual arguments when the macro is expanded.

C is one of the few higher-level languages that has a good macro processor. As the name implies, a *macro* is a shorthand way of writing a piece of code. The abbreviated version is expanded by the preprocessor into its long form. Unlike other language macros, C macros do not need to be defined to be complete language constructs; however, they must contain complete C tokens. The only criteria is that when all macros have been expanded, the resulting stream of tokens is acceptable to the other preprocessor directives that use them, or to the compiler itself.

6.1.1   Object-Like Macros

In Chapter 3, an example contained the directive:

```
#define MAXLEN 20
```

Here, the symbol `MAXLEN` was assigned the string value 20. (We say "string" value because all macro names are symbolic constants for strings. Macros have no type per se.) Once this symbol has been defined, every subsequent occurrence of the token `MAXLEN` following in the same source file (or in subordinate source files included via the `#include` directive) is replaced by the string 20 before that source is processed by the compiler.

Object-like macros have several purposes: They allow meaningful names to be assigned to constants, expressions or text and therefore can help document the code; their existence or value can be tested mechanically to help make the routine portable by isolating compiler implementation dependencies; and their use can reduce the size of source code files and the time and thought it takes to create them.

Let's look at some simple macro examples:

```
#define BELL 7                    /* the ASCII bell char */
#define TAB '\t'                  /* the tab char */
#define EOS '\0'                  /* end-of-string terminator */
#define NL putchar('\n')          /* print new-line to stdout */
#define PI 3.1415926              /* value of PI */
#define CTRL_C 3                  /* ASCII control/C char */
#define CLR_SCR printf("\033[2J") /* ANSI clear screen */


#define FALSE 0
#define TRUE !FALSE
```

```
        #define MIN 10
        #define MAX 100
        #define RANGE_INCLUSIVE (MAX - MIN + 1)
        #define RANGE_EXCLUSIVE (MAX - MIN - 1)
        #define MID_POINT (MIN + (RANGE_EXCLUSIVE/2))
        #define TEXT "This is some text"


        #include <stdio.h>

        main()
        {

        /* Clear screen */

                CLR_SCR;
                puts("At top of cleared screen");

        /* display PI */

                printf("PI =%c%f", TAB, PI);
                NL;


        /* display a few values */

                printf("TRUE = %d, FALSE = %d\n", TRUE, FALSE);
                printf("MIN = %d, MAX = %d, MID_POINT = %d\n", MIN, MAX,
                        MID_POINT);
                printf("RANGE_I = %d, RANGE_E = %d\n",
                        RANGE_INCLUSIVE, RANGE_EXCLUSIVE);
                printf("TEXT = >%s<\n", TEXT);
        }


        <<screen is cleared>>
        At top of cleared screen
        PI =    3.141593
        TRUE = 1, FALSE = 0
        MIN = 10, MAX = 100, MID_POINT = 54
        RANGE_I = 91, RANGE_E = 89
        TEXT = >This is some text<
```

Macro names are identifiers, so they may contain alphanumeric characters and underscores with the first character being non-numeric. However, traditionally, macro names have been written in uppercase letters (possibly with digits and underscores as well) while all other identifiers (such as variable and function names) are written using lowercase letters. Of course, you are permitted to invent identifier names containing any combination of valid characters you wish (except that ANSI C reserves certain name space beginning with underscore characters); however, adopting this widespread naming convention is highly recommended.

The advantage of the case distinction is that if you use uppercase names for macros, you make the code a little more self-documenting. That is, if you see the expression:

```
temp = f(i + 10 - COUNT) * (j - SIZE)
```

you immediately know that `COUNT` and `SIZE` are macros that each potentially can expand into huge and/or complex expressions. What you see here in the source is not what the compiler (or the debugger) actually sees. In fact, unless you have completely debugged the definitions of `COUNT` and `SIZE`, they may cause you some grief. For example, what if `COUNT` expands into some expression containing `j++`? In this case, the resultant expression is unsafe because the order of evaluation of the operands is undefined.

If, however, the macros had lowercase names, you would not be able to distinguish them from variable and function names. For example:

```
temp = f(i + 10 - count) * (j - size)
```

If `count` expanded into an expression that resulted in undefined behavior, it may take you quite some time to locate the problem, particularly if you had not written the code initially. And, once you did find the problem, you might never trust the actual source code again since you can't tell which names designate macros. Instead, you always would look at the output produced by the preprocessor because, by then, macros no longer exist. However, this approach may be far from ideal because many preprocessors remove comments and all or most white space from the source given to the compiler. In short, it may be quite unreadable. Either way, debugging and maintenance may be less efficient.

It was suggested above that you might be able to view or retain the output produced by the preprocessor. And while it is quite often possible, it is not required by ANSI C. Some preprocessors write their output to a temporary disk file for subsequent use by the compiler, in which case, saving the output simply involves making that file permanent. Other implementations do not permit a preprocessor-only mode of operation so the preprocessor output exists only temporarily. However, if a compilation source listing file is produced by the compiler, it may be possible to have it include both the original source lines and the source output by the preprocessor. (VAX C provides a compiler switch to enable both intermediate and final macro expansions to be shown, which is very useful when macro definitions involve other macros.)

The output produced by one preprocessor from the program above is as follows:

```
<<
The expanded contents of stdio.h appeared here.
These included the function prototypes of all
the Standard I/O library functions.
>>
```

```
main()
{



        printf("\033[2J");
        puts("At top of cleared screen");



        printf("PI =%c%f", '\t', 3.1415926);
        fputc(('\n'),(&_iob[1]));



        printf("TRUE = %d, FALSE = %d\n", !0, 0);
        printf("MIN = %d, MAX = %d, MID_POINT = %d\n", 10, 100,
                (10 + ((100 - 10 - 1)/2)));
        printf("RANGE_I = %d, RANGE_E = %d\n",
                (100 - 10 + 1), (100 - 10 - 1));
        printf("TEXT = >%s<\n", "This is some text");
}
```

For the most part, we get what we might have expected—all of our macros are replaced with their corresponding definitions. In fact, even our tabs and new-lines used to format the code have been preserved. (This often is not the case with preprocessors.) However, our comments each have been replaced with white space. The only other discernable difference is that, while NL expanded to a call to the library routine putchar with one argument, the preprocessed output contains a call to fputc containing two arguments. So, putchar actually is defined as a function-like macro in stdio.h. Instead of providing putchar to write to standard output and fputc to write to any output file (including standard output), putchar has been defined in terms of fputc to the standard output file. This approach often is taken by implementers and applications programmers alike.

Another preprocessor produced almost identical output except that comments were retained. (In fact, the preprocessor provided an option to do this explicitly.) However, the expansion of NL resulted in quite a different set of tokens:

```
/* display PI */

        printf("PI =%c%f", '\t', 3.1415926);
        (--((&_iob[1]))->_cnt >= 0 ? 0xff &
                (*((&_iob[1]))->_ptr++ = (char)(('\n')))
                : _flsbuf((('\n')),((&_iob[1]))));
```

The meaning of this is quite implementation-defined and involves knowing just how this implementation does buffered character I/O. And, since this macro is provided by the implementer, we hope they have adequately tested it. As such, we never need to concern ourselves about its meaning. That's another advantage of macros and headers (such as stdio.h): They permit us to deal with things logically without having to delve into the physical implementation techniques.

If a macro definition contains the whole or trailing part of a C statement such as in NL above, it is a good idea not to include the statement-terminating colon in the macro definition. Then you can use NL; in the code to make it look more like a C statement. (A problem common with beginning C programmers is to terminate #define directives with semicolons. Then, when the macro is expanded, strange errors result. For example:

```
/* 1*/   #include <stdio.h>
/* 2*/
/* 3*/   #define MAX 10; /* note presence of semicolon */
/* 4*/   #define STEP 3; /*         "              "     */
/* 5*/   #define VAL 10; /*         "              "     */
/* 6*/
/* 7*/   main()
/* 8*/   {
/* 9*/           int i;
/*10*/           int j = VAL;
/*11*/
/*12*/           for (i = 0; i <= MAX; i++)
/*13*/                   printf("i*STEP = %d\n", i * STEP);
/*14*/
/*15*/           if (j > 10)
/*16*/                   j = -VAL;
/*17*/           else
/*18*/                   j = 5 - VAL;
/*19*/   }
```

produces the following compilation errors:

```
Error q.c 12: Expression syntax in function main
Error q.c 12: Statement missing ; in function main
Error q.c 13: Expression syntax in function main
Error q.c 17: Misplaced else in function main
```

The output from the preprocessor is:

```
/* 7*/   main()
/* 8*/   {
/* 9*/           int i;
/*10*/           int j = 10;;
/*11*/
/*12*/           for (i = 0; i <= 10;; i++)
/*13*/                   printf("i*STEP = %d\n", i * 3;);
/*14*/
/*15*/           if (j > 10)
/*16*/                   j = -10;;
/*17*/           else
/*18*/                   j = 5 - 10;;
/*19*/   }
```

The errors in lines 12 and 13 should be fairly obvious. However, that on line 17 may take a little thought. In the absence of a brace-delimited block, the true path of an `if` is taken to be the next one statement; in this case, the assignment of -10 to j. However, the true path contains two statements and no braces. The second semicolon, added when `VAL` was expanded, represents the null statement. Therefore, the compiler deduces that no `else` clause can follow and, when it does encounter one, it doesn't belong to an `if`.

Two other "errors" exist, yet they are not reported by the compiler. Lines 10 and 18 contain extra semicolons. However, each is considered to be (a superfluous) null statement and, as such, is accepted and produces no code. In such cases, a macro can appear to work fine for a long time but still not be correct in all possible legitimate or intended expansions.

The use of macros can be overdone. For example, the macros `TAB` and `EOS` defined earlier are nothing more than synonyms for the character constants `'\t'` and `'\0'`, respectively. The symbolic names give you no more information than their respective definitions and they are no easier to write. In short, they serve no useful purpose and their use may, in fact, detract from, rather than enhance, the code.

As demonstrated above, macro definitions may contain the names of other macros. The only requirement is that all macros referred to must already have been defined.

ANSI C allows a macro to be redefined, provided the definitions are the same. This is known as *benign redefinition*. Just what does "the same" mean? Basically, it requires that the macro definitions be spelled exactly the same and, depending on how white space between tokens is processed, multiple consecutive white-space characters may or may not be significant.

Consider the following example:

```
/*1*/   #define MACRO a macro
/*2*/   #define MACRO a macro
/*3*/   #define MACRO a<TAB>macro
/*4*/   #define MACRO a    macro
/*5*/   #define MACRO example
```

Macros 1 and 2 are the same. Macros 3 and 4 also may be the same as 1 and 2 depending on the handling of the white space. Macro 5 definitely should be flagged as an error. This does not solve the problem of having different definitions, which are not in the same scope for the same macro.

To assign the same macro a different value, you first must remove that macro's definition using the `#undef` directive as follows:

```
#define ABC 123
#undef ABC
#define ABC 456
```

While this is permitted, it is not recommended because it generally is illogical to use the same macro for two different purposes (just as it is with variable names). Also, some implementations do not require the intervening `#undef`—they merely continue with the macro now having the new value.

Macros can be used to "customize" your programs as follows:

```
#define then             /* add a dummy keyword then */

        if (condition) then
               ...


#define begin {          /* define a begin procedure keyword */
#define end }            /* and an end procedure keyword */

        while (condition)
                begin
                  ...
                end
```

However, such use is not recommended because it suggests you are not happy with the keywords and/or facilities C has to offer. And, if that is the case, hiding its "inadequacies" behind vacuous macros will do little to convince you otherwise, even if doing so does make the program look "cute." (The macros have lowercase names, so they look like keywords.)

As we see with the macro **then**, a macro can be defined to have no string value. Therefore, all occurrences of the token **then** are removed from the source. One particular use of this technique is to remove non-standard keywords from source written for one implementation but being compiled on another.

Sometimes certain limits or values are unknown or may vary once programming of a project has been started. If these limits are defined as macros, it becomes a simple matter to change them later without affecting the programs. For example, the following code is dependent on the value of the macros NAMELEN and MAXPAIRS. However, when either or both of these has their definitions changed, all references to them are resolved by the preprocessor.

```
#define NAMELEN 30
#define MAXPAIRS 100

f()
{
        char name[NAMELEN + 1];
        int value1[MAXPAIRS];
        int value2[MAXPAIRS];

        /* ... */
}
```

In the first example in this chapter, you may have noticed that several of the macro definitions were enclosed in parentheses. Let's take the case of MID_POINT which was defined as follows:

```
#define MID_POINT (MIN + (RANGE_EXCLUSIVE/2))
```

In the program shown, MID_POINT is used simply as an argument to printf; however, it is conceivable that it could be used in other contexts. For example, what result would the following code produce:

```
i = 10 * MID_POINT;
```

if the parentheses had been omitted? Quite obviously, a different answer would be obtained because the assignment would become:

```
i = 10 * MIN + (RANGE_EXCLUSIVE/2)
```

instead of:

```
i = 10 * (MIN + (RANGE_EXCLUSIVE/2))
```

Whenever you define a macro whose value is a valid C expression involving an operator, always place the definition inside a pair of grouping parentheses so the enclosed operator precedence is not impacted by any operators present in the expanded context.

6.1.2   Function-Like Macros

Like most assembly language macros, C preprocessor macros can have arguments; for example:

```
#include <stdio.h>

#define isdigit(c) ((c) >= '0' && (c) <= '9')
#define islower(c) ((c) >= 'a' && (c) <= 'z') /* ASCII */
#define TRACEMSG(s) printf("TRACE entered function %s.\n",(s))


sub1()
{
        int ch = 10;
        int m = 100;
        int k = 5;

        TRACEMSG("sub1");

        if (isdigit(m))
                /* ... */;

        if (islower(ch + m - k))
                /* ... */;
}
```

The macro isdigit has one formal argument c. When isdigit is referenced with an actual argument of m, each occurrence of the token c in the macro is replaced with m. Likewise, in islower, c is replaced by the expression ch + m - k. The formal arguments are merely place-holders that indicate where actual arguments are to be substituted. They have no name space of their own and exist only within the preprocessor. Therefore, their names do not conflict with other identifiers having the same name.

An object-like macro's definition begins with the first non-blank character following the blank after the macro name. In the case of a function-like macro, the value begins after the white space following the parenthesis terminating the formal argument list. This means that function-like macros can not have a space between the macro name and the argument list opening parenthesis.

For example, the macro definition:

```
#define A (c) putchar(c)
```

would assign the string `(c) putchar(c)` to `A`. In this case `A` has no formal argument and `A(x);` would be expanded to `(c) putchar(c)(x);` instead of `putchar(x);`.

The correct macro definition would be:

```
#define A(c) putchar(c)
```

Once the opening parenthesis is seen in a function-like macro definition, white space is permitted between any subsequent tokens in the formal argument list. In the case of an invocation of that macro, white space is also permitted before the opening parenthesis.

When the `TRACEMSG` macro is expanded, the `s` in `%s` is not expanded. The macro processor ignores the contents of literal strings and character constants when searching for formal arguments to replace, because it can never find a token inside another token: Tokens are the fundamental unit of C source.

The preprocessor output from the above example is:

```
sub1()
{
        int ch = 10;
        int m = 100;
        int k = 5;

        printf("TRACE entered function %s.\n",("sub1"));

        if (((m) >= '0' && (m) <= '9'))
                ;

        if (((ch + m - k) >= 'a' && (ch + m - k) <= 'z'))
                ;
}
```

Simple sequences of code such as `isdigit` and `islower` can be defined as in-line macros rather than as functions. This eliminates the overhead of a function call at the expense of duplicating the macro expansion in-line, once for each such macro reference. Note that these two macros have lowercase names. This allows a programmer to be oblivious as to whether they are macros or functions. Later, the programmer may change from a function to a macro or vice versa without need for changes to the source as would be required if `ISLOWER` and `ISDIGIT` were used as the macro names.

When writing macros, consider the context in which they might be used. As stated earlier, placing grouping parentheses around expressions in a macro's definition often is a good idea. When writing function-like macros, it also is generally a good idea to put parentheses around each occurrence of the formal arguments in the definition, as was done with isdigit, islower and TRACEMSG above. You may question the need for parentheses in TRACEMSG since the only argument that seems possible is a string literal. However, as we learn about pointers, you will find that the actual argument given to this macro can be a more complex expression.

Despite all attempts to "bullet-proof" a macro by using parentheses, it is possible that the macro is still "unsafe." That is, given a valid set of arguments, the macro may expand so that it produces undesired behavior.

Consider calling isdigit with an argument of of m++ instead of m. The expanded macro would become:

```
if (((m++) >= '0' && (m++) <= '9'))
```

and, depending on the value of m, m++ may be evaluated once or twice. If m contains the value '9', then (m++) >= '0' will be true and m will be incremented by one. Now, (m++) <= '9' is false and we are told that '9' is not a digit, which obviously is not true. Given the way this macro is defined, there is no way to make it perfectly safe in the presence of arguments with such side effects. (That is why the macro versions of these functions in ctype.h are implemented differently so that they only evaluate their formal arguments once, at most.)

In Chapter 4, we saw some function versions of various ANSI terminal escape sequences. Here are the equivalent macro versions:

```
#define scr_cub(ncolms)     printf("\033[%dD", ncolms)
#define scr_cuf(ncolms)     printf("\033[%dC", ncolms)
#define scr_cuu(nlines)     printf("\033[%dA", nlines)
#define scr_cud(nlines)     printf("\033[%dB", nlines)
#define scr_cup(line,colm)  printf("\033[%d;%dH", line, colm)
#define scr_ed(parm)        printf("\033[%dJ", parm)
#define scr_el(parm)        printf("\033[%dK", parm)
#define scr_sgr(attrib)     printf("\033[%dm", attrib)
```

It is possible to implement some of these in a simpler manner. By calling printf and having it check its arguments at run-time, we incur certain overheads. However, some of these sequences have only a few possible values. For example, scr_ed can be used with one of three arguments to clear the whole screen or the leading or trailing part of the screen.

It may be more efficient performance-wise to provide three separate macros as follows:

```
#define scr_edwh() fputs("\033[2J", stdout) /* clr screen */
#define scr_edfs() fputs("\033[1J", stdout) /* clr from beg */
#define scr_edte() fputs("\033[0J", stdout) /* clr to end */
```

The string to be output is known completely at compile-time and the function call becomes quite a bit cheaper because fputs doesn't have to work out what to do and how to format its output. It just does the only thing it can do: write the string to standard output.

These macros have argument lists that are empty, and that is permissible. Defining them that way makes them look like functions, making it easier to replace them with actual functions, if necessary. And, if you wished to have all three macros actually call `scr_ed` as described earlier, you simply could change these macros as follows and recompile without otherwise changing the code:

```
#define scr_edwh()      scr_ed(2)
#define scr_edfs()      scr_ed(1)
#define scr_edte()      scr_ed(0)
```

Occasionally, a macro definition may be too long to fit comfortably on one source line, in which case you may continue it by ending the line with a backslash, immediately followed by a new-line. Each subsequent line likewise can be continued, except for the last line of the definition.

ANSI C requires a conforming implementation to handle up to 1,024 concurrent macro definitions. It also requires support for macros with at least 31 arguments. (An implementation need not support 1,024 macros each with 31 arguments, however, since this is impossible for systems running on small memory configurations. ANSI C simply requires that the implementer be able to demonstrate it can compile a program that meets each of the translation limit minimums individually. It doesn't have to be able to handle arbitrary combinations of the limits in the same source file.)

ANSI C also requires the number of actual arguments in a macro call to match the number of formal arguments in the corresponding definition.

6.1.3   The # Stringize Operator

ANSI C provides a preprocessor-only operator **#** which can be used only in a function-like macro definition. It is used as follows:

```
#include <stdio.h>

#define PR(id) printf("The value of " #id " is %d\n", id)

main()
{
        int i = 10;
        int k = -2345;

        PR(i);
        PR(k);
        PR(k * 10);
        PR(i + k - 25);
}
```

The output produced is:

```
The value of i is 10
The value of k is -2345
The value of k * 10 is -23450
The value of i + k - 25 is -2360
```

Let's see how the macro expands on its fourth call. The original definition is:

```
#define PR(id) printf("The value of " #id " is %d\n", id)
```

and the call is:

```
PR(i + k - 25);
```

The expanded macro produced is:

```
printf("The value of " "i + k - 25" " is %d\n", i + k - 25);
```

The second occurrence of `id` in the definition is replaced by the actual argument as you would expect. However, the first occurrence is not, due to the presence of the `#` operator preceding it. This operator causes the text of the actual argument to be placed in quotes. That is, the actual argument is converted to a string containing the text of the argument.

ANSI C also has endorsed the idea of concatenation of adjacent string literals. Specifically, if two string literal tokens are separated only by white space (or nothing), the compiler treats them as one big string literal without the intervening white space.

The expanded macro is treated as if it had been written as:

```
printf("The value of i + k - 25 is %d\n", i + k - 25);
```

6.1.4   The ## Token Pasting Operator

Another preprocessor-only operator invented by ANSI C is `##`. This is used to create new tokens during the preprocessing phase and its use is relatively advanced. As such, it will not be discussed further here except to show how it is used. The macro definition and call:

```
#define PRN(x) printf("%d", value ## x)
```

```
PRN(3);
```

expands to:

```
printf("%d", value3);
```

The `##` operator can be used only within a macro definition. Although a construct of the form `a ## b ## c` is permissible, the order of evaluation of the two operators is unspecified.

6.1.5   Defining Macros at Compile-Time

Most hosted implementations permit one or more macros to be defined external to the source code. They do this via a compiler switch or option something like:

```
cc file.c -dTEST=10
```

The option `-dTEST=10` is treated so that it is equivalent to having the directive:

```
#define TEST 10
```

at the beginning of the source file `file.c`. Using this approach, you can vary the value of a macro without altering the source. And, as we will see later in the discussion of conditional compilation directives, you can test the value or existence (or non-existence) of a macro using preprocessor directives.

While compilers generally permit two or three (or possibly more) object-like macros to be so defined, few implementations permit function-like macros to be defined in this manner. Also, numerous aspects of this approach (including whether or not it is even available) are implementation-defined. For example, is the case of the macro name and its definition preserved? What happens to white space embedded in the macro's definition? How many macros can be defined this way?

Exercise 6-1: Determine if your preprocessor is a program separate from your compiler. Are you able to save and/or inspect the output generated by the preprocessor? If so, can you preserve comments and white space so the output is readable?

Exercise 6-2: In directives, is white space permitted before the # and between the # and the directive name?

Exercise 6-3: Determine the maximum number of concurrent macros you may have in a source file. Do so for both object-like and function-like macros. Does the maximum number depend on the length of macro definitions or the number of formal arguments? How many arguments can be present in function-like macro definitions? Does your preprocessor permit you to call a macro with less arguments than were defined for it?

Exercise 6-4: Does your preprocessor permit a macro to be redefined identically and differently without the use of an intervening `#undef` directive?

Exercise 6-5: Check the compiler-supplied headers for examples of both object-like and function-like macros. Often, `stdio.h` contains some safe function-like macro versions of standard library routines. `ctype.h` almost always contains a series of function-like macros.

Exercise 6-6*: Define a macro called `isupper` which evaluates to true or false based on the value of its `int` argument. Define another macro called `tolower` which calls `isupper` and evaluates to the lowercase equivalent of its `int` argument. If that argument is not an uppercase letter, no conversion is done. Note that the `int` argument passed to `tolower` is not altered. Write a program to test `tolower` for the characters A-z, inclusive, displaying each character and its (possibly) converted version as graphic characters using `printf` with `%c`. Make the macros as safe as you can. Are there any restrictions on what operators the integral argument expressions may contain for the macro to be safe?

Exercise 6-7: Look at the size and content of the code generated by the above example, using both macro and function versions. (ANSI C standard libraries are required to provide real function versions of these. If they don't, it is a simple matter to write them yourself based on the discussion and examples in Chapter 4.) Also time the program's execution for a large number of iterations. The intent of this exercise is to get a "feel" for the trade-offs of in-line macro generation versus function call overhead.

Exercise 6-8*: If your preprocessor permits the listing of macro expansions, look at the expanded output from the `tolower` problem above. When macros expand to other macro calls, etc., can you look at intermediate stages of expansion as well as final stages?

Exercise 6-9: Does your preprocessor support the `#` and `##` operators? Does your compiler support adjacent string concatenation? (If so, this should be in any part of the language, not just within preprocessor directives.)

Exercise 6-10: Can you define macros with and without arguments at compile-time? How many can be defined? Is the case of the macro name and its definition preserved? What happens to white space embedded in the macro's definition?

6.2 Removing Macro Definitions

Once a macro has been defined, it is known for the rest of that source file unless its definition is removed from the preprocessor symbol table. Symbols can be removed using the `#undef` directive as follows:

```
#define HIGH 1000
#define MAX(a, b) ((a) < (b) ? (b) : (a))

#undef HIGH
#undef MAX
```

Each compiler's preprocessor symbol table has some limit on the maximum number of macro definitions and their total string size. Therefore, a program with many macros, particularly large ones, may cause the symbol table to overflow. In this case, macros can be removed, once they are no longer needed, to make room for new definitions.

If you `#undef` a name that currently is not defined as a macro, the implementation is supposed to ignore the `#undef` directive. However, in such cases some preprocessors issue a warning or information message while others have been known to generate (incorrectly) a fatal compilation error.

Just as some implementations permit macros to be defined at compile-time, they also may permit macros to be "undefined." For example:

```
cc file.c -uUNIX
```

causes the predefined macro `UNIX` to be removed from the preprocessor's symbol table (assuming it existed there). Implementations often predefine one or macros which indicate the CPU and/or host operating environments. DEC's VAX C, for example, predefines the macros `VAX`, `vax`, `VMS` and `vms` among others. Many PC-based compilers predefine `MS-DOS`, `I8086`, `I80286`, etc., and most also have a series of macros that identify the Intel memory model being used. Unlike the `-d` compiler switch used to define macros, `-u` (or its equivalent) does not remove macro definitions from your source code—it merely removes the specified macro definitions from the list of those predefined by the implementation itself, exclusive of those macros explicitly defined in the supplied headers.

The value of this capability is that if your code contains conditional compilation directives, you can compile and possibly test various compilation paths by disabling and/or predefining various macros at the compilation level without having to modify the source code.

> **Exercise 6-11:** Does your preprocessor ignore attempts to #undef non-existent macros?

> **Exercise 6-12:** Does your implementation provide a mechanism to remove predefined macro definitions at compile-time?

6.3 Source File Inclusion

When programming non-trivial projects, you may find it useful to be able to share certain information between multiple source files. For example, function prototypes, external data declarations and macro definitions all may have some use beyond one particular source file. These shareable items can be placed in their own source file(s). Such a file is referred to as a *header* and usually has a file type of h. All implementations come with a set of headers and all ANSI C-conforming kits must contain at least 15 standard headers. One example is stdio.h (which we have been using from the beginning) which contains prototypes and macros used by the standard I/O library.

The ANSI C Standard headers and their purposes are:

Standard C Library Headers	
Header	*Purpose*
assert.h	program diagnostic purposes
ctype.h	character testing and conversion
errno.h	various error checking facilities
float.h	floating type characteristics
limits.h	integral type sizes
locale.h	internationalization support
math.h	math functions
setjmp.h	nonlocal jump facility
signal.h	signal handling
stdarg.h	variable argument support
stddef.h	miscellaneous
stdio.h	input/output functions
stdlib.h	general utilities
string.h	string functions
time.h	date and time functions

The headers errno, float, limits, locale and stdarg are ANSI C inventions. (Actually, stdarg is a revamped version of the UNIX varargs header.)

Headers may contain any valid C source code token or preprocessor directive and they are accessed via the #include preprocessor directive. This directive causes header records to be considered as part of the original source code file at the line at which they are included. A header may not contain part of a token, and its last line must be terminated by a new-line.

Moving common symbolic definitions to a header reduces the need to modify source files when porting programs to different environments or otherwise changing the value of any macro. Any changes necessary need only be made to the header files with these changes being implemented when the source files are recompiled.

ANSI C declares each standard library routine in a corresponding header and requires you either to #include that header or to duplicate the prototype, support macros, etc., in your own code. (The former approach is far simpler and less error prone.) Since ANSI C added function prototypes, you should include a routine's parent header, even if that routine returns an int value (the default for undeclared functions). For this reason, we have been including stdio.h from the beginning.

The physical location of a header depends on the way you specify the #include directive. Two principal methods are available. They are:

```
#include <header>
```

and:

```
#include "header"
```

ANSI C has provided a third method, #include ID, where ID is a macro that ultimately expands to one of the first two formats. (This approach allows the header name to be constructed by the preprocessor using the # and ## operators and macros defined at compile-time via a -d switch [or similar].)

If the <...> method is used, the compiler searches in a set of "system" places. (Most multiuser operating systems have specially named disks and directories for placing shareable files.) Usually, you use this format for the standard library headers, and those provided by your implementation to give you access to your host hardware and software environments.

The "..." format indicates that a system-specified set of places is to be searched, generally starting with the user's default device/directory. Some implementations also search the <...> place if the header otherwise can not be found.

Many implementations provide a compile-time switch (such as -i or /include) to specify a hierarchy of places to search for headers included with either "...", <...> or both. This capability eliminates the need to hard-code device and directory information in the source thus providing more flexibility in moving headers, or in compiling against different sets of headers (production and test, for example).

Headers may be nested up to an implementation-defined level (ANSI C requires at least eight levels). When you design your own headers, you should make sure they cause no problems if they are included multiple times in the same compilation. Also, a header that relies on things in another header should explicitly #include that other header. This is better than forcing the programmer to know which headers are related to which other headers. However, in doing this, it is possible that one compilation can include the same header five or six times. To save the preprocessor from doing so more than once, you can place a conditional compilation envelope around the whole header. (This will be shown in a later section.)

> **Exercise 6-13:** How many of the ANSI Standard headers are provided with your implementation? If any other headers are also provided, find out their purpose. Get hard-copies of some of these headers to see what they contain.

> **Exercise 6-14:** Does your preprocessor support the #include ID format where ID is a macro that expands to either the <...> or the "..." form?

Exercise 6-15: Does your implementation provide a mechanism to specify a set of header inclusion paths to be searched at compile-time?

Exercise 6-16: What is the depth of header nesting permitted by your implementation?

6.4 Conditional Compilation Directives

A series of preprocessor directives is available to allow source code to be compiled on a conditional basis. Examples of each of them follow:

```
/* testing if macros are defined */

#include <stdio.h>

#define DEBUG

main()
{
        int c;

        printf("Please enter a printable character: ");
        c = getchar();


#ifdef DEBUG
        printf("\nChar %c with value %d.\n", c, c);
#else
        printf("\nSymbol DEBUG is not defined.\n");
#endif

#ifndef TEST
        printf("\nMacro TEST is not defined.\n");
#endif
}
```

which produces the output:

```
Please enter a printable character: A

Char A with value 65.

Macro TEST is not defined.
```

The directives `#ifdef` and `#ifndef` check whether a macro is or is not currently defined, respectively. The true path for these directives includes all source lines between the `#if`*xxx* and its corresponding `#else` or `#endif` (if no `#else` exists). The false path (if any) includes all lines between the `#else` and `#endif`.

Note that `DEBUG` is defined without any particular value. Its value is irrelevant for these directives—they simply test if it is defined or not.

If your implementation permits macros to be defined at compile-time, then the definition of `DEBUG` can be removed from the source altogether.

When header inclusion was discussed earlier in this chapter, it was suggested you ensure that headers were included only once per compilation. The following technique does this:

```
/* header head.h */

#ifndef HEAD_H
#define HEAD_H

/* contents of header go here */

#endif
```

Each header contains a condition compilation envelope based on the presence or absence of a macro. In this case, the macro name is a function of the header name. The first time this header is included, HEAD_H presumably will not be a defined macro. However, as a result of this inclusion, HEAD_H becomes defined. On subsequent inclusions, this macro is already defined, so the body of the header is skipped.

Sometimes it is desirable to check for specific macro values or combinations of macro values; for example:

```
/* using the #if directive */

#include <stdio.h>

#define TRACE 1
#define TRACEMSG(s) printf("TRACE entered function %s.\n",s)

main()
{
#if TRACE
        TRACEMSG("main");
#else
        printf("TRACE is off.\n");
#endif


#if TEST
        printf("TEST is true\n");
#else
        printf("TEST is false\n");
#endif
}
```

which produces the output:

```
TRACE entered function main.
TEST is false
```

The #if directive evaluates the arithmetic expression following it using long int arithmetic. The true and false paths selected for compilation are the same as those for the #ifdef and #ifndef directives discussed above.

Note the use of TEST here. We are attempting to use the value of a macro that has not been defined. In such cases, the preprocessor pretends that macro has the value zero and continues. However, this is only true in #if directive expressions.

#if expressions may contain almost all of C's operators; for example:

```
/* #if expressions and #elif */

#define VAX 1
#define UNIX 101
#define VMS 102

#if CPU == VAX
        #if OPSYS == UNIX
                /* ... */
        #elif OPSYS == VMS
                /* ... */
        #else
                /* ... */
        #endif
#else
        #if CPU == M68000 && OPSYS != UNIX
                /* ... */
        #endif
#endif
```

As shown, conditional directives may be nested. ANSI C added the #elif directive, which is simply a more elegant way of nesting #if directives.

The main limitations on the contents of #if expressions are that they contain no floating-point expressions, type casts or enumeration constants. And, while ANSI C permits a preprocessor to recognize the sizeof operator here, it is not required to. (Enumerated data types are discussed in Chapter 10.)

In Chapter 1, we learned that comments do not nest and the problem arose, "How do I comment out a section of code that already contains comments?" The following example provides a solution:

```
/* "commenting out" code containing comments */

#if 0
        i = 10;
        printf("Has initialized i\n"); /* ... */
#endif
```

Since 0 is false, the enclosed block is never compiled.

ANSI C added a preprocessor-only operator defined. This adds no new value except to make Boolean criteria much simpler to read and write; for example:

```
#if defined M1 && !defined M2
        /* ... */
#endif
```

is equivalent to:

```
#ifdef M1
        #ifndef M2
                /* ... */
        #endif
#endif
```

Optional parentheses are permitted around the macro name operand of the `defined` operator.

While it may not be immediately obvious, you conditionally can compile down to the source token level. For example:

```
int i =
#if SYS == 1
25
#else
50
#endif
;
```

While this works fine, it is not very readable. Perhaps a better approach would be to use:

```
#if SYS == 1
int i = 25;
#else
int i = 50;
#endif
```

Exercise 6-17*: Conditionally compile one of two `printf` function calls based on whether or not the macro TEST is defined. If it is defined, display its value using the `%d` mask (assuming it has an `int` type); otherwise, print a message saying that it is not defined. If it is defined, use `#if` to print conditionally a message saying whether it does or does not have a value less than 100. Rather than `#define` the macro TEST in the source code to test this, define it using the compilation command-switch (assuming one is supported). Define the macro both with and without a value. What is the value of a macro that has been defined without being given an explicit value?

Exercise 6-18: Check whether the headers provided with your implementation are protected from being included more than once.

Exercise 6-19: Does your preprocessor support the `#elif` directive and `defined` operator?

Exercise 6-20: ANSI C defines two standard headers, `limits.h` and `float.h`. These contain a series of macros that define the integral and floating-point properties, respectively, of your target environment. They can be used conditionally to compile code based on various arithmetic magnitude and representational properties of your system(s). If your implementation provides these headers, study them in detail to see how you might be able to use them.

6.5 Miscellaneous Directives

Several other directives are defined. They are: `#line`, `#`, `#pragma` and `#error`.

6.5.1 The `#line` Directive

The `#line` directive is used to change the current file name and/or line number used by the preprocessor and compiler to report errors. For example, if `#include "abc.h"` is encountered during preprocessing, you would want any messages that pertained to it to be reported based on that file's name and line number, not on that of your source file. Much of this is transparent to application programmers and this directive rarely (if ever) needs to be used by them. It is used mostly by programs that directly generate C source code.

Nevertheless, its format is:

>   `#line` *line-number*

or:

>   `#line` *line-number file-name*

Examples of its use are:

>   `#line 100`
>   `#line 123 "test.c"`

6.5.2 The `#` Directive

The `#` (or null) directive is a relic and has absolutely no effect. Therefore, you should never use it.

6.5.3 The `#pragma` Directive

ANSI C invented the implementation-defined directive `pragma`. Essentially, an implementation can invent any pragmas it wishes. If an implementation comes across a pragma it does not recognize, it ignores it. Pragmas are being used for all sorts of things. Examples include definition of page format for compilation listings, controlling optimization and function call mechanisms. For the most part, the format and purpose of pragmas are pretty well up to the imagination of the implementers. There are no standard pragmas in ANSI C.

The format of a pragma is:

>   `#pragma` *preprocessor-tokens*

6.5.4 The `#error` Directive

ANSI C also invented the `#error` directive. Its format is:

>   `#error` *preprocessor-tokens*

and it causes the implementation to issue a diagnostic message made up of the pre-processor tokens in the directive. Here is one example of its use:

```
#ifdef M
        /* ... */
#else
        #error "Macro M is not defined"
#endif
```

6.6 Predefined Macros

As stated earlier, some implementations have one or more predefined macros indicating their host CPU and operating system, etc. ANSI C defines only five such standard macros and they cannot be the subject of an **#undef** directive. They are:

- __FILE__ – a string literal containing the name of the source file being compiled.

- __LINE__ – a numeric literal containing the number of the source line being compiled.

- __DATE__ – a string literal containing the date of compilation in the form "Mmm dd yyyy" where days less than 10 have a leading space.

- __TIME__ – a string literal in the form "hh:mm:ss" containing the time of compilation.

- __STDC__ – is set to 1 if the implementation conforms to the ANSI C Standard.

These macros (assuming they are defined) can be used in any context where literals of their type are allowed. For example:

```
char compile_date[] = __DATE__;
char compile_time[] = __TIME__;

printf("File is %s, line is %d\n", __FILE__, __LINE__);
```

Exercise 6-21: If your implementation provides any pragmas, study them in detail, because they could be used to provide small and/or more efficient code. They even may provide for in-line assembly code or the implementation of some of the simpler library functions as in-line code. (For example, memcmp and memcpy can be implemented trivially as block compare and block move instructions, respectively, on many modern machines.)

Exercise 6-22: Is the #error directive implemented by your compiler?

Exercise 6-23: Which of the standard predefined macros (if any) is implemented in your compiler? Are their formats exactly the same as ANSI C's? (Some versions of __DATE__ use different formats.) Note that a non-conforming implementation can choose either not to define __STDC__ at all or to define it with a value other than 1.

6.7   Chapter Summary

- The preprocessor is a program that scans a C source file, looking for lines beginning with a # character. Such lines are assumed to be directives to the preprocessor indicating some action to be taken before the resulting source code lines are handed off to the compiler proper.

- Preprocessor directives are organized by lines. Directives typically end at the new-line terminating the source line on which the directive occurs.

- The preprocessor is not statement-based, so no semicolons are needed to terminate directives. Preprocessor directives have their own defined scope. They are not subject to C's block structure or linkage mechanism.

- ANSI C permits white space both before and after the # in directives. However, this is not universally supported.

- There are two types of macros. An object-like macro has a name and a corresponding definition. A function-like macro has these attributes plus a formal list of arguments that are replaced with actual arguments when the macro is expanded.

- Macro names are identifiers and traditionally are spelled using all uppercase letters and underscores.

- Some implementations provide the ability to save the output they produce. Some also preserve comments and white space.

- If a macro definition contains the whole or trailing part of a C statement, it is a good idea not to include the statement-terminating colon in the macro definition.

- Macro definitions may contain the names of other macros, provided those macros already have been defined.

- ANSI C allows a macro to be redefined, provided the definitions are the same. To assign the same macro a different value, you first must remove that macro's definition using the #undef directive.

- A macro can be defined without a value.

- Whenever you define a macro whose value is a valid C expression involving an operator, always place the definition inside a pair of grouping parentheses so the enclosed operator precedence is not impacted by any operators present in the expanded context.

- An object-like macro's definition begins with the first non-blank character following the blank after the macro name. In the case of a function-like macro, the value begins after the white space following the parenthesis terminating the formal argument list.

- Despite all attempts to "bullet-proof" a macro by using parentheses, it is possible that the macro is still "unsafe" if it is given an actual argument containing side effects, such as the ++ and -- operators or a function call.

- Long macro definitions may be continued across lines using a backslash/new-line continuation sequence.

- ANSI C requires a conforming implementation to handle up to 1,024 concurrent macro definitions. It also requires support for macros with at least 31 arguments.

- ANSI C requires the number of actual arguments in a macro call to match the number of formal arguments in the corresponding definition.

- The `#` operator in a function-like macro definition causes the text of the actual argument to be placed in quotes. That is, the actual argument is converted to a string containing the text of the argument.

- ANSI C has endorsed the idea of concatenation of adjacent string literals.

- The operator `##` is used to create new tokens during the preprocessing phase.

- Many hosted implementations permit macros to be defined external to the source code via a compiler switch or option. They also may permit a set of inclusion paths to be specified.

- Headers may contain any valid C source code token or preprocessor directive and they are accessed via the `#include` preprocessor directive.

- Headers may be nested up to an implementation-defined level. (ANSI C requires at least eight levels.)

- A series of preprocessor directives is available to allow source code to be compiled on a conditional basis. These are `#if`, `#ifdef`, `#ifndef`, `#else`, `#elif` and `#endif`. The `defined` operator is used with `#if`.

- `#if` expressions may contain almost all of C's operators and are evaluated using `long int` arithmetic.

- `#if 0` can be used to disable a block of code containing comments.

- `#line` is used to change the current file name and/or line number used by the preprocessor and compiler to report errors.

- `#pragma` is an implementation-defined directive.

- `#error` causes the implementation to issue a diagnostic message made up of the preprocessor tokens in the directive.

- ANSI C defines five predefined macros. They are `__FILE__`, `__LINE__`, `__DATE__`, `__TIME__` and `__STDC__`.

Standard C Preprocessor Directives	
Name	*Purpose*
`#define`	define a macro
`#undef`	remove a macro definition
`#include`	include a header
`#if`	compile based on expression
`#ifdef`	compile based on macro defined
`#ifndef`	compile based on macro not defined
`#else`	conditional compilation false path
`#elif`	compound if/else
`#endif`	end conditional compilation path
`#line`	override line number and/or source file name
`#error`	generate a translation error
`#pragma`	implementation-defined action
`#`	null directive

Standard C Preprocessor Operators	
Name	*Purpose*
`#`	stringize
`##`	token pasting
`defined`	short-hand for multiple `#ifdef`s

Chapter 7

Pointers

Much of what we have covered so far has involved the C-specific syntax for doing things already possible in most high-level languages. However, for many of you, pointers will be a whole new concept. And, even if you have used pointers in other languages, the syntax required to declare and use them in C can take some mastering.

Pointers are powerful and easy to use, but without care, they can make code unreadable, difficult to debug, unmaintainable and difficult to port to other systems. In short, pointers can provide a lot of capability and trouble. And, if your system includes a symbolic debugger, you'll probably get to know it rather well at this stage. The only way to really understand pointers is to use them again and again.

7.1 Introduction

What are pointers and why do we need them? Simply stated, a *pointer* is a variable that contains the address of another variable. And, if the address of a variable is stored in a pointer, the contents of that variable can be accessed indirectly through the pointer. In fact, accessing an object via a pointer to it is known as *dereferencing* that pointer. That is, when you dereference a pointer, you get the value of the object it currently points to.

In Chapter 4, we showed various examples of functions that implemented simple ANSI terminal escape sequences. However, we did not have sufficient information to implement others. For example, to interrogate the terminal to see what the cursor's current line and column position are, we need to have a function return two values, the line and column. The problem is that a function can return only one value, and all scalars are passed in by value, by default. To have a function give us more than one value, we must pass in arguments by address allowing the function to deal directly with objects rather than copies of objects. In this case, we must pass in pointers to the variables into which we want the function to store the line and column values.

C always passes arrays by address. That is, when we use the name of an array as an argument to a function, the address of the first element in the array is actually passed by value. As such, a pointer to the first element is passed in. And, because a string literal is implemented as an array of `char`, every example we have used of passing string literals to functions has involved the use of pointers. (The first argument to `printf` is one common example.)

Rarely, if ever, are we interested in the actual address of an object. We simply store its address so we can get at it indirectly. In fact, for objects having automatic storage duration, they may have different addresses each time they are created dynamically. (Certainly this would be true for such objects defined in a function called recursively.)

Let's look at a simple example to see how pointers are declared and used. The task is to define an int variable var and to store its address in a pointer pvar. Then, var will be accessed indirectly via pvar and its value will be copied to another int, newvar:

```
#include <stdio.h>

main()
{
        int var = 10;
        int *pvar;
        int newvar;


        pvar = &var;    /* find var's address */

        newvar = *pvar; /* access var indirectly */

        printf("Value of var is %d\n", var);
        printf("Value of newvar is %d\n", newvar);
        printf("Address of var is %p\n", pvar);
        printf("Address of pvar is %p\n", &pvar);
}
```

which produces the output:

```
Value of var is 10
Value of newvar is 10
Address of var is 364E:0FD2
Address of pvar is 364E:0FD4
```

The declaration int *pvar; declares pvar to be a pointer to an int. That is, at any time, pvar may contain the actual address (absolute or virtual, depending on your system) of an int object. However, at the time of declaration, we have not said which particular int object it points to. And, as we learned in Chapter 1, automatic objects have undefined initial values by default. Therefore, pvar initially points "into the wild blue yonder." In fact, the "address" it contains may not even be part of our program's address space. On a real-memory (as opposed to virtual) machine, such a memory location may not even physically exist. Of course, this is irrelevant, unless you try to access that (possibly) non-existent memory location. The rule, therefore, is to not dereference a pointer until it has been initialized to point to some predictable memory location and one you have appropriate access to.

The declaration int *pvar can be read in one of two ways, both of which are equivalent. You can read "pvar is a pointer to an int" or "the contents of the location pointed to by pvar is an int."

Note that a pointer declaration specifies the type of the object pointed to; in this case, to an int. Other than this, a pointer has no type of its own, per se. Once a pointer is declared, it may point only to objects of the specified type. Attempting to make pvar point to a double, for example, should cause a compilation error.

(Numerous pre-ANSI compilers are quite lenient in this respect and freely permit the mixing of "apples and oranges.") However, in systems programming, it is sometimes useful to be able to make a pointer point to arbitrary type objects. This is possible, although ANSI C requires it to be done overtly, as we shall see later.

Like several other punctuation characters we have seen, & is used for different purposes. We have seen it used as the binary bit-wise AND operator (and in the &= assignment operator) and in the logical AND operator &&. It also can be used as a unary operator in the prefix position as in this example. The expression &var is read as "take the address of var." (Note, though, that you can not apply & to a variable declared with class register.) Hence:

```
pvar = &var;
```

assigns the address of var to pvar so that pvar now points to var. Note that we do not write:

```
*pvar = &var;
```

When we are assigning an address to a pointer as in this case, the * must not be used. Because var is an automatic variable, its address is not known until run-time. However, because pvar is also an automatic object, its initializer can be any run-time expression of the appropriate type. Therefore, we could have declared pvar as follows:

```
int *pvar = &var;
```

Although the * is part of the declaration of pvar, it takes no part in the initialization. The initializer always applies to the identifier being declared; in this case, to pvar.

Assignment requires both operands either to have the same type or to be assignment-compatible. In this case, pvar is declared to be a pointer to an int, and var is an int. By definition, the type of the expression &var is also "pointer to int," so it is compatible with pvar.

The statement newvar = *pvar; causes pvar to be dereferenced. That is, it takes the int value stored at the location pvar points to and copies it to the variable newvar. The type of newvar is int and that of pvar is pointer to int.

The unary * prefix operator is used to get at the object pointed to indirectly and, by definition, the expression:

```
*pointer-to-type-T
```

has type *T*. Therefore, *pvar has type int and its value can be assigned to newvar directly.

Perhaps the most difficult thing to remember when learning pointers is when to use or omit the * in pointer expressions. The * prefix operator should be used only when you wish to get at the object the pointer points to. If you wish to get at the value of the pointer itself, the * must be omitted.

If we omitted the * in the assignment of newvar, we should get a compilation error. However, many pre-ANSI compilers were very liberal and treated pointers and integral expressions as being assignment-compatible. ANSI C does not, and any attempt to do so will result in a compilation error. If your compiler does not enforce such strict compatibility checking and it provides a compilation switch to enable such checking, you are advised always to enable that switch. To do otherwise almost certainly will cost you hours of needless debugging.

Occasionally, it is useful to display the value of a pointer, so ANSI C provided a special edit mask %p for this purpose. The output format, however, is implementation-defined, since addressing notation and memory layout details are quite system-specific. (The example shown actually was run on an MS-DOS system and, because the Intel 80x86 chip series has a segmented architecture, a reasonable way to display an address is with a segment base address and offset in the format *bbbb:oooo*. Implementations running on machines such as a VAX or M68K might display an address as a hexadecimal or octal number.)

Prior to the invention of %p, it was commonplace to see pointers displayed using %u or %lu. While this will work on many implementations, it does require that pointers have the same size and representation as an unsigned int or unsigned long int. (Note that on some systems, addresses are signed. In any event, you should never deal with addresses as signed or unsigned integers.)

We have said that pvar is itself a variable, so we can change its value at run-time. (In fact, we can make it point to any int object we wish.) It also means that pvar itself is allocated some storage space which has an address. Therefore, we can take the address of a pointer with the expression &pvar. However, what is the type of this expression? pvar has type pointer to int and & creates a new level of indirection, so the resulting type must be pointer to pointer to int. If we were to declare an identifier of this type, we would use:

```
int **ppi;
```

This makes sense. Since a pointer is a variable that contains the address of another variable, it can contain the address of another pointer. (Actually, there is no limit on the number of levels of indirection; however, beyond two, it is difficult for a programmer to keep track of it in his mind.) Knowing this, we even could initialize a pointer with its own address.

The amount of storage allocated to a pointer is implementation-defined. For example, on VAX C it is 32 bits, on Cray machines, it is 64 bits, and on MS-DOS machines, it can be either 16 or 32 bits. (In fact, on DOS-class machines, a program may contain both 16- and 32-bit pointers simultaneously.) Also, all pointers are not necessarily created equal. For example, a pointer to type *T1* might have a different representation than a pointer to type *T2*.

Pointers may point to objects of any type that you legitimately can declare. (Pointers even may point to executable code, in which case, they are known as pointers to functions. These are discussed in Chapter 10.)

The following example can be used to display the amount of space allocated to various types of pointers for any implementation:

```
#include <stdio.h>

main()
{
        unsigned long int size;

        size = sizeof(char *);
        printf("Size of char * = %lu\n", size);

        size = sizeof(int *);
        printf("Size of int * = %lu\n", size);


        size = sizeof(double *);
        printf("Size of double * = %lu\n", size);

        size = sizeof(long int **);
        printf("Size of long int ** = %lu\n", size);

        size = sizeof(float ***);
        printf("Size of float *** = %lu\n", size);
}
```

The output produced from one implementation is:

```
Size of char * = 4
Size of int * = 4
Size of double * = 4
Size of long int ** = 4
Size of float *** = 4
```

As we learned in earlier chapters, the type of `sizeof` is implementation-defined. (It is either `unsigned int` or `unsigned long int`.) So, to make this program maximally portable, we assign the size to an `unsigned long int` and display that value using `%lu`.

Exercise 7-1: Does your implementation warn you if you assign a pointer of one type to a pointer of another type? What about when assigning integral values to pointers or vice versa? Does your version of `printf` support the `%p` edit mask?

Exercise 7-2: Are pointers on your implementation like `unsigned ints` or `unsigned longs`? How much storage space do pointers take up and can or must you have different sizes for different types? What is the internal representation of a pointer?

Exercise 7-3: Does your hardware have any object alignment requirements? If not, can it benefit from certain object alignment anyway?

7.2   Pointers and Casts

In the previous section, we showed an example that displayed the size of various pointer types. Each part of that example could have been written in a simpler way:

```
#include <stdio.h>

main()
{
        printf("Size of char * = %lu\n",
                (unsigned long) sizeof(char *));
}
```

Since pointers are types, you may cast from and to pointer types. Be careful, though, since dereferencing a pointer that was created via a cast can be catastrophic. For example:

```
main()
{
        char c;
        int i;
        int *pi;

        pi = (int *) &c;
        i = *pi;          /* ??? */
}
```

Here we have taken the address of the `char` c resulting in an expression of type pointer to `char`. By casting this to type pointer to `int`, pi thinks it is pointing to an `int`, when in fact it is not. On subsequent attempts to access the "int" pointed to, the program's behavior may vary from actually producing an `int` value to causing a fatal run-time error. Assuming an `int` and a `char` have different representations (they almost always do), using the pointer to access more bits than exist in the `char` causes either adjacent bytes (or words) to be interpreted as well, or some kind of access violation if these extra bytes don't belong to this program, or are otherwise inaccessible. (On the PDP-11, for example, if the address of c was odd, all attempts to access that address via a non-`char` pointer result in a fatal "odd address trap.")

7.3   Incrementing and Decrementing Pointers

In Chapter 2, the `++` and `--` operators were introduced. Since that time, we have used them with arithmetic operands simply to mean increment by one or, in the case of floating-point operands, by 1.0. However, these operators also can be used with pointer operands as follows:

```
#include <stdio.h>

main()
{
        static char name[40];
        char *pc;

        printf("Please input a string (39 chars max): ");
        scanf("%39s", name);      /* get string from stdin */

        pc = &name[0];            /* point to start of name */
        while (*pc != '\0') {     /* end of string found? */
                putchar(*pc);     /* if not, display char */
                ++pc;
        }

        putchar('\n');
}
```

One set of input produced the following:

```
Please input a string (39 chars max): Some_test_data!!
Some_test_data!!
```

The array name has been initialized using the library function scanf. This function uses edit masks much like printf. However, because scanf returns values back through its argument list, every argument must be a pointer. The %s mask accepts characters until white space is detected or the limit (in this case, 39) is reached. scanf automatically adds a null character terminator. With %s, scanf ignores any leading white space.

The expression &name[0] is the address of the first character in this array. Therefore, it has type pointer to char and can be assigned to pc. If pc has type pointer to char, then *pc has type char, and in the first iteration of the loop, has value 'S'. The loop body executes until pc points to the terminating null character. During each iteration, the character currently pointed to is written to standard output and the pointer is incremented to point to the next char in the array.

By definition, when a pointer is incremented (or decremented), the increment (or decrement) amount is scaled by the size of the object being pointed to. Therefore, if pt points to an object of type T, pt + 1 points to the object of type T immediately following in memory. (This is guaranteed on all C implementations regardless of the size and representation of any pointer type.)

The loop body also can be written as follows:

```
while (*pc != '\0')
        putchar(*pc++);
```

Here we have combined the pointer dereference and increment into one expression. This combination of unary operators is common in pointer expressions; however, it is less overt than the first approach. According to the precedence table, the unary operators * and ++ have the same precedence. However, they associate right to left. Therefore, ++ is evaluated first. The expression is equivalent to *(pc++). By definition, the value of pc++ is pc before it is incremented, so the pointer dereferenced is actually pc, not one more than pc. So, while the ++ has precedence, it does not change the operand of *.

It also is common practice to further abbreviate this loop as follows:

```
while (*pc)
        putchar(*pc++);
```

Since '\0' has a value of zero by definition, a comparison of != '\0' is the same as testing for true, so the controlling expression can be written as a logical test instead. You explicitly should write in the '\0' comparison to make the expression's meaning obvious. Any compiler worth its price should generate the same code from either approach, in which case, readability should take precedence.

Consider the following example in which a double pointer is decremented:

```
#include <stdio.h>

main()
{
        static double da[] = {0.0, 1.1, 2.2, 3.3, 4.4, 5.5};

        double *pd = &da[5];

        while (*pd > 0.0)
                printf("%6.2f\t", *pd--);

        putchar('\n');
}
```

The output produced is:

```
     5.50    4.40    3.30    2.20    1.10
```

The while loop terminates when it gets to the first element, da[0]. Consider the case where you want to print that element as well. A common suggestion for doing this would be to change the loop test criteria to be while (*pd >= 0.0). Nice try, but no cigar.

Let's look at what results when this was run with one compiler:

```
5.50    4.40    3.30    2.20    1.10    0.00  3969690.64 76345.23
```

We got the first element and a few other numbers as well. Where did they come from? You may recall that C has no run-time array bounds-checking. There is no facility to check if a pointer such as pd is incremented or decremented beyond an array's bounds. The reason we see two extra values printed is that, by chance, that is what was stored in the two double values in memory immediately before the storage area that contained the array da. The double immediately prior to them must have had a negative value, causing the controlling expression to test false. To process all elements in an array, you must know the number of elements in that array or know the value of the first or last element values. The only special case is when you are processing char arrays in the forward direction and the array is terminated by a null character.

Exercise 7-4*: Use the precedence table in Appendix A to explain the meaning of the following expressions. In each case, state the type and value of the expressions. Assume that in each case pc points to the first char in an array containing "axjr".

```
---------------------
| a | x | j | r | \0|
---------------------
  ^
   pc
```

```
a)   *pc++
b)   (*pc)++
c)   *++pc
d)   ++*pc
e)   ++(*pc)
f)   ++(*pc++)
g)   ++(*++pc)
```

7.4   The strcpy Function

This commonly used library function is trivial to implement using pointers; for example:

```
#include <stdio.h>

main()
{
        char str[30];
        void strcpy(char *, char *);

        strcpy(str, "The C Programming Language");
        printf("str = >%s<\n", str);
}


void strcpy(char *pdest, char *psource)
{
        while ((*pdest = *psource) != '\0') {
                ++psource;
                ++pdest;
        }
}
```

The output produced is:

```
str = >The C Programming Language<
```

The strcpy function copies one char array (including the trailing '\0') to another `char` array and it expects its arguments to be pointers to the destination and source arrays, respectively. Therefore, the formal arguments are declared correspondingly.

In this example, we manipulate both the pointers and the objects they point to, so in one case the `*` operator is required and in the other it is not. `*pdest = *psource` causes one `char` to be copied from the address `psource` points to, to the address `pdest` points to.

A more common way of writing the `while` loop is:

```
while ((*pdest++ = *psource++) != '\0')
        ;
```

and, because all the work is done in evaluating the controlling expression, a null statement is needed. As shown in an earlier example, this loop could be condensed even further to:

```
while (*pdest++ = *psource++)
        ;
```

Actually, the library version of `strcpy` declared in `string.h` does return a value. However, that is irrelevant at this stage. A complete implementation of `strcpy` will be shown later in this chapter.

Let's look at a version of `strcpy` that uses arrays rather than pointers:

```
void strcpy(char dest[], char source[])
{
        unsigned i = 0;

        while ((dest[i] = source[i]) != '\0')
                ++i;
}
```

For programmers new to pointers, this version makes much more sense. However, it requires the creation of the temporary variable `i` and its initialization. The variable `i` must be incremented separately because neither `dest[i++] = source[i]` nor `dest[i] = source[i++]` guarantee the correct result. (Remember that C, like most languages, makes no promises about the order of evaluation of expressions such as these.)

Note, then, in the context of formal argument lists, pointer and array notation can be interchanged freely. For example, all of the following function definitions are equivalent:

```
void strcpy(char dest[], char source[]) { /* ... */ }
void strcpy(char dest[], char *source)  { /* ... */ }
void strcpy(char *dest, char source[])  { /* ... */ }
void strcpy(char *dest, char *source)   { /* ... */ }
```

The manner in which `dest` and `source` are declared has no bearing on whether or not these identifiers can be used with pointer or array notation in the function body. However, it is common practice to use either all pointer notation or all array notation. (In earlier chapters, we used array notation because we had not yet learned about pointers. However, all of those earlier examples could be rewritten using pointer notation.)

7.5 Functions Returning Pointers

Functions can return objects of any type except arrays. Therefore, a pointer can be returned. Earlier, it was stated that the library routine `strcpy` returns a value. A complete implementation of `strcpy` follows:

```
#include <stdio.h>

main()
{
        char str[30];
        char *strcpy(char *, char *);

        printf("return value = >%s<\n", strcpy(str, "abc"));
        printf("str = >%s<\n", str);
}


char *strcpy(char *pdest, char *psource)
{
        char *pcopy = pdest;

        while ((*pdest++ = *psource++) != '\0')
                ;

        return (pcopy);
}
```

The output produced is:

```
return value = >abc<
str = >abc<
```

We must declare that `strcpy` returns a pointer to `char` in both the function prototype and the function definition. When the `printf` edit mask `%s` was introduced in an earlier chapter, it was stated that the argument expected was a null-terminated array of `char`. However, because such arrays are passed by address, a pointer to a null-terminated string is really what is expected. And, because `strcpy` returns such an object, the return value can be used directly to display the string it points to.

The fact that `strcpy` returns the address of its first argument is purely a matter of convenience. If we wish to embed a call to `strcpy` within an expression, we can do so as shown. If, however, we wish simply to call `strcpy` using an expression statement, that, too, is possible. Many of the *strxxx* and *memxxx* library routines declared in `string.h` have this capability.

The following example contains a function called `stoupper` which accepts a pointer to a null-terminated string and converts each lowercase letter in that string to its uppercase equivalent.

```
#include <stdio.h>
#include <ctype.h>

main()
{
        char *ptext = "ABCdefghij!@#$%wxyz";
        char *stoupper(char *);

        printf("  Original version: >%s<\n", ptext);
        printf("Upper case version: >%s<\n", stoupper(ptext));
}


char *stoupper(char *pc)
{
        char *pcopy = pc;

        while ((*pc = toupper(*pc)) != '\0')
                pc++;

        return (pcopy);
}
```

The output produced is:

```
  Original version: >ABCdefghij!@#$%wxyz<
Upper case version: >ABCDEFGHIJ!@#$%WXYZ<
```

A lowercase version `stolower` can be written simply by calling `tolower` instead of `toupper`. Neither `stoupper` nor `stolower` is part of the standard C library.

The following declaration is worthy of a comment:

```
char *ptext = "ABCdefghij!@#$%wxyz";
```

The identifier `ptext` is being declared as an automatic object that can point to a `char`. Because `ptext` is a scalar, its initializer list may contain only one expression. That expression is a string literal. We have seen on numerous occasions that when the compiler comes across a string literal used in an expression, it allocates space for it and adds a terminated '\0'. The type of that expression is array of n `char` (where n is the number of `chars` in the array, including the '\0') and the value of the expression is a pointer to the first `char` in the array. Therefore, `ptext` is being initialized with the address of the letter A. The string is not being copied to `ptext` as you might first believe because C does not support string assignment.

The library function `strchr` locates the first occurrence of a given character in a given string. The prototype for this function is:

```
char *strchr(char *pstring, int chr);
```

An implementation of this function might look something like the following. (Note that by definition, in this library function the null character terminating the string is considered to be part of the string. That is, you can search a string looking for the terminating '\0'. However, the same result also can be achieved via `strlen` and some pointer arithmetic.)

```c
char *strchr(char *pstring, int chr)
{
        while (*pstring != '\0') {
                if (*pstring == chr)
                        return (pstring);

                ++pstring;
        }

        return (0);
}


#include <stdio.h>

main()
{
        char *pc;

        pc = strchr("ABCDEF", 'C');
        if (pc == 0)
                printf("Character C not found\n");
        else
                printf("Trailing substring is >%s<\n", pc);

        if ((pc = strchr("ABCDEF", 'X')) == 0)
                printf("Character X not found\n");
        else
                printf("Trailing substring is >%s<\n", pc);
}
```

The output produced is:

```
Trailing substring is >CDEF<
Character X not found
```

The only new aspect introduced here is the use of 0 in pointer comparisons and as a pointer return value; i.e., we are mixing pointers and integers, something you generally should avoid. The reason is simple: C guarantees that it will never store an object or function at an address of 0. Therefore, we have a value that can be given to a pointer so it can take on a special meaning. In this example, a pointer value of zero is returned if the character being searched for does not exist. Likewise, the library function `strstr` returns this special null pointer if a substring can not be found in another string. ANSI C permits the value 0 to be assigned and/or compared with pointer expressions without using a cast. This is the only integral value that you can use with pointers in a portable fashion.

In fact, numerous standard library routines use the *null pointer* in this way. Consequently, the null pointer has been given a special name NULL. This macro is defined in numerous standard headers; although, traditionally, it usually was only defined in `stdio.h`.

Use the name `NULL` instead of 0 in pointer expressions because that is `NULL`'s purpose and its meaning is well understood and obvious. You should understand that the specific definition of `NULL` is not given by ANSI C. The Standard only requires that `NULL` expand to an implementation-defined null pointer constant. Specifically, the Standard states, "An integral constant expression with the value 0, or such an expression cast to type `void *`, is called a null pointer constant. If a null pointer constant is assigned to or compared for equality to a pointer, the constant is converted to a pointer of that type. Such a pointer, called a null pointer, is guaranteed to compare unequal to a pointer to any object or function."

`NULL` could be defined as 0 or 0L or, perhaps, something else. On some implementations, different pointer types can have different sizes and you must take care that `NULL` can be used with all of them. The null pointer constant need not be represented by all-bits-zero.

> **Exercise 7-5*:** Write a function called `reverse` that accepts one argument, a pointer to a null-terminated string. It reverses the characters in the input string in place and returns the address of the string to the caller. `reverse` must be able to handle an arbitrary length string without allocating storage for that string locally. Test the function with various length strings, including both odd and even lengths. Also reverse a null (empty) string. Can you use a string literal as an argument to `reverse`; after all, its type is `char *`? The prototype for `reverse` is:
>
> ```
> char *reverse(char *);
> ```
>
> **Exercise 7-6:** How does your implementation represent the null pointer?

7.6   Pointer Arithmetic Revisited

Pointers may be involved in limited arithmetic operations (We already have seen pointers being used with the `++` and `--` operators.) Given the similarity between `++i` and `i = i + 1`, we might expect that we can add arbitrary integral expressions to, or subtract them from, pointer expressions. That is, indeed, the case. For example, the following code is an implementation of the library function `strrchr`, which searches a string for a given character. `strrchr` is almost identical to `strchr` except that `strrchr` searches from the end of the string backwards.

```
#include <stdio.h>
#include <string.h>

char *strrchr(char *pstring, int chr)
{
        char *pc;

        pc = pstring + strlen(pstring) - 1;
        while (pc >= pstring) {
                if (*pc == chr)
                        return (pc);

                --pc;
        }

        return (NULL);
}


main()
{
        char *pc;

        pc = strrchr("CBCDCF", 'C');
        if (pc == NULL)
                printf("Character C not found\n");
        else
                printf("Trailing substring is >%s<\n", pc);

        if ((pc = strrchr("ABCDEF", 'X')) == NULL)
                printf("Character X not found\n");
        else
                printf("Trailing substring is >%s<\n", pc);
}
```

The output produced is:

```
Trailing substring is >CF<
Character X not found
```

The statement:

```
pc = pstring + strlen(pstring) - 1;
```

makes pc point to the char immediately preceding the trailing '\0'. And, in the case of a null string, pc points to the char before the start of the string. However, in this case, pc would be less than pstring, the loop would never be entered and NULL would be returned as required.

Another arithmetic operation that can be performed on pointers is that one pointer can be subtracted from another. However, the pointers have to point to the same type of object for this to be syntactically correct. Also, to be strictly portable, both pointers must point to elements in the same array, otherwise, the result usually will be meaningless; for example:

```
#include <stdio.h>

main()
{
        double d[25];
        double *pd1 = &d[5];
        double *pd2 = &d[22];
        double e;

        long int diff;


        diff = pd2 - pd1;
        printf("pd2 - pd1 = %ld\n", diff);

        diff = pd1 - pd2;
        printf("pd1 - pd2 = %ld\n", diff);

        diff = pd2 - &e;          /* ??? */
        printf("pd2 - &e  = %ld\n", diff);
}
```

The output produced is:

```
pd2 - pd1 = 17
pd1 - pd2 = -17
pd2 - &e  = -3
```

As we see, the difference between two pointers is n objects, not n bytes. That is, the difference between the two addresses is scaled by the size of the object being pointed to (as with all pointer arithmetic). Therefore, the first result is as expected—17 double objects do indeed separate these two addresses. However, 17 is neither the inclusive nor exclusive number of objects separating d[5] and d[22]. So, depending on what you want the pointer subtraction to mean, you may need to add or subtract one from the result.

If a pointer with a larger value is subtracted from one with a smaller value, a negative result is produced. Therefore, the difference provides both magnitude and direction information.

In the third case, a useless result probably is obtained because we have no control over where e is allocated in memory and we don't know what lies between it and any other object we have allocated.

Note that we have gone to the trouble of creating a temporary variable of type long int. This is because the type of the difference between two pointers is implementation-defined. ANSI C calls this type ptrdiff_t and, in many respects, it is just like size_t, the type of the sizeof operator. By definition, ptrdiff_t is a signed integral type capable of storing the difference between two pointers. The only candidates realistically available for this type are int and long int. Therefore, the example stores the difference in the largest of these and displays it using the %ld mask. This is the only guaranteed way to make the program portable.

All other arithmetic operations are syntactically illegal when applied to pointers. However, as with numerous other aspects of C, there is a back door through which you can perform other operations. For example, for certain programs you may wish to know the base address of a particular segment of memory. On VAX/VMS, each address belongs to a memory page, while on MS-DOS, each belongs to a paragraph. Perhaps you wish to find out what that page (or paragraph) base address is; for example:

```
/* locate the page base address of a variable */

#include <stdio.h>

main()
{
        double d;
        unsigned long int u;

        printf("                    &d = %lx\n", &d);
        u = (unsigned long int) &d;
        u &= ~511;
        printf("page base address = %0lx\n", u);
}
```

The output is:

```
              &d = 374c0fce
page base address = 374c0e00
```

By masking off the nine low-order bits, the 512-byte page base address is determined. Similarly, the % modulus operator can be used to determine the offset within a page. And once we have cast the pointer to an integral type, we can perform any arithmetic operation on it that makes sense. Of course, all this is quite implementation-defined because it relies on the implementation having an integral type large enough to hold a pointer representation. It also requires us to know what that integral type is and whether or not it is signed or unsigned. You also must be careful when casting pointers to and from integer types on word architectures since the behavior may be different from that on byte machines.

7.7 Array Subscripts and Pointers

As mentioned earlier, when the name of an array is used as a function argument, it behaves like a pointer to the first element. In fact, this is true whenever an array designator (such as an array name) appears in an expression. For example, if name is a char array and pc is a pointer to char, pc = &name[0] is equivalent to pc = name. And, because the latter is simpler to write, it is much more commonly used.

While it is true that an array name can be thought of as a pointer to the first element in that array, the array name itself is not, strictly speaking, a pointer. Pointers are variables and, therefore, their value may change. However, the address of the first element of an array is static: Once an array is allocated space, its address remains constant and can not be changed.

While there is a very close relationship between arrays and pointers, they are not completely interchangeable. In particular, in the scope of an array definition, that array name can not be used in all respects as a pointer. However, once the address of an array is passed to a function, within that function, the array's identity has been lost. The array can be manipulated using either array or pointer notation, or even both of them at the same time. This is also true once the address of an array element is stored in a pointer. From that point on, the pointer is ignorant of the fact that it is pointing into an array. In fact, this aspect is one that makes C as powerful as it is.

Consider the following example:

```
#include <stdio.h>

main()
{
        static float fa[] = {2.34, 3.45, 4.56, 5.67, 6.78};

        float *fp = fa;
        int i;

        for (i = 0; i < (sizeof(fa)/sizeof(fa[0])); ++i)
                printf("fa[%d] = %5.2f\t*(fp + %d) = %5.2f\n",
                        i, fa[i], i, *(fp + i));
}
```

which produces the output:

```
fa[0] = 2.34    *(fp + 0) = 2.34
fa[1] = 3.45    *(fp + 1) = 3.45
fa[2] = 4.56    *(fp + 2) = 4.56
fa[3] = 5.67    *(fp + 3) = 5.67
fa[4] = 6.78    *(fp + 4) = 6.78
```

If you think about it, an array subscript is nothing more than an offset from a base address. As such, we can think of `fa[0]` as being that element at offset 0 from the start of the array. That is why arrays in C begin at subscript 0 instead of 1.

The meaning of expressions of the form `fa[i]` is obvious. However, that of `*(fp + i)` may not be. Let's take a closer look at this expression. Since, in an expression, the name of an array is treated as a pointer to its first element, this expression can be rewritten as:

```
*(&fp[0] + i)
```

We also know that when an integer expression having value v is added to a pointer, the result is a pointer that points to a location v objects beyond the original pointer. That is, `&fp[0] + i` points to the *ith* object beyond `fp[0]`. And, if we dereference that pointer, we get that *ith* object. Simply stated, then, the formula for converting between array and pointer notation is:

```
a[i]   is equivalent to   *(a + i)
```

Because of this rule, array subscript expressions always can be rewritten as pointer expressions and vice versa. This is possible because in C, [] is an operator, not a punctuator. As such, its only requirements are that, of its two operands, one must be a pointer expression and the other must be an integral expression. Therefore, it is possible to use subscripting even when no arrays have been declared; for example:

```
char *strcpy(char *dest, char source[])
{
        unsigned i = 0;

        while ((dest[i] = *source++) != '\0')
                ++i;

        return (dest);
}
```

Not only are we subscripting dest when it was declared as a pointer, we are dereferencing and incrementing source when it was declared as an array. While this code is legitimate, it's not good style.

Programmers new to C generally will stay with the subscripting method as it is used in most other high-level languages. However, seasoned C programmers generally go the pointer route.

It is easy to recognize an array subscript expression and to convert it to its pointer equivalent. However, the opposite is not always so obvious. Consider the following program:

```
#include <stdio.h>

main()
{
        double d = 1.234;
        double *pd = &d;

        printf("*pd = %6.3f, pd[0] = %6.3f\n", *pd, pd[0]);
}
```

The output produced is:

```
*pd =  1.234, pd[0] =  1.234
```

The expression *pd is equivalent to *(pd + 0). By the conversion rule, this is equivalent to pd[0]. That is, we can deal with d indirectly through pd as an array of one element, and isn't that what a scalar is? (Of course, we also could use pd[1], but that would result in undefined behavior.) Voila! We have discovered something "magic" about C. You arbitrarily can subscript any pointer to one level no matter what, and the resulting expression will have meaning.

If we apply this new-found knowledge to multidimensional arrays, we gain some more insight into how they can work. For example, a[2][3] declares an array of two rows, each having three objects. Since [] is an operator and operators at this precedence level associate left to right, the expression a[1][2] is equivalent to (a[1])[2].

a[1] designates the second row of the array. That is, it is an array of three objects. However, when an array designator is used in an expression, it is treated as a pointer to the first element, so the value of a[1] is a pointer to the first object in the second row. And, by subscripting this pointer using [2], we get the object at offset two from that pointer, namely, the third object in the second row. Now we see why multidimensional arrays are written using [i][j]...[k] notation instead of [i, j, ..., k]. Also, we have explained how an n-dimensional array can be referenced using anywhere between zero and n subscripts.

7.8   Arrays of Pointers

Pointers are variables and, because we can have arrays of variables, we can have arrays of pointers. For example:

```
double d1 = 1.2;
double d2 = 2.3;
double d3 = 3.4;
double *pd[] = {&d1, &d2, &d3};
```

pd is an array of three pointers to double and it is initialized with the addresses of three double variables.

```
#include <stdio.h>

char *table[] = {
        "Summer",
        "Fall",
        "Winter",
        "Spring",
        ""
};


main()
{
        int i = 0;

        while(*table[i] != '\0') {
                printf("table[%d] points to >%s<\n",
                        i, table[i]);
                ++i;
        }
}
```

The output is:

```
table[0] points to >Summer<
table[1] points to >Fall<
table[2] points to >Winter<
table[3] points to >Spring<
```

In this case, `table` is an array of five pointers to `char`. Each element is initialized to point to a null-terminated array of `char` that is allocated space by the compiler. The empty string is used as a terminator so we can traverse the array without knowing its size. The loop stops when `table[i]` points to a byte containing `'\0'`. That is what an empty string contains.

Exercise 7-7*: Write a program that gets strings from standard input using the `scanf` library function, until the string `END` is entered. Compare the input string against a list of valid strings. If a match is found, display "Match found at subscript[*xx*]"; otherwise display, "Invalid string". Make the comparison case-insensitive. The list of valid strings is "ADD", "DELETE", "LIST" and "REPLACE" and should be implemented as an array of pointers to `char`. The string `END` is not part of the list. (Hint: You can use the function `stoupper` defined earlier in this chapter.)

Exercise 7-8*: Consider the following declaration:

```
char *list[] = {"abc", "defghijkl", "wxyz"};
```

What does `list[1][5]` mean? What is its type and value? Seeing that it is possible to subscript `list` to two levels, discuss the pros and cons of arrays of pointers over multidimensional arrays.

7.9 Command-Line Arguments

To date, every `main` function has had zero arguments. However, standard C permits `main` to have either zero or two arguments and, if two are present, they can be used to access arguments entered on the command-line when the program is invoked; for example:

```
#include <stdio.h>

main(int argc, char *argv[])
{
        int i;

        for (i = 0; i < argc; ++i)
                printf("arg #%2d is >%s<\n", i, argv[i]);
}
```

When this program is invoked on PC-DOS V3.3 using the command- line:

```
test ABC def "ABC" "AB DE"
```

the results obtained from one compiler were:

```
arg # 0 is >C:\WRITING\LETSCNOW\TEST.EXE<
arg # 1 is >ABC<
arg # 2 is >def<
arg # 3 is >ABC<
arg # 4 is >AB DE<
```

A formal argument, `argv` is an array of pointers whose elements point to null-terminated command-line strings. `argc` contains the number of the strings found at program startup. By definition, `argv[0]` points to the name of the program and the format of this string is implementation-defined (as are numerous other aspects of command-line processing). In this case, the program startup code provided by this particular compiler translated the program name to its full device and directory specification. Also, the case of arguments and any white space embedded in double quotes were preserved. (This is not guaranteed by ANSI C.)

Because `argc` and `argv` are formal arguments, they may have any name the programmer wishes. However, it is common practice to use the names `argc` and `argv`.

Many implementations (including UNIX, VAX C and most MS-DOS compilers) also provide a third argument to `main`. This generally is called `envp` and, like `argv`, it is an array of pointers to `char`. Each element points to a string describing some environment variable whose format is operating system-specific. The array contains a dummy last element with a value of `NULL`. ANSI C does not support `envp`.

Command-line argument processing can be used to make user-written programs look more like those utilities provided with the operating system. In fact, on UNIX, the operating system utilities are implemented exactly in this manner using C.

If `main` is defined without arguments, then any values passed to it by the startup code will be inaccessible by the program.

> **Exercise 7-9:** Learn how to run a program on your system so that command-line arguments can be passed. (On systems that require something like a RUN command, accompanying arguments may not be possible.)

> **Exercise 7-10:** Does your implementation preserve the casing of command-line arguments? Is white space embedded in double quotes preserved? Can you modify `argc` and `argv` and the strings pointed to by `argv`?

> **Exercise 7-11:** Does your implementation support the `envp` argument to `main`? If so, write a program to use it.

7.10   Generic Pointers

On machines with word architectures, pointers to `char` generally have a different representation than pointers to other types do. However, library routines such as `memcpy` (in `string.h`) require arguments that are pointers to arbitrary objects. How, then, can the prototype for `memcpy` be written given that we don't know the type of the pointer that will be given to it at compile-time? Historically, `char *` was used because that was considered to be equivalent to a generic pointer. However, this was a little misleading. Also, functions such as the dynamic memory allocation routines in `stdlib.h` need to return generic pointers.

As a result of these and other reasons, ANSI C invented a generic pointer type called pointer to void. It is written as `void *`; however, it has nothing to do with `void` functions or `void` in prototype argument lists. This is the third different use for the `void` keyword.

You can create `void` pointer objects and arrays of such objects and you can pass them to functions and return them from functions. In short, you can treat them in every way like "real" pointers except that you can not dereference a `void` pointer or perform arithmetic on it. A `void` pointer is simply an address and it has no other attributes. To get at the location pointed to by a `void` pointer, you first must assign it or cast it to a non-`void` pointer.

All pointer types are assignment-compatible with a `void` pointer. If you assign a pointer of type T into and then out of a `void` pointer, you are guaranteed to point to the same object you started out pointing to. However, the results are undefined if you assign a pointer of more strict alignment criteria to a `void` pointer and then assign it out to a pointer of less strict alignment, and dereference the final pointer.

Examples of `void` pointer use follow:

```
#include <string.h>

f()
{
        void *pv;
        char c1[10];
        char c2[50];
        double d1 = 1.2;
        double d2;
        double *pd = &d1;
        char *pc = c1;
        void **abc[10][23];


        pv = memcpy(c1, c2, 5);

        pv = pd;                /* OK */
        pd = pv;                /* OK */
        d2 = *((double *) pv);  /* OK */
        pv = pc;                /* OK */
        pd = pv;                /* ??? */
}
```

The `memcpy` library routine is given two `char` pointers when it expects two `void` pointers. However, these pointer types are compatible. To dereference `pv`, it is first cast a pointer to `double`. The final assignment is questionable because `pd` contains an address that is not necessarily aligned suitably for a `double` object on certain machines. The assignment itself might be OK, but attempts to dereference `pd` may fail. `abc` is a two-dimensional array of pointers to `void` pointers.

If you examine the headers of an implementation that is tracking the ANSI Standard, you will see numerous examples of `void *` argument and function return declarations. In fact, `NULL` even may be defined as `(void *)0`.

Exercise 7-12: Does your implementation support `void` pointers? If so, inspect the standard library headers looking for uses of `void *` as function argument and return types.

7.11   Common Pointer Problems

One very common error made when dealing with pointers is to allocate space for the
pointer itself, but not for the space it is to point to; for example:

```
/* Incorrect pointer use */

#include <stdio.h>
#include <string.h>

main()
{
        char *txt;

        strcpy(txt, "A literal string");
        printf("txt points to >%s<\n", txt);
        printf("txt points to address %p\n", txt);
}
```

which produces the output:

```
txt points to >A literal string<
txt points to address xxxx
```

Because `txt` has an undefined initial value, `strcpy` copies its source string to
an unknown location, possibly overwriting critical areas of memory. In fact, when
this program was run on an MS-DOS system using the large memory model (which
provides access to all memory including that occupied by the operating system), part
of MS-DOS was overwritten causing a file on disk to be trashed. Then the system
hung and had to be rebooted. When run on VAX/VMS, an access violation occurred
because the address `txt` pointed to was outside the program's address space. On
another implementation, the program ran to completion.

Another problem occurs when arrays of `char` are not null-terminated and their
address is given to `printf` with a mask of `%s`, or to `strcpy`, `strlen`, etc., all of which
expect to find a `'\0'`. Two outcomes can result. Either a `'\0'` is found somewhere
in memory and the process completes after having run too far, or the `char` pointer is
incremented so far that it produces an address outside the program's address space,
causing the program to abort (at least on multitasking systems).

As mentioned earlier, initially it can be confusing as to whether or not a * is needed in a pointer expression. Consider the following:

```
#include <stdio.h>
#include <string.h>

void f()
{
        char array[100];
        char *pc;

        /* ... */

        strcpy(array, *pc);
        printf("text is >%s<\n", *pc);
}
```

In both function calls, *pc is used instead of pc. That is, we have passed a char rather than the pointer to char expected by strcpy and printf. And, because the value of a char (on an eight-bit machine) can range from 0 to 255, that is the magnitude of the address actually used by these routines. On MS-DOS systems using the large memory model, this maps into the interrupt vector table. On VAX/VMS, the first page of address space (addresses 0–511) can not be accessed by the user program, resulting in an access violation.

If you are programming on a multiuser (or maybe even on a single-user, multi-tasking) system, memory access violations are generated when you attempt to access memory not allocated to your executable image. And, hopefully, your system provides some traceback mechanism to help locate the erroneous statement. However, on simple-minded systems such as MS-DOS, there is no memory protection and any address is accessible. Therefore, problems can go undetected for a long time and about the only safeguard you have is to compile using small memory models, so when something gets trashed, at least you restrict the damage to your own memory segment. That way, you can not cause any serious (and possibly permanent) damage to the operating environment.

> **Exercise 7-13:** Does your system provide a way to detect and trap attempts to write outside your program's address space?

7.12 Chapter Summary

- A pointer is a variable that contains the address of another variable.

- Accessing an object via a pointer to it is known as dereferencing that pointer.

- C always passes arrays by address. And, because a string literal is implemented as an array of char, such literals are passed as pointers to char. (The first argument to printf is one common example.)

- Rarely, if ever, are we interested in the actual address of an object. We simply store its address so we can get at it indirectly.

- Uninitialized automatic pointers point "into the wild blue yonder."

- The & unary operator is used to find the address of an object. The * unary operator is used to dereference a pointer.

- The value of a pointer can be displayed in an implementation-defined format by printf using %p.

- Because a pointer is a variable that contains the address of another variable, it can contain the address of another pointer.

- The amount of storage allocated to a pointer is implementation-defined.

- Pointers may point to objects of any type that you legitimately can declare. Pointers even may point to executable code, in which case, they are known as pointers to functions.

- Because pointers are types, you may cast from and to pointer types. Be careful, though, because dereferencing a pointer that was created via a cast can be catastrophic if object alignment requirements are violated.

- scanf is a standard library function that reads from standard input. It uses edit masks much like printf. However, because scanf returns values back through its argument list, every argument given to it must be a pointer. The %s mask accepts characters until white space is detected.

- In the context of formal argument lists, pointer and array notation can be interchanged freely.

- Functions can return pointers of any type.

- C guarantees that it will never store an object or function at an address of 0. Therefore, we have a value that can be given to a pointer so it can take on a special meaning. This null pointer is given the name NULL, which is a macro defined in stdio.h (among other headers).

- Pointers may be involved in limited arithmetic operations. Specifically, you can add integral expressions to, or subtract them from, a pointer expression and you can subtract one pointer from another, provided both have the same type.

- The type of the difference between two pointers is implementation-defined. ANSI C calls this type ptrdiff_t.

- While an array name can be thought of as a pointer to the first element in that array, the array name itself is not, strictly speaking, a pointer.

- The formula for converting between array and pointer notation is "a[i] is equivalent to *(a + i)".

- Array subscript expressions always can be rewritten as pointer expressions and vice versa.

- You arbitrarily can subscript any pointer to one level no matter what, and the resulting expression will have meaning.

- Standard C permits main to have either zero or two arguments. If two are present, they can be used to access arguments entered on the command-line when the program is invoked. These arguments traditionally are called argc and argv. argv is an array of pointers whose elements point to null-terminated command-line strings. `argc` contains the number of the strings found at program startup.

- ANSI C invented generic pointers. They are like "real" pointers except that you can not dereference a `void` pointer or perform arithmetic on it. A `void` pointer is simply an address and it has no other attributes. To get at the location pointed to by a `void` pointer, you first must assign it or cast it to a non-`void` pointer.

- All pointer types are assignment-compatible with a `void` pointer.

Chapter 8

Standard Library
I/O Routines

When learning a language, one of the first things you typically learn is to perform rudimentary file and terminal I/O. Until now, we have read only from the keyboard and written only to the screen. (Of course, if your operating system supports I/O redirection, as do UNIX and MS-DOS systems, among others, you indirectly could have done disk I/O as well.) The reason for deferring file I/O until now is that the syntax required involves the use of pointer notation, something covered only in the previous chapter.

In this chapter, we will show how to interface with files and will outline the other capabilities available in the standard I/O library. In particular, we will summarize all of the edit masks available to the formatted input and output function families of scanf and printf.

Note that the standard I/O library supports only sequential files. It does, however, permit random positioning within those files. Support for other file types and file positioning operations is implementation-defined.

8.1   Introductory File I/O

Since I/O is part of the run-time library, it is the programmer's responsibility to establish and manage the interface between the program and any I/O files. In Standard C, the logical channels on which we perform I/O are called *streams*. In previous chapters, three standard streams were mentioned. They are called stdin, stdout and stderr and they refer to standard input, standard output and standard error, respectively. They are opened for you at the start of each program (unless you take special steps to disable them) and they are closed when the program terminates.

The stdin stream generally is mapped to the standard input device such as a terminal's keyboard. stdout generally is mapped to a video screen or terminal printer, and stderr usually is mapped to the same place as stdout. Systems that support I/O redirection provide a means to redirect stdin and stdout. They also may provide a way to redirect stderr.

Ever since we began using printf, we have been performing I/O to the stream stdout. However, because printf can write only to that stream, there is no need to state it explicitly. As we shall see later, another member of the printf family can write to any given output stream.

Let's consider the following fairly simple program that reads characters from the file text.dat, counting the number of characters, new-lines and form-feeds it contains.

```c
/* wc1 - count characters, lines and pages in a file. */
/* hard-coded filename version */

#include <stdio.h>
#include <stdlib.h>

main()
{
        int c;
        unsigned long numlines = 0;
        unsigned long numchars = 0;
        unsigned long numpages = 0;
        FILE *infile;

        infile = fopen("text.dat", "r");
        if (infile == NULL) {
                printf("Can't open input file\n");
                exit(2);
        }
        else
                printf("Input file opened OK\n");

        while ((c = fgetc(infile)) != EOF) {
                ++numchars;
                if (c == '\n')
                        ++numlines;
                else if (c == '\f')
                        ++numpages;
        }

        fclose(infile);

        printf("Char count: %lu\n", numchars);
        printf("Line count: %lu\n", numlines);
        printf("Page count: %lu\n", numpages);
}
```

Possible outputs from this program could be:

```
Can't open input file
```

and:

```
Input file opened OK
Char count: 610
Line count: 33
Page count: 0
```

The header `stdio.h` is included so that prototypes for all the I/O library routines are made available and so that macros such as `NULL` and `EOF` are defined; `stdlib.h` contains a prototype for the `exit` library routine.

The key part of this program is the declaration of `infile`. It has the type `FILE *`, which is "a pointer to FILE." This is the type of a stream and is defined in `stdio.h`; however, to fully understand the definition, you will need more information than we have covered at this stage. In any case, the specific technical details are unimportant, provided you understand the idea behind them. In fact, the actual definition of `FILE` varies widely from one implementation to another; hence the use of the pseudo-type `FILE` because this allows each implementation to map `FILE` to the structure needed by the underlying file system.

When you open a file using `fopen`, a file context block (of type FILE) is established that contains the current context information for that file, while it is open. For example, it may contain the address of the I/O buffer, the size of that buffer, whether the file currently is at end-of-file or in an error condition. It also records whether the file is currently being used in read, write or update mode. Apart from a few standard requirements, the implementer is free to record any other information they think will be useful.

If `fopen` successfully opens the given file, it returns a pointer to the file context block. That is, the return type of `fopen` is `FILE *`. Specifically, the prototype for `fopen` is:

```
FILE *fopen(char *filename, char *mode);
```

If the file can not be opened for any reason, `fopen` returns the null pointer value `NULL`. `fopen` provides no way to indicate the source of the error. Error-handling involves the use of `errno` and will be discussed later. You always should check the return value of `fopen` against `NULL`.

In this example, the function call and the test are separate; however, they often are combined as follows:

```
if ((infile = fopen("text.dat", "r")) == NULL)
```

Note that in this case the extra grouping parentheses are absolutely necessary, because without them, equality has precedence over assignment, in which case, the result of `fopen` is compared with `NULL`, and the `int` result of true or false is then assigned to `infile` causing all subsequent I/O operations on that stream almost certainly to fail. (An ANSI Conforming compiler should generate an error in this case because you would be assigning an integer to a pointer and, except for the integer constant expression 0, the two types are not assignment-compatible.)

The second argument to `fopen` indicates the open mode. The simplest form is one of `"r"` (read), `"w"` (write) and `"a"` (append). If a file is opened for write and a file by the same name exists, it is implementation-defined as to what happens. It may be overwritten, a new version might be created, or an error may result, or some other action might be taken. Opening for append writes beyond the end of an existing file, or creates a new file if none exists by that name.

If the mode character is followed by a `"+"`, this indicates that the file is opened for update. Therefore, the modes `"r+"`, `"w+"` and `"a+"` are possible. Only the lowercase versions of these mode characters are recognized. All six of these modes access the stream as a text stream. If the second or third mode character is a `"b"`, the stream is accessed as a binary stream. On some systems, most noticeably UNIX, the two are the same. However, on other systems, text and binary streams are handled differently. For example, in text mode a carriage-return/line-feed record terminator character pair might be translated to a '\n' on input and the reverse may happen on output, whereas reading these characters in binary mode might result in both characters being read, untranslated. Numerous aspects of text versus binary modes are implementation-defined, since underlying file systems may vary considerably.

Characters are read using `fgetc` whose argument is the input stream name. And, because we know that `stdin` represents the standard input stream, `fgetc(stdin)` is equivalent to `getchar()`. (In fact, `getchar` often is implemented as a macro which expands to a call to `fgetc`, or some other library routine.)

To disconnect from a stream, we call `fclose`. This flushes the buffer (if output is being performed) and otherwise closes the file in an orderly manner, releasing the `FILE` object in the process. Even though files are closed properly by the implementation when a program terminates normally, you alway should explicitly close them yourself, particularly output files, so you guarantee their buffers are flushed properly.

The program exit value of 2 was not chosen for any particular reason and may, in fact, be ignored unless you have a mechanism to check it at the operating system level and you choose to do so.

Clearly, `wc1` is limited to reading from one specific file. To make the program more useful, the `wc2` version prompts the user for an input filename.

```
/* wc2 - count characters, lines and pages in a file. */
/* version to handle any file */

#include <stdio.h>
#include <stdlib.h>

main()
{
        /* ... */
        FILE *infile;
        char filename[81];

        printf("Please enter filename (80 chars max): ");
        gets(filename);

        infile = fopen(filename, "r");
        if (infile == NULL) {
                printf("Can't open input file %s\n", filename);
                exit(2);
        }

        /* ... */
}
```

Here, `gets` is used to get the string and it appends a null character at the end. Note, though, that `gets` blindly reads in characters until a new-line or end-of-file is encountered. To limit the number of characters read (in this case, to 80), you should use `fgets` instead. However, `fgets` does retain the new-line at the end of the string, whereas `gets` does not.

In this example, the first argument to `fopen` is the name of an array, which, as we know, is converted to the address of its first element. And, because `fopen` is expecting a pointer to `char` here, we can give it a string literal, the name of a `char` array or a `char` pointer that points to a null-terminated string.

The following version, `wc3`, adds the ability to specify the filename on the command-line when it is run. If no filename is present, `wc3` prompts for one just like `wc2`.

```
/* wc3 - count characters, lines and pages in a file. */
/* command-line version */

#include <stdio.h>
#include <stdlib.h>
#include <string.h>

main(int argc, char *argv[])
{
        /* ... */
        FILE *infile;
        char filename[81];

        if (argc < 2) {
                printf("Please enter filename (80 chars max): ");
                gets(filename);
        }
        else
                strcpy(filename, argv[1]);

        infile = fopen(filename, "r");

        /* ... */
}
```

Possible outcomes are:

```
>wc3
Please enter filename (80 chars max): abc.dat
Can't open input file abc.dat


wc3 text.dat
Input file text.dat opened OK
Char count: 610
Line count: 33
Page count: 0
```

Here we use `argc` and `argv` as defined in Chapter 7. Because arrays in C begin as subscript zero, `argv[0]` points to the name used to invoke the program (in this case, to "wc3"). `argv[1]` points to the second command-line argument provided one exists. If `argc` is less than 2, we know that no filename was given, so we prompt. If one is given, we copy it to the array `filename` and continue as before.

Using C's built-in command-line argument facility, it is relatively simple to design utility programs that manipulate one or more text files, for example. In fact, as stated before, many of UNIX's utilities are written in just this manner.

Exercise 8-1: Look at `stdio.h` and see how FILE and FILE * are declared. See if you can deduce the purpose of each of the data items in a FILE object for your implementation. How are `stdin`, `stdout` and `stderr` defined? Some implementations (such as MS-DOS) also provide other std*xxx* file pointers—`stdaux` and `stdprn` are examples.

Exercise 8-2: How many files can you concurrently have open? Can you prove this using a program? Does this number include the three standard file pointers?

Exercise 8-3: Does your implementation distinguish between text and binary files? If so, read the manuals to find the differences.

Exercise 8-4: Does your implementation's version of `fopen` provide any non-standard modes or extra arguments to allow you to open other than sequential files? It might, for example, permit extra arguments to define indexed sequential file attributes.

Exercise 8-5*: The spelling of filenames is implementation-defined. If you need to port programs onto different file systems, how can you handle filenames portably? One approach would be to compile conditionally a set of `fopen` calls, but that would make the source very messy. (Hint: Use macros for filenames in a header.)

8.2 More on Command-Line Processing

Next, let's look at a "filter" program that copies a file converting all uppercase characters to lowercase in the process. (A filter program is one that performs one or more simple operations on some input data, creating a new file in the process. That is, it filters the data somehow.)

```
/*
lower.c - a program to convert all upper-case characters in
a file to lower-case.  To run, type:

      lower [input-file [output-file]]

The output filename is optional and if omitted, output is
written to the terminal.  If the input filename is omitted,
then the output filename should also be omitted and input
defaults to the keyboard.  If the compiler supports I/O
redirection it can be used as follows:

          lower input-file >output-file
          lower <input-file >output-file
*/
```

```
#include <stdio.h>
#include <stdlib.h>
#include <ctype.h>

main(int argc, char *argv[])
{
        FILE *ifp, *ofp;
        int c;                          /* input character */

        if (argc > 3) {                 /* # of args valid? */
                printf("\nERROR: Invalid # of arguments. ");
                printf(" Command-line format is:\n");
                printf("\n\tlower [[<]input-file ");
                printf("[[>]output-file]]\n");
                exit (2);
        }


        if (argc == 3) {          /* both files specified */
            if ((ifp = fopen(argv[1], "r")) == NULL) {
                printf("\nERROR: Can't open input file %s\n",
                        argv[1]);
                exit (3);
            }


            if ((ofp = fopen(argv[2], "w")) == NULL) {
                printf("\nERROR: Can't open output file %s\n",
                        argv[2]);
                exit (4);
            }
        }
        else if (argc == 2) {               /* input file only? */
            if ((ifp = fopen(argv[1], "r")) == NULL) {
                printf("\nERROR: Can't open input file %s\n",
                        argv[1]);
                exit (5);
            }

            ofp = stdout;       /* use standard output */
        }
        else {                          /* no files specified */
                ifp = stdin;    /* use standard input */
                ofp = stdout;   /* use standard output */
        }
```

```
        while ((c = fgetc(ifp)) != EOF) {
                fputc(tolower(c), ofp);
        }

        fclose(ifp);
        fclose(ofp);
}
```

In this example, we may need to open two files, hence the definition of `ifp` and
`ofp`. If either or both filenames are not supplied, `stdin` and/or `stdout` are used
by default. (These and `stderr` are streams and, as such, have type `FILE *`. Note,
though, that they are constants and any attempt to modify them should result in a
compilation error.) `fputc` writes the character represented by its first (`int`) argument
to the stream pointed to by its second. As with `fgetc` and `getchar`, `putchar` can be
defined in terms of `fputc`. `ctype.h` is needed to use `tolower` and `stdlib.h` to use
`exit`. Again, the exit values chosen have no particular significance, except that they
are all different, so the specific exit path can be deduced, if necessary.

If your system supports command-line I/O redirection, `lower` can be written far
more simply, as follows:

```
#include <stdio.h>
#include <ctype.h>

main()
{
        int c;

        while ((c = getchar()) != EOF) {
                putchar(tolower(c));
        }
}
```

8.3   The `stdio.h` Header

We have been including this header from almost the first example. However, apart
from defining `EOF` and `NULL`, and providing prototypes for the few I/O routines we
have seen, this header contains many more macros and prototypes. A summary of
their names and purposes follows:

stdio.h Library Routines	
Name	*Purpose*
_IOFBF	Buffer type macros used with `setvbuf`
_IOLBF	Buffer type macros used with `setvbuf`
_IONBF	Buffer type macros used with `setvbuf`
BUFSIZ	Macro, specifying the size of the setbuf buffer
clearerr	Clears both error and end-of-file flags
EOF	Macro representing end-of-file
fclose	Closes an open stream

stdio.h Library Routines (continued)	
Name	*Purpose*
feof	Test if end-of-file flag set
ferror	Test if error flag set
fflush	Flush output stream buffer
fgetc	Read character from a stream
fgetpos	Read stream's current character position
fgets	Read a string from a stream
FILE	The (derived) type of a file object
FILENAME_MAX	Maximum length of a filename for this system
fopen	Opens a stream
FOPEN_MAX	The number of streams that can be simultaneously open
fpos_t	A (derived) type used by `fgetpos` and `fsetpos`
fprintf	Formatted write to a stream
fputc	Write a character to a stream
fputs	Write a string to a stream
fread	Read binary data from a stream
freopen	Recycles an open stream's FILE pointer
fscanf	Formatted input from a stream
fseek	Position stream to a specific character position
fsetpos	Position stream to a specific character position
ftell	Read stream's current character position
fwrite	Write binary data to a stream
getc	Macro, to read a character from a stream
getchar	Reads a character from `stdin`
gets	Reads a string from `stdin`
L_tmpnam	Macro, the size of a temporary filename
NULL	Macro, representing the null pointer
perror	Maps an `errno` error number to a message
printf	Formatted write to `stdout`
putc	Macro, writes a character to a stream
putchar	Writes a character to `stdout`
puts	Writes a string to `stdout`
remove	Removes (deletes) a file
rename	Renames a file
rewind	Resets a file to its start character position
scanf	Formatted input from `stdin`
SEEK_CUR	Macro, for positioning with `fseek`
SEEK_END	Macro, for positioning with `fseek`
SEEK_SET	Macro, for positioning with `fseek`
setbuf	Sets a stream's buffering type
setvbuf	Sets a stream's buffering type
size_t	Integral type returned by various functions
sprintf	Formatted write to a character array
sscanf	Formatted input from a character array
stderr	Standard error stream
stdin	Standard input stream
stdout	Standard output stream
tmpfile	Create and open a temporary file

| stdio.h Library Routines (continued) ||
Name	*Purpose*
tmpnam	Construct a unique temporary filename
TMP_MAX	Number of unique temporary filenames available
ungetc	Pushback (unread) a character to an input stream
vfprintf	Special formatted write to a stream
vprintf	Special formatted write to stdout
vsprintf	Special formatted write to a string

Some of these macros and functions are ANSI C inventions and, as such, may not be supported universally.

Exercise 8-6: Many implementations define clearerr, ferror and feof as macros that directly access FILE objects. See if these are functions or macros in stdio.h.

Exercise 8-7: See if your library supports the new capabilities provided by ANSI C. Examples are fgetpos, fsetpos, fpos_t, FILENAME_MAX and FOPEN_MAX.

Exercise 8-8: ANSI C's fflush only works with output files. However, some versions also work for input files. Does yours? Can you flush all output (and/or input) files with one call to fflush?

8.4   Formatted Output

We have been using printf to write formatted output to stdout. All that we have learned about printf also applies to the other members of the printf family, fprintf and sprintf. fprintf performs formatted writes to streams while sprintf does likewise to strings.

The prototypes for all three functions are:

```
int printf(char *mask, ...);
int fprintf(FILE *stream, char *mask, ...);
int sprintf(char *string, char *mask, ...);
```

The only difference between printf and fprintf is that fprintf has an extra (first) argument that indicates the stream being written to. Therefore:

```
printf("...");
```

is equivalent to:

```
fprintf(stdout, "...");
```

Note, though, that unlike getchar and fgetc, printf can not be a macro defined in terms of fprintf, because macros can not have a variable number of arguments. sprintf is like FORTRAN's ENCODE. It formats the argument list as requested and writes the output into a char array pointed to by the first argument. A null character is appended to the output string.

For example:

```
#include <stdio.h>

main()
{
        char buffer[30];
        int length;

        length = sprintf(buffer, "|%4d%6.2f %s %x|",
                23, 34.567, "abc", 123);

        printf("buffer = >%s<, length = %d\n", buffer, length);
}
```

which produces the output:

```
buffer = >|  23 34.57 abc 7b|<, length = 19
```

As you might expect, the arguments are formatted according to the edit mask and other text in the mask is passed straight through. The value returned by sprintf (and by printf and fprintf) is the number of characters written out, in this case, 19. This is particularly useful when using sprintf, because you may wish to make a temporary copy of the buffer by allocating just enough space for it at run-time.

The general format of an output edit mask is as follows:

%[flags][width][.precision][modifier]specifier

The following flags are permitted:

- - The field is left-justified.

- + Signed output has a plus or minus sign.

- *space* If a signed value is positive or results in no output, a leading space is added. The space flag is ignored if + is also present.

- # Results in an alternate output form. For o, a leading zero is added; for x (or X) a leading 0x (or 0X) is added; for e, E, f, g and G, a decimal point always appears; for g and G, trailing zeros are not removed from the fraction.

- 0 For d, i, o, u, x, X, e, E, f, g and G, leading zeros are used to pad the field width. The 0 is ignored if the - flag is also present. For d, i, o, u, x and X, a precision causes the 0 flag to be ignored.

The field width specifies the minimum width. More characters are used if necessary. By default, space padding is used.

The precision specifies the minimum number of digits to appear for d, i, o, u, x and X. For e, E and f, it specifies the number of decimal places. For g and G, it specifies the number of significant digits. It also can be used with s to limit the number of characters displayed.

Certain edit masks may have modifiers. For d, i, o, u, x and X, the h modifier indicates a short int (or unsigned short int). With n, h indicates a pointer to short int. The l modifier indicates a long int (or unsigned long int) when used with d, i, o, u, x or X; l with n means pointer to long int; and L with e, E, f, g or G, indicates a long double argument.

Either or both of the width and precision may be *, in which case, the corresponding value is taken from the next int argument instead.

The complete set of specifiers follows:

- d, i, o, u, x, X The int argument is converted to signed decimal (d or i), unsigned octal (o), unsigned decimal (u) or unsigned hexadecimal (x or X). The letters a–f are used with x and A–F are used with X. The precision indicates the minimum number of digits to appear with leading zeros added if necessary. The default precision is 1. A value of 0 displayed with an explicit precision of 0 produces no output.

- f The double argument is converted to decimal notation in the style *[-]ddd.ddd*, where the precision indicates the number of fractional decimal places. The default precision is 6. If the precision is 0, no decimal point appears. If a decimal point appears, at least one digit preceded it. Rounding occurs as necessary to fit into a given (or default) precision.

- e, E The double argument is converted to the style *[-]d.ddd±dd*. e and E behave much like f in all other respects regarding precision, etc. E uses an E in the exponent while e uses e. The exponent always contains at least two digits and is zero if the value is zero.

- g, G Uses either f or e (or E in the case of G). Style e is used if the exponent is less than -4 or greater than or equal to the precision. A decimal point appears only if it is followed by a digit.

- c The int argument is converted to unsigned char and the resulting character is written out.

- s The string pointed to by the char * argument is written out. The precision specifies the maximum number of characters to write. If no precision is specified, the string must be null-terminated.

- p The void * argument is displayed in an implementation-defined manner.

- n The argument is a pointer to an integer into which the number of characters output thus far by this printf call is written. No conversion takes place.

- % Causes a % character to be written.

Exercise 8-9: Does your printf support the masks i, X, E, G, p and n? If X is not supported, does x produce upper- or lowercase hex letters? If E and G are not supported, are exponents displayed with e or E?

8.5 Formatted Input

The scanf library family is used to perform formatted input and, in many ways, works the opposite to the printf family. scanf reads from stdin, fscanf reads from a given stream, and sscanf decodes the contents of a null-terminated string pointed to a given char pointer. sscanf is like FORTRAN's DECODE.

Their prototypes are:

```
int scanf(char *mask, ...);
int fscanf(FILE *stream, char *mask, ...);
int sscanf(char *string, char *mask, ...);
```

The only difference between `scanf` and `fscanf` is that `fscanf` has an extra (first) argument that indicates the stream being read. Therefore:

```
scanf("...", arg_list);
```

is equivalent to:

```
fscanf(stdin, "...", arg_list);
```

Note, though, that unlike `getchar` and `fgetc`, `scanf` can not be a macro defined in terms of `fscanf`, because macros can not have a variable number of arguments.

There is one very important requirement for the `scanf` family: All arguments passed to them must be pointers. Because scalars are passed by value by default, their original value can not be changed from within the called function. To do this requires passing by address. Forgetting to pass a pointer not only means the field converted is not returned to the caller, it is a likely recipe for a fatal error such as a memory access violation or random memory trashing because the value passed in will be interpreted as an address. And, if the argument is an uninitialized object of automatic storage duration, some random address will be generated and propagated from that point on.

```
#include <stdio.h>

main()
{
        char name[31];
        int quantity;
        int value;

        printf("Enter name and quantity: ");
        value = scanf("%30s %d", name, &quantity);

        printf("name: %s, quantity: %d\n", name, quantity);
        printf("value = %d\n", value);
}
```

Some sample outputs follow:

```
Enter name and quantity: frames 123
name: frames, quantity: 123
value = 2

Enter name and quantity: frames 1234567890123
name: frames, quantity: -1
value = 2

Enter name and quantity: frames stuff
name: frames, quantity: -32
value = 1
```

The `scanf` family separates input fields either by determining that a specified input field width has been reached or by white space between fields. In this example, a multiword name can not be entered because s stops scanning when white space is seen. (Embedded white space can be handled by the c and [masks.)

The value returned indicates the number of input items assigned to argument list members. It also can return `EOF` if an input failure occurs before any conversion is done. In the first example above, `value` is 2 because two fields were converted. However, as is shown by the second example, successful conversion does not necessarily mean the results of the conversion are usable. In this case, the number entered can not be represented as a signed `int`.

In the third example, the second conversion fails and `value` is set to 1. `quantity` contains -32 because that was its (undefined) initial value.

It is easy to break `scanf` by giving it unexpected input. And, because it is very difficult to write industrial strength validation routines to recognize such errors and to backup and reprompt, it is strongly suggested you not use `scanf` to get input from end users in production programs. Once you have gotten valid data into a file or string, then use `fscanf` and `sscanf`, because they can prove quite valuable.

The general format of an input edit mask is:

%[*][width][modifier]specifier

The optional * represents the assignment-suppression character. That is, you wish to read in the corresponding field, but you do not wish to assign it. You merely wish to skip over that field and continue. The return value from `scanf` does not include such fields in its count because they do not result in a conversion. Because * is already in use with `scanf`, it can not be used to supply run-time widths as with `printf`.

The field width specifies the maximum width. For some masks, less characters are used if white space is seen.

Certain edit masks may have modifiers. For d, i and n, the h modifier indicates the argument is a pointer to a `short int`. For these masks, l implies a pointer to a `long int`. Likewise, h and l indicate pointers to `unsigned int` and `unsigned long int`, respectively, when used with o, u and x. When l is used with e, f or G, it indicates a pointer to `double` rather than a pointer to `float`, and L indicates a pointer to `long double`. (Note that with `scanf`, f maps to `float`, not `double` as does `printf`.)

The complete set of specifiers follows:

- d Matches an optional signed decimal number; expects a pointer to integer argument.

- i Matches an optional signed integral number (possible with a base specifier); expects a pointer to an integer argument.

- o Matches an optional signed octal number; expects a pointer to an unsigned integer argument.

- u Matches an optional signed decimal number; expects a pointer to an unsigned integer argument.

- x Matches an optional signed hexadecimal number; expects a pointer to an unsigned integer argument.

- e, f, g Matches an optionally signed floating-point number; expects a pointer to a floating-point type argument.

- s Matches a sequence of non-white-space characters; expects the address of a char array large enough to hold the sequence plus the terminating null character.

- [Matches a non-empty sequence of characters from a set of expected characters; expects the address of a char array large enough to hold the sequence plus the terminating null character. The set is specified between [] and if the first character contained therein is a ^, the set contains those characters that terminate the scan rather than continue it. An implementation is permitted to use a hyphen to indicate ranges such as %[A-Z] to mean "the whole uppercase alphabet"; however, this is implementation-defined. For this reason, if your set includes the hyphen character, it should be the first or last where it can not be interpreted as part of a range.

- c Matches a sequence of characters with the given width (or 1 by default); expects the address of a char array large enough to hold the sequence. No terminating null character is added.

- p Matches an implementation-defined displayable pointer value of the same format generated by printf using %p; expects a pointer to pointer to void argument.

- n Causes the number of characters read to be written into the integer pointed to by the next argument; expects a pointer to an integer argument. No input characters are processed.

- % Matches a % character and no assignment occurs.

If an input edit mask contains any amount of contiguous white space, any white space in the input is skipped, provided there is still input. Otherwise, white space on input is skipped by edit masks other than [, c or n. Any non-white space, non-edit masks sequences in the format must match exactly with input characters.

Most of the input masks are straightforward. However, [warrants an example:

```
#include <stdio.h>

main()
{
        char name[31];

        printf("Please enter your name. (30 chars max): ");
        scanf("%30[^\n\f\v]", name);
        printf("name: >%s<\n", name);

        printf("Please enter another name. (30 chars max): ");
        scanf("%30s", name);
        printf("name: >%s<\n", name);
}
```

An example of some output follows:

```
Please enter your name. (30 chars max): John Smith
name: >John Smith<
Please enter another name. (30 chars max): Thomas Jones
name: >Thomas<
```

The s stops scanning at the white space, separating the first and last names while [gets the whole name. In the case of [, scanf is directed to continue inputting characters while they were not new-lines, form-feeds or vertical tabs.

A couple of final tips are worth mentioning: Always check scanf's return value to see if it equals the same number you think it should; and remember that for most edit masks, scanf skips leading white space, so entering multiple new-lines can make it appear that scanf has hung when it is really ignoring those characters as leading white space.

Exercise 8-10: Does your scanf support the masks i, p and n? Does [permit ranges to be specified using notation such as %[A-Za-z]?

Exercise 8-11*: Write a program that loops from -5 to 5. For each loop value, write a record to the file TEST.DAT that you have just created. Each record should contain the loop value, the value squared and the value cubed and should be terminated with a new-line. Separate each output field with a horizontal tab. Use the fprintf library function to write the records. After the file has been closed, reopen it and read and display to the screen the fields in each record. Use fscanf to read the fields.

8.6   Library Error Handling

Introduction to errno

The header errno.h contains the declaration of a macro errno and a number of macros against which the value of errno can be compared.

Historically, errno has been declared as an extern int; however, ANSI C requires that errno be a macro. (The macro could, however, expand to a call to a function of the same name.) ANSI C requires that errno be defined in errno.h so that it immediately becomes available when errno.h is included. Some implementations' version of errno.h contain only the errno value macros, requiring the programmer to declare errno explicitly in his own code. Still other implementations declare errno in the header math.h (not endorsed by ANSI C) and don't even have a header called errno.h.

Various standard library functions are documented as setting errno to a nonzero value when certain errors are detected. ANSI C requires that this value be positive. It also states that no library routine is required to clear errno (giving it the value 0) and, certainly, you should never rely on a library routine doing so. (However, ANSI C guarantees that errno is cleared during program startup.) Unfortunately, during the evolution of the UNIX C Standard library, errno was used as a scratch work area by various library (and other) functions. This has lead to the rule that you shouldn't assume a function leaves errno alone just because it isn't documented as changing it.

It is the programmer's responsibility to clear errno each time immediately before calling a library routine that is documented as having the ability to set it. They also must test the value of errno immediately after the library function returns, or they must save the value of errno in another variable. This is to ensure that the value of errno doesn't get overwritten by the next documented (or undocumented) library routine call.

The ANSI C library functions perror and strerror can be used to process messages corresponding to the documented values for errno. Note that to implement these functions, some libraries declare an external array sys_errlist as an array of pointers to char. This is a table of pointers to the message strings. Also, a macro sys_nerr defines the maximum errno message number stored in the table sys_errlist. While support for this table and macro are common (particularly with UNIX systems), they are not part of ANSI C.

Often, implementations have a secondary error storage location whose value is inspected when errno contains a specific value. The name of this location varies widely—VAX C uses vaxc$errno, Microtec C uses local_errno, and various DOS compilers use _doserrno. The notion of an implementation-defined secondary error status code is not addressed by ANSI C.

The following ANSI C library functions are documented as setting or using errno: acos, asin, cosh, exp, fgetpos, fsetpos, ftell, ldexp, log, log10, perror, pow, signal, sinh, strtod, strtol and strtoul.

The errno Value Macros

Historically, macros that define valid values for errno have been named starting with E. Although a standard set of names has evolved for UNIX systems and one is emerging for DOS systems, there is otherwise wide divergence on the spelling and meaning of such names. As a result, ANSI C defines only two macros: EDOM and ERANGE. EDOM is used to indicate a domain error, while ERANGE indicates a range error.

The list of standard macros in UNIX SVID follows (the POSIX Standard may be slightly different):

```
        E2BIG    /* arg list too long */
        EACCES   /* permission denied */
        EAGAIN   /* no more processes */
        EBADF    /* bad file number */
        EBUSY    /* mount device busy */
```

```
ECHILD  /* no children */
EDEADLK /* deadlock avoided */
EDOM    /* math argument */
EEXIST  /* file exists */
EFAULT  /* bad address */
EFBIG   /* file too large */
EINTR   /* interrupted system call */
EINVAL  /* invalid argument */
EIO     /* i/o error */
EISDIR  /* is a directory */
EMFILE  /* too many open files */
EMLINK  /* too many links */
ENFILE  /* file table overflow */
ENODEV  /* no such device */
ENOENT  /* no such file or directory */
ENOEXEC /* exec format error */
ENOLCK  /* no locks available */
ENOMEM  /* not enough core */
ENOSPC  /* no space left on device */
ENOTBLK /* block device required */
ENOTDIR /* not a directory */
ENOTTY  /* not a typewriter */
ENXIO   /* no such device or address */
EPERM   /* not owner */
EPIPE   /* broken pipe */
ERANGE  /* result too large */
EROFS   /* read-only file system */
ESPIPE  /* illegal seek */
ESRCH   /* no such process */
ETXTBSY /* text file busy */
EXDEV   /* cross-device link */
```

Note that other macros are possible for network and operating system-specific purposes, and it is expected more will be added in future product releases. This is permitted by ANSI C, which has reserved the space of identifier names beginning with E followed by an uppercase letter or digit for just this purpose.

A number of implementations define a macro EZERO with a value of 0. We presume that this can be used instead of the constant 0. However, this is not required by ANSI C, and it is suggested you use 0 instead.

ANSI C requires that EDOM and ERANGE (and presumably any implementation-defined macros) be distinct nonzero integral constant expressions. In fact, they also should be positive.

As mentioned above, a secondary error status location also may exist. If it does, it is inspected based on some implementation-defined value of errno indicating some implementation-specific error. For example, on VAX C, if errno is set to EVMSERR, vaxc$errno is inspected. Other implementations use a macro called ELOCAL. There is no standard name for, or guarantee that, the secondary storage actually exists.

Since errno is available to the programmer, you may wish to use it for your own error-reporting purposes. While this is not encouraged, you probably will be safe if you stick to macros with negative values.

Some Examples of errno Use

As stated above, ANSI C defines only two macros, **EDOM** and **ERANGE**. However, ANSI C does not define any macro values of **errno** that pertain to I/O errors. That is, there is no standard way to handle I/O errors except for end-of-file. The main reason for this is that there are very few things you can say about I/O errors without getting deep into a discussion of the implementation-defined details of each specific file system. The set of **errno** macros defined by UNIX provides a base to build on, but even this is incomplete for many problems and is not universally emulated. However, two file open examples follow, each of which is specific to a particular implementation.

```c
/* VAX C V2.3 on VAX/VMS */

#include <stdio.h>
#include <errno.h>
#include <perror.h>      /* VAX~C extension */

main()
{
        FILE *fp;
        char filespec[100];

        printf("Enter filespec of file to open for read: ");
        scanf("%99s", filespec);

        errno = 0;
        fp = fopen(filespec, "r");
        if (fp != NULL) {
                printf("File opened sucessfully\n");
                fclose(fp);
        }

        printf("errno = %d\n", errno);
        perror("Error");

        if (errno == EVMSERR) {
                printf("We have a VAX/VMS error\n");
                printf("vaxc$errno = %d\n", vaxc$errno);
        }
        else
                printf("Message: %s\n", sys_errlist[errno]);
}
```

The standard library routine **perror** displays a message pertaining to the current value of **errno**. It prefixes this message with the user-supplied text, a colon and a space, as shown. The UNIX-based approach of using **sys_list** has been subsumed by the new function **perror** to allow implementations to handle these messages in any way they wish without tying them down to a specific named array of pointers to char. VAX C supports both the old and the new approaches. To get at VAX/VMS-specific error codes and messages, it provides **vaxc$errno** as well as **errno**.

```
/* Turbo C V1.5 on MS-DOS */

#include <stdio.h>
#include <errno.h>

main()
{
        FILE *fp;
        char filespec[100];

        printf("Enter filespec of file to open for read: ");
        scanf("%99s", filespec);

        errno = 0;
        fp = fopen(filespec, "r");
        if (fp != NULL) {
                printf("File opened sucessfully\n");
                fclose(fp);
        }

        printf("errno = %d\n", errno);
        perror("Error");

        printf("Message: %s\n", sys_errlist[errno]);
}


Enter filespec of file to open for read: abc.dat
errno = 2
Error: No such file or directory
Message: No such file or directory

Enter filespec of file to open for read: z:abc.dat
errno = 2
Error: No such file or directory
Message: No such file or directory

Enter filespec of file to open for read: \\\abc.dat
errno = 5
Error: Permission denied
Message: Permission denied
```

Turbo C behaves much like VAX C except it does not use the extra header
perror.h. However, it can not distinguish between a file not found and a non-existent
disk drive. In both cases, errno is set to 2. In the third case, an invalid directory specification is used resulting in a seemingly unrelated message. With Turbo C, an errno
value of 2 corresponds to the UNIX errno macro ENOENT. An errno of 5 corresponds
to EACCES.

Exercise 8-12: Does your implementation supply the errno.h header?
If so, does it contain a declaration for errno? Does it define the set of
UNIX standard errno macros?

8.7   Chapter Summary

- `stdio.h` contains macros, prototypes and other information needed to interface with the standard I/O library. The standard I/O library supports only sequential files. It does, however, permit random positioning within those files.

- The logical channels on which we perform I/O are called streams.

- The three standard streams are `stdin`, `stdout` and `stderr` and they refer to standard input, standard output and standard error, respectively. You need not explicitly open these streams.

- The type of a stream is `FILE *`, read as "a pointer to FILE." The actual definition of `FILE` can and does vary widely from one implementation to another to allow each implementation to map `FILE` to the structure needed by the underlying file system.

- If `fopen` successfully opens a file, it returns a pointer to the file's "context block." If the open fails, `NULL` is returned.

- The second argument to fopen indicates the open mode and the simplest form is one of `"r"` (read), `"w"` (write) and `"a"` (append).

- If the mode character is followed by a `"+"`, this indicates the file is opened for update. Therefore, the modes `"r+"`, `"w+"` and `"a+"` are possible.

- Standard C supports both text and binary file modes using (or not using) the mode character `"b"`.

- The only difference between `printf` and `fprintf` is that `fprintf` has an extra (first) argument that indicates the stream being written to.

- `sprintf` is like FORTRAN's `ENCODE`. It formats the argument list as requested and writes the output into a `char` array pointed to by the first argument. A null character is appended to the output string.

- The general format of an output edit mask is:

$$\%[\textit{flags}][\textit{width}][.\,\textit{precision}][\textit{modifier}]\textit{specifier}$$

- The value returned by `printf` indicates the number of characters written out. If negative, it indicates an error.

- The `scanf` library family is used to perform formatted input.

- The only difference between `scanf` and `fscanf` is that `fscanf` has an extra (first) argument that indicates the stream being read from.

- There is one very important requirement for the `scanf` family—all arguments passed to them must be pointers.

- `scanf` separates input fields either by determining a specified input field width has been reached or by white space between fields.

- The value returned by scanf indicates the number of input items assigned to argument list members. It also can return EOF if an input failure occurs before any conversion is done.

- It is easy to break scanf by giving it unexpected input. And, because it is very difficult to write industrial strength validation routines to recognize such errors and to backup and reprompt, do not use scanf to get input from end users in production programs. Once you have gotten valid data into a file or string, use fscanf and sscanf because they can prove quite valuable.

- The general format of an input edit mask is:

  %[*][width][modifier]specifier

- Various standard library functions are documented as setting errno to a nonzero value when certain errors are detected.

- It is the programmer's responsibility to clear errno each time immediately before calling a library routine that is documented as having the ability to set it.

- The following ANSI C library functions are documented as setting or using errno: acos, asin, cosh, exp, fgetpos, fsetpos, ftell, ldexp, log, log10, perror, pow, signal, sinh, strtod, strtol and strtoul.

- ANSI C defines only two macros: EDOM and ERANGE. EDOM is used to indicate a domain error, while ERANGE indicates a range error. Neither can be used to resolve I/O errors. A standard set of errno macro names has evolved for UNIX systems and this is in widespread use.

Chapter 9

Structures, Bit-Fields
and Unions

In some applications, it is natural for an object to have more than one attribute at the same time. That is, the object is a group object rather than a scalar. Examples of group objects include an employee's personnel record, a data entry form definition and a library book's index card. So far, the only group object (or aggregate) type we have seen is an array. However, in an array, each element must have exactly the same type and this is not always the case with group objects. Clearly, we need another aggregate type and one in which the types of its elements can vary. In C, such an object is called a *structure*, and each of its elements is called a *member*.

9.1 Structure Templates

Before a structure object can be declared, a *template* for that structure must be defined. This template indicates the name, type and ordering of the members within that structure. It must be defined before any reference to it and it must be defined only once in a given program scope.

Let's look at a template definition:

```
/* template for a rectangular box */

struct box {
        int xpos;        /* x-coord of bottom left corner */
        int ypos;        /* y-coord of bottom left corner */
        unsigned xlen;   /* horizontal side length */
        unsigned ylen;   /* vertical side length */
};
```

The template is defined using the keyword **struct** along with a user-defined structure *tag* name, in this case, **box**. The tag is an identifier and, because it always must be prefixed by the keyword **struct**, it will not conflict with variable and function names of the same spelling. However, you can not have different structures with the same tags in the same scope. (In fact, as we shall see later, structure, union and enumerated template tags all share the same identifier namespace.)

The braces delimit the set of members and, although the template can be written in a free format, it is typically written one member per line and indented as shown. The type we have invented is `struct box`, not simply `box`. The keyword `struct` is part of the type and always must be included whenever the type is used (in declarations, for example). The four members in such a structure are named `xpos`, `ypos`, `xlen` and `ylen` and they have the types indicated in the template. As we shall see, the member names can be used only in conjunction with their parent structure name so they do not conflict with other identifiers of the same name, even in other structure templates. That is, each structure has its own unique member namespace, and the only requirement on member names is that there be no duplicates within a given template.

9.2   Structure Objects

A template definition does not cause any storage to be allocated. For that to happen, you must define an object of that structure type. For example, if we wished to define some particular boxes, we could write the following code:

```
struct box mybox;
struct box box1, box2, box3;
```

These variable definitions look just like any other we have seen in previous chapters, except that `struct box` is used as the type instead of `char`, `int`, `double`, etc. In all other respects, the format of structure declarations and definitions is the same, including initializer lists.

The term structure is really used in two contexts: to refer to the layout or mapping of a structure type and to refer to an object of that type. To disambiguate these, we will refer to the first use by the name template, and the second using structure (or structure object or variable).

As stated earlier, structure members are referenced by name and are qualified by their parent structure name; for example:

```
#include <stdio.h>

/* use template definition from above */

struct box boxa;

main()
{
        struct box boxb;
        double xpos = 1.234;
        double ylen = 3.456;

        boxa.xpos = 10;
        boxa.ypos = 12;
        boxa.xlen = 3;
        boxa.ylen = 5;

        boxb.xpos = 20;
        boxb.ypos = 22;
        boxb.xlen = 4;
        boxb.ylen = 7;

        ++boxa.xpos;

        printf("boxa.xpos = %d\n", boxa.xpos);
        printf("boxb.ylen = %u\n", boxb.ylen);
        printf("xpos = %.3f, ylen = %.3f\n", xpos, ylen);
}

boxa.xpos = 11
boxb.ylen = 7
xpos = 1.234, ylen = 3.456
```

Two structures are defined: boxa is a global structure because it is defined outside all functions and it has no static or extern class keyword. On the other hand, boxb has automatic storage duration. All of the information regarding linkage and storage duration discussed in Chapter 5 is applicable to structures as well as arrays and scalars. You even can assign the register class to a structure. However, because most structures are too big to fit into hardware registers (or wherever register variables are stored), the register class is ignored and auto is assumed instead, as with any register object that is "too big."

Note that class applies only to objects or functions; it can not be applied to a member within a template. In fact, class can not be applied to the template as a whole. It can be applied only to a declaration of a structure itself. For example, all members in a static structure inherit the static class attribute. However, you can not define a structure where only some of its members are static.

Note that the automatic variables xpos and ylen have the same names as members in the two structures. However, as stated earlier, there is no naming conflict.

To reference a member in a particular structure, the expression must include the parent structure name, the *dot* operator and the member name. For example, `boxa.xpos` is an expression that refers to the `int` member `xpos` within the structure `boxa`. We call `boxa.xpos` an expression because the period represents the dot operator. (If you refer to the precedence table in Appendix A, you will see the dot has the highest precedence possible.) And, because dot is an operator its operands are expressions: In this case they are the names of the structure and member. (Actually, the expression to the left of the dot does not have to be a structure name. It must be an expression that designates a structure, but so far, the only way we know how to do that is to use its name.)

The type of a dot expression is the type of the right-most expression, the member named. That is, `boxa.xpos` has type `int` because the member `xpos` was declared with `int` type. The left expression and dot only qualify which member you are referring to. They do not affect the type of the expression.

This is demonstrated by the following statements taken from the example above:

```
boxa.xpos = 10;
++boxa.xpos;
printf("boxa.xpos = %d\n", boxa.xpos);
printf("boxb.ylen = %u\n", boxb.ylen);
```

In the first three statements, `boxa.xpos` is used as a "regular" `int` expression. In the last, `boxb.ylen` has type `unsigned int` and, accordingly, is displayed with a `%u` edit mask. The increment case is worth further mention because, at first glance, it appears we are incrementing `boxa` rather than the member `xpos`. A quick check of the operator precedence table, however, will show that the dot has a higher precedence than `++`. That is, if we include the default grouping parentheses, the expression becomes `++(boxa.xpos)`. And while you may find this more clear, it is rarely, if ever, actually written that way. As you would expect, the value of the expression `++boxa.xpos` is different from that of `boxa.xpos++`, even though both result in the member being incremented.

Exercise 9-1*: Consider the following example in which all objects are global:

```
char name_of_the_item[30];
double multiplication_value;

struct tag {
        char name_of_the_item[30];
        double multiplication_value;
} G;
```

What are the advantages of each approach; that is, of having individual global declarations versus having one global structure, which contains all the other objects as members?

9.3 Nested Structures

On occasion, you may find that an object not only has members, but that one or more of those members is itself an aggregate. This would be implemented using nested structures as follows:

```
#include <string.h>

struct box {
        int xpos;       /* x-coord of bottom left corner */
        int ypos;       /* y-coord of bottom left corner */
        unsigned xlen;  /* horizontal side length */
        unsigned ylen;  /* vertical side length */
};

struct window {
        char xlabel[30];
        char ylabel[30];
        char title[30];
        struct box winbox;
};


main()
{
        struct window win1;

        strcpy(win1.xlabel, "X Label");
        win1.winbox.xpos = 23;
        win1.winbox.ylen = 5;

        if (win1.winbox.ylen > 3)
                /* ... */;
}
```

In this case, we define a window object that consists of some text and graphic attributes. And, because the dot is an operator and it associates left-to-right, we can have expressions involving multiple dot operators. (In fact, there is no limit to the depth of such nesting, except for your memory capacity.) The expression `win1.winbox.ylen` is evaluated as if it were written `((win1.winbox).ylen)`. That is, the member `winbox` of the structure `win1` is selected and, within that structure, member `ylen` is selected. And, because the type of `ylen` is `unsigned`, that is the type of the whole expression.

Three of the members in `struct window` are arrays, and this is permitted. In fact, a structure can contain members of any type except functions and structures of the same type as that being defined. That is, a structure can not contain an instance of itself. (It can, however, contain a pointer to an instance of itself, as we shall see.) Since the `xlabel` member is a `char` array, it can be used in any appropriate context as shown by its use as a destination argument to `strcpy`. As you might expect, to get at the fourth `char` within such an array, you would use the expression `win1.xlabel[3]`. Note that the dot and subscript operators have the same precedence, but they associate left-to-right. Therefore, this expression behaves as `(win1.xlabel)[3]`.

The two templates used here could have been combined into one definition, but still defining two templates as follows:

```
struct window {
        char xlabel[30];
        char ylabel[30];
        char title[30];
        struct box {
                int xpos;
                int ypos;
                unsigned xlen;
                unsigned ylen;
        } winbox;
};
```

In this case, the second template is defined when it is first used rather than having it defined earlier. It's largely a matter of style which approach you use, but it can matter. For example, if two different structure types both contain a common substructure, that common structure template should be defined external to those structures so it can be shared. It really doesn't "belong" to either structure, so it shouldn't be defined within one of them.

For this particular example, you could argue that there is no need for nested structures. Why not simply put all the members at the same level as follows?

```
struct window {
        char xlabel[30];
        char ylabel[30];
        char title[30];
        int xpos;
        int ypos;
        unsigned xlen;
        unsigned ylen;
};
```

This is possible and desirable for some applications. However, if the box attribute structure also exists in other structures or we wish to manipulate box objects as a whole, we would need to retain the nested approach.

9.4   Initialization

As we have seen, when an object is defined, it can contain an optional initialization list and, if the list is missing, some default initial value results depending on the storage duration of the object. Specifically, objects of static storage duration take on a default value of zero (cast to their respective type) while the initial value of automatic storage duration objects is undefined. In the case of an aggregate type (i.e., arrays and structures), the initial value is applied to each element within the aggregate (and recursively for nested aggregates).

Let's revisit some of the examples above, and initialize the structures using initializer lists instead of assignment expressions.

```
struct box {
        int xpos;
        int ypos;
        unsigned xlen;
        unsigned ylen;
};

struct box boxa = {10, 12, 3, 5};

main()
{
        struct box boxb = {20, 22, 4, 7}; /* ?? */
}
```

When an aggregate is being initialized, the braces delimiting the initializer list are required. (They are optional for scalars.) The second initializer list is questionable not because it is wrong, but because automatic aggregates have not always been able to be initialized. And, while this capability is in the ANSI C Standard, not all implementations support it.

While the template's members have been written one per line, the initializer list has been written all on one line. This is often the case when the initializing expressions are few and simple. In other cases, it is more convenient and easier to read if each initializer is on a separate line in the same style as the template definition.

```
/* use box template from above */

struct window {
        char xlabel[30];
        char ylabel[30];
        char title[30];
        struct box winbox;
};

main()
{
        static struct window win1 = {
                "X Label",
                "Y Label",
                "Title",
                {23, 12, 4, 5}
        };
}
```

In the case of nested structures, the initializer list contains subinitializer lists. That is, the list initializing `win1` contains four initializers separated by commas. However, the fourth member is another structure, so it needs its own initializer list and the brace pairs are nested accordingly. In fact, if you really think about it, the first three members are also aggregates—they are arrays. In Chapter 3 we learned that

C provides a shorthand way of initializing `char` arrays. Instead of spelling out each element initializer as a separate expression, a string literal can be used as shown above.

The longhand method follows:

```
/* use the box and window templates from above */

main()
{
        static struct window win1 = {
                {'X', ' ', 'L', 'a', 'b', 'e', 'l', '\0'},
                {'Y', ' ', 'L', 'a', 'b', 'e', 'l', '\0'},
                {'T', 'i', 't', 'l', 'e', '\0'},
                {23, 12, 4, 5}
        };
}
```

These two versions are equivalent, and the first is considerably easier to read. Therefore, it is the one almost always used.

Just as with arrays, when initializing structures and nested structures, you must specify the complete leading part of any initializer list. In partial initializer lists, unspecified trailing members take on the value zero cast to their respective type. (This is true even for automatic structures, as discussed with arrays in Chapter 3.)

There are a number of different ways in which to define templates and structures of that type. Technically, all are equivalent, but some have style merits over others. For example, the preferred case is:

```
struct box {
        int xpos;
        int ypos;
        unsigned xlen;
        unsigned ylen;
};

struct box box1 = {1, 2, 3, 4}; /* ... */
struct box box2 = {9, 8, 7, 6}; /* ... */
```

Here, the template is separate from the structure definitions because it isn't "owned" by either of them. And, because you can define structures of type `box` in any source file in which you have declared the template, it makes sense to put template definitions inside user-written headers. Then, by using the `#include` pre-processor directive, you can "define" the template in any source file you wish. (One common example of this is the type `FILE` defined in the standard header `stdio.h`. This type is almost always a structure. The ANSI Standard headers contain other types that are explicitly defined to be structures: `struct lconv` in `locale.h` and `struct tm` in `time.h` are examples.) The danger of hard-coding the same template in multiple places is that if you ever need to change it, you run the risk of not finding all the places, resulting in some troublesome bugs.

In this case, both structures are defined separately, permitting them to be manipulated (by a text editor, for example) independent of each other. This provides
more editing flexibility than if they were combined, as in the next example:

```
struct box {
        int xpos;
        int ypos;
        unsigned xlen;
        unsigned ylen;
};

struct box box1 = {1, 2, 3, 4}, box2 = {9, 8, 7, 6};
```

This approach is harder to read and leaves no appreciable room for comments on
the declaration line. Of course, you always could write:

```
struct box box1 = {1, 2, 3, 4},
           box2 = {9, 8, 7, 6};
```

but that also has its stylistic problems. The worst version is the next example where
the template and structure definitions are combined:

```
struct box {
        int xpos;
        int ypos;
        unsigned xlen;
        unsigned ylen;
} box1 = {1, 2, 3, 4}, box2 = {9, 8, 7, 6};
```

In this case, the template definition can not be placed in a header because it
includes object definitions which can not be shared.

> **Exercise 9-2:** Does your compiler permit structures with automatic stor-
> age duration to have initializer lists?

> **Exercise 9-3:** Inspect all of the headers that come with your compiler
> to see which of them, if any, contain structure templates and/or structure
> object declarations. Start with `stdio.h` and look at the definition of `FILE`.
> Also look at `tm` in `time.h` and `lconv` in `locale.h`.

9.5   Structure Expressions

In the late 1970s, AT&T added structure expressions to its C compilers. Prior to that,
an expression containing the name of a structure (except when used as the argument
of `sizeof`) was converted to a pointer to that structure, just like array names were
(and still are). As such, it was not possible to generate an expression that designated
a structure without it's being converted to a pointer. ANSI C includes structure
expressions and almost all mainstream C compilers now support them.

There are numerous ways to create and use a structure expression, but perhaps the simplest is with assignment. Consider the following example:

```
/* use box template from above */

struct box box1 = {1, 2, 3, 4};
struct box box2;

main()
{
        box2 = box1;
}
```

Since both expressions in the assignment are structure expressions, the result is that the whole of the structure box1 is copied to box2. (Because this is not true with arrays, arrays become the only object type in C that can not be manipulated as a whole.)

As it happens, there seldom is a need to copy whole structures; however, when the need arises, it is much more elegant and simpler than assigning each individual member. In modern (and some not so modern) machines you typically have a block-move instruction which makes structure assignment a trivial task to implement. A down side of this elegance is that it hides a possibly expensive operation behind a very simple-looking expression. What if the structure is 10,000 bytes long or the machine does not have a block-move capability? In any case, the capability is in the language if you need it, but you should understand its implementation cost (if any) if you decide to rely on it heavily.

Because most modern machines also have block-compare instructions, you also might expect that structures can be compared. However, they can not. It would make little sense to perform a relational test, although testing for equality or inequality might be useful. (The reasons for not implementing structure compares is discussed in a later section regarding member alignment and holes.)

Once structure assignment was added, you got other capabilities as well. Since argument passing and function returning are modelled on assignment, they, too, became possible. For example:

```
struct box {
        int xpos;
        int ypos;
        unsigned xlen;
        unsigned ylen;
};

main()
{
        static struct box box1 = {1, 2, 3, 4};
        struct box box2;
        struct box movebox1(struct box, int, int);

        box2 = movebox1(box1, 2, -1);
}
```

```
struct box movebox1(struct box s, int x, int y)
{
        struct box tmp;

        tmp.xpos = s.xpos + x;
        tmp.ypos = s.ypos + y;
        tmp.xlen = s.xlen;
        tmp.ylen = s.ylen;

        return (tmp);
}
```

In this example, a structure is passed to movebox1 which returns a new structure containing the contents of the structure passed, except that the origin has been moved by the x and y amounts specified. The structure is passed in by value and so is not altered in the process.

Depending on the ability of your compiler and your machine's instruction set, the following version of movebox1 may be more efficient. It likely would be if the structure contained quite a few members and only a few of them were altered.

```
struct box movebox1(struct box s, int x, int y)
{
        struct box tmp;

        tmp = s;
        tmp.xpos += x;
        tmp.ypos += y;

        return (tmp);
}
```

In this case, the whole input structure is copied to the output one with only those members that change actually being assigned individually.

Passing and returning structures by value may place an undue burden on some implementations particularly for other than quite small structures. Some environments, such as VAX/VMS, have a limit on the size of an argument or on the total size of all arguments. With VMS, this total limit is 1,020 bytes (or more precisely, 255 long-words each of which is four bytes). That is, the sum of the sizes of all arguments to a function can not exceed 1,020 and, if there is only one argument and it is a structure, it can be no larger than 1,020 bytes. (It actually is possible to pass larger structures on the VAX, but doing so violates VMS's standard calling conventions. Ultrix [DEC's implementation of UNIX] does not have this limitation.)

In the case of function return values, they often are passed back in one or more adjacent hardware registers. However, few machines have enough registers to return a 1,000-byte structure. Such things are left up to the implementer to devise a game plan if one is not suggested or provided by the operating system and/or hardware. (In the case of VAX/VMS, the VAX hardware definition provides a way to return an unlimited size object.)

There are several ways to designate a structure apart from naming it. The following example demonstrates a few:

```
struct box {
        int xpos;
        int ypos;
        unsigned xlen;
        unsigned ylen;
};


struct window {
        char xlabel[30];
        char ylabel[30];
        char title[30];
        struct box winbox;
};


main()
{
        struct window win1;
        struct window win2;
        struct window frs(void);
        char *pc;
        int i = 5;

        win1 = win2;
        win1.winbox = win2.winbox;
        win1 = frs();
        win1 = i ? win2 : frs();
}
```

Structure expressions can be used as operands to a very few operators and casting is not one of them. You can not cast a structure expression into any type nor cast any expression into a structure type. However, you can use pointers to structures with the cast operator.

Exercise 9-4: Does your compiler support structure assignment and passing and returning by value? If so, look at the code generated to see what the cost of these operations is. Are there limits on the size of the structure that can be passed or returned?

9.6 Templates Without Tags

The tag on a structure template is optional, in which case, the type of the resulting
structure is "structure of unknown type"; for example:

```
struct {
        int xpos;
        int ypos;
        unsigned xlen;
        unsigned ylen;
} box1, box2;


struct {
        int xpos;
        int ypos;
        unsigned xlen;
        unsigned ylen;
} box3;

main()
{
        box1 = box2;    /* OK */
        box1 = box3;    /* error */
}
```

In this case, box1 and box2 have the same "unknown" type by definition and,
consequently, are assignment-compatible. However, box3 is a different "unknown"
structure type despite the fact that the templates for each are identical.

As you perhaps can deduce, tagless structure templates have limited usefulness.
The most obvious aspect is that objects of that type must be declared along with the
template, meaning the template can not be shared. Also, you can not refer to that
type in any other context. Specifically, you can not declare or define other variables of
that type at some later point, have functions taking or returning objects of that type
since there is no way to write the corresponding prototype, nor have casts involving
pointers to that type. Also, you can not use the type with sizeof (although you can
use sizeof with expressions of that type).

What, then, is the value of tagless structures? If you have a local structure type
that is never used outside some limited scope and you easily can define all objects
along with the definition, then you don't have to use a unique tag name. Of course,
you also must be prepared to live with the restrictions stated earlier as well. There is
no hard and fast rule for this. Good arguments can be made for both using and not
using tags. If you were to choose just one rule, then it must be always to use a tag.

9.7   Arrays of Structures

Since structures behave much like other types it is reasonable to want to have arrays of structures. Consider the following example:

```
#include <string.h>

struct box {
        int xpos;
        int ypos;
        unsigned xlen;
        unsigned ylen;
};


struct window {
        char xlabel[30];
        char ylabel[30];
        char title[30];
        struct box winbox;
};


main()
{
        static struct window win1[3];
        static struct window win2[] = {
                {"xlab1", "ylab1", "title1", {1, 2, 3, 4}},
                {"xlab2", "ylab2", "title2", {5, 6, 7, 8}},
                {"xlab3", "ylab3", "title3", {3, 4, 5, 6}}
        };
        static struct window win3;

/*1*/   strcpy(win1[0].xlabel, "New label");
/*2*/   win1[0].winbox.xpos = 3;
/*3*/   win1[1].ylabel[2] = 'X';
/*4*/   *(win1[1].ylabel + 2) = 'X';
/*5*/   win3.ylabel[0] = 'X';
}
```

In case 1, win1[0].xlabel has type "array of 30 char." When that array designator is used, it is converted to type "pointer to char." That is the type expected by strcpy as its first argument. Note that the subscript is applied to win1 because that is the array. We must qualify which element in the array of structures we want before we can identify the member in that element. Also, the [] operator takes precedence over dot because these operators associate left-to-right. Redundant parentheses may make it clearer to see the default precedence, but they are rarely seen.

The expression win1[0].winbox.xpos in case 2 has type int and is used in an assignment. Again, the three operators have the same precedence, so they associate left-to-right. A common error is to want to put the subscript to the far right of the whole expression instead of after the array-designating expression. (At this point, you should remember that dot is implemented as an operator, not as a punctuator as some languages implement its equivalent.)

Since the member `ylabel` is an array, it is permissible to have expressions such as `win1[1].ylabel[2]` where both expressions are subscripted. The whole expression has type `char` and the letter `X` is stored at that location. Case 4 is equivalent to case 3 by reason of the array/pointer identity described in Chapter 7. That is, `a[i]` can be rewritten as `*(a + i)`, and vice versa. The parentheses are necessary, so the addition gets higher precedence than the indirection. Without them, the expression would mean something quite different. Specifically, `*(win1[1].ylabel + 2)` designates the third `char` offset into the `ylabel` array while `*win1[1].ylabel + 2` is two more than the value of the `char` designated by the first `char` in `ylabel`. As it happens, the latter version would generate an error in this context because it does not designate a memory location and, as such, can not be assigned to.

Case 5 uses `win3.ylabel[0]` to reference the first `char` in the `ylabel` array in the structure `win3`. Because `win3` is a single structure, it is not subscripted in the member expression.

> **Exercise 9-5*:** Write a program that gets strings from standard input using the `scanf` library function until the string `"END"` is entered. Compare the input string against a list of valid strings. If a match is found, display "Match found with value *xx*"; otherwise display "Invalid string". Make the case comparison case-insensitive. The list of valid strings is `"ADD"`, `"DELETE"`, `"LIST"` and `"REPLACE"`. Strings in the list have corresponding values 73, -7, 256 and -100. Use an array of structures to store the list. `"END"` is not to be stored in the list of valid strings. (Hint: The structure template will contain two members, a pointer to `char` and an `int`.)

9.8   Pointers to Structures

A structure is an object and, as such, occupies one or more consecutive memory locations. Because these locations have to be addressable, we can have pointers to structures. The notation for doing so simply combines that for pointers and member references. However, a new operator is available for use specifically with structure pointers. It is called the *arrow operator* and it has the same precedence as dot, subscripting and function call.

Consider the following example:

```
struct box {
        int xpos;
        int ypos;
        unsigned xlen;
        unsigned ylen;
};
```

```
main()
{
        static struct box box1 = {1, 2, 3, 4};
        void movebox2(struct box *, int, int);

        printf("box1.xpos = %d\n", box1.xpos);
        printf("box1.ypos = %d\n", box1.ypos);

        movebox2(&box1, 2, -1);

        printf("box1.xpos = %d\n", box1.xpos);
        printf("box1.ypos = %d\n", box1.ypos);
}


void movebox2(struct box *ps, int x, int y)
{
        ps->xpos += x;
        ps->ypos += y;
}

box1.xpos = 1
box1.ypos = 2
box1.xpos = 3
box1.ypos = 1
```

The argument box1 is passed by address. That is, the address of the structure in memory is passed rather than the whole structure, so the formal argument must be declared as a pointer to a structure. When arguments are passed by address, their contents can be modified directly because the called function is not dealing with a copy of the argument, but the real object itself. As such, movebox2 can modify directly the xpos and ypos members in the structure whose address was passed.

The expression ps->xpos contains the arrow operator which consists of a dash immediately followed by a greater-than symbol. Like dot expressions, both operands here are expressions in their own right and the first expression must be a pointer to a structure of a type containing a member of the name indicated by the right operand. Again, like dot, the type of an arrow expression is that of the right-most expression. (Because dot and arrow are operators, and therefore tokens, you can put white space on either side of them. This is not normally done, although you may need to use a new-line there if the dot or arrow expression is too long for a source line in your editor.)

Dot and arrow expressions always can be rewritten in terms of each other. In fact, when structures first were added to C, only the dot operator was defined, despite the fact that pointers to functions also were added. The following two examples demonstrate this:

```
struct box movebox1(struct box s, int x, int y)
{
        struct box tmp;

        tmp = s;
/*1*/   tmp.xpos += x;
/*2*/   (&tmp)->xpos += x;

/*3*/   tmp.ypos += y;
/*4*/   (&tmp)->ypos += y;

        return (tmp);
}
```

Here, cases 1 and 2 are equivalent, as are cases 3 and 4. If you know the name of a structure you can take its address and therefore use the arrow operator. Note, though, that the grouping parentheses are necessary because arrow has higher precedence than indirection.

```
void movebox2(struct box *ps, int x, int y)
{
/*1*/   ps->xpos += x;
/*2*/   (*ps).xpos += x;

/*3*/   ps->ypos += y;
/*4*/   (*ps).ypos += y;
}
```

This example demonstrates the converse of the rule applied in the previous example. Again, the statements in each pair of cases are equivalent. If you have a pointer to a structure, by indirecting on that pointer expression, you get an expression that designates the object being pointed to, by definition. In this example, *ps designates a structure of type struct box and, as such, can be used with the dot operator as shown.

The approach you use is purely one of style. The most obvious approach is to use dot when you know the structure's name, and arrow when you know only its address. Not only is this easy to remember, it is much easier to read and write the corresponding expressions.

Now that we have seen arrays of structures, and pointers to structures, you should be able to work out how to define an array of pointers to structures; for example:

```
#include <stdio.h>

struct box {
        int xpos;
        int ypos;
        unsigned xlen;
        unsigned ylen;
};
```

```
struct box box1 = {1, 2, 3, 4};
struct box box2 = {9, 8, 7, 6};
struct box box3 = {1, 9, 3, 7};

struct box *boxes[] = {&box1, &box2, &box3};

main()
{
        printf("boxes[0]->xpos = %d\n", boxes[0]->xpos);
        printf("boxes[2]->xlen = %u\n", boxes[2]->xlen);
}

boxes[0]->xpos = 1
boxes[2]->xlen = 3
```

It is also possible and sometimes necessary to have both dot and arrow operators in the same expression; for example:

```
struct box {
        int xpos;
        int ypos;
        unsigned xlen;
        unsigned ylen;
};


struct window {
        char xlabel[30];
        char ylabel[30];
        char title[30];
        struct box winbox;
};


struct group {
        struct window *w1;
        struct window *w2;
};


main()
{
        struct window win1;
        struct window *pw = &win1;
        struct group g = {&win1, 0};

        pw->winbox.xpos = 5;
        g.w1->winbox.xpos = 7;
}
```

Exercise 9-6: Look at how `feof`, `ferror` and `clearerr` are defined in stdio.h. In many implementations, one or more of them are macros rather than functions. If this is the case, their macro definitions should include pointers to structures and the arrow operator. See if you can determine what each definition means and how it works.

Exercise 9-7: Look over the following program and make sure you understand the meaning of all the expressions used. Walk through the program to verify the output is correct:

```
/* some structure/operator puzzles */

#include <stdio.h>

struct s {
        int i;
        int *pi;
};

struct s st[5];


main()
{
        struct s *ps = st;

        int j = 10;
        int k = 25;

        st[0].i = 5;
        st[0].pi = &j;
        st[1].i = 9;
        st[1].pi = &k;


        printf("    ps->i = %2d\n", ps->i);
        printf("  ++ps->i = %2d\n", ++ps->i);
        printf("++(ps->i) = %2d\n", ++(ps->i));
        printf("  ps->i-- = %2d\n", ps->i--);
        printf("(ps->i)-- = %2d\n", (ps->i)--);
        putchar('\n');


        printf("        j = %2d\n", j);
        printf("  *ps->pi = %2d\n", *ps->pi);
        printf("*(ps->pi) = %2d\n", *(ps->pi));
        putchar('\n');
```

```
                    printf("(++ps)->i = %2d\n", (++ps)->i);
                    printf("(ps--)->i = %2d\n", (ps--)->i);
                    printf("(ps++)->i = %2d\n", (ps++)->i);
                    printf("  ps--->i = %2d\n", ps--->i);
                    putchar('\n');

                    ps = st;
                    printf("(ps+1)->i = %2d\n", (ps+1)->i);
                    printf("  st[1].i = %2d\n", st[1].i);
            }
```

```
            ps->i  =  5
          ++ps->i  =  6
        ++(ps->i)  =  7
          ps->i--  =  7
        (ps->i)--  =  6


                j  = 10
          *ps->pi  = 10
        *(ps->pi)  = 10


        (++ps)->i  =  9
        (ps--)->i  =  9
        (ps++)->i  =  5
          ps--->i  =  9

        (ps+1)->i  =  9
          st[1].i  =  9
```

9.9   Linked Lists

A common data structure is that of a singly- or doubly-linked list. Let's define a
structure template suitable for use in a doubly-linked list. For example, each link of a
chain will describe a box and will contain forward and backward pointers to the next
and previous boxes, respectively.

```
            #include <stdio.h>

            struct box {
                    int xpos;
                    int ypos;
                    unsigned xlen;
                    unsigned ylen;
            };
```

```
struct link {
        struct link *pfwd;
        struct link *pbwd;
        struct box abox;
};


struct link link1;
struct link link2;

main()
{
        link1.pbwd = NULL;        /* no backward link */
        link1.pfwd = &link2;
        link1.abox.xpos = 3;
        link1.abox.ypos = 3;
        /* ... */

        link2.pbwd = &link1;
        link2.pfwd = NULL;        /* no forward link */
        /* ... */
}
```

Structure type `link` contains forward and backward pointers to objects of type
`struct link`. This is possible even though at that stage in the template definition,
`struct link` is not yet defined. The compiler certainly will know by that time how
big a pointer to the type will be, even if it doesn't know how big the actual structure
will be.

Initializing the links at run-time seems a waste considering all the contents are
known at compile-time. The following example shows a much more compact version,
and one that contains no executable code:

```
#include <stdio.h>

struct box {
        int xpos;
        int ypos;
        unsigned xlen;
        unsigned ylen;
};


struct link {
        struct link *pfwd;
        struct link *pbwd;
        struct box abox;
};

struct link link2;        /* tentative definition */
struct link link1 = {NULL, &link2, {3, 3, 0, 0}};
struct link link2 = {&link1, NULL, {5, 3, 0, 0}};
```

The multiple definition of link2 is worth a comment because this capability has not been widely implemented prior to ANSI C, which now requires it. We have two links that reference each other, yet we can not define both of them first. However, the compiler requires that all variables be declared before they are used. To resolve this common situation, ANSI C permits tentative definitions as shown. Here, link2 is defined with all its attributes and it is initialized at a later point, using the same attributes.

In either of these two examples, a circular list can be implemented by making the last link's forward pointer point to the first link, and the first link's backward pointer point to the last link.

9.10   Dynamic Memory Allocation

There are several problems with the above solutions. First, when a chain has many links, the ordering of links may not be known until run-time (it usually isn't) and it may change over the life of the chain. Second, you may not know how many links the chain will need (as often is the case) and you may not wish to allocate space for links unless they actually are used. The first problem can be solved using the information provided thus far, so we will not pursue it further. The second problem leads us to the general topic of dynamic memory allocation; that is, the ability to allocate (and free) a given amount of address space at run-time at a time specified by the programmer. This is quite different from objects of static storage which are allocated space often by the compiler or linker, and automatic objects which are allocated space (and deleted) at very specific times at run-time.

There are four dynamic memory manipulation routines in the standard library. While malloc, calloc and realloc allocate space, free releases it. All are declared in the standard header stdlib.h. (Prior to ANSI C, there was wide discrepancy as to the header [if any] in which they were declared.)

Before we solve the linked list problem, let's show a very simple example of the use of each of these four functions:

```
#include <stdio.h>
#include <stdlib.h>
#include <string.h>

main()
{
        char *pc;
        double *pd, *pd1;

        pc = malloc(10);
        if (pc == NULL) {
                fprintf(stderr, "Can't allocate memory #1\n");
                exit(2);
        }

        strcpy(pc, "abcdef");
        printf("pc points to >%s<\n", pc);
        free(pc);
```

```
            pd = calloc(20, sizeof(double));
            if (pd == NULL) {
                    fprintf(stderr, "Can't allocate memory #2\n");
                    exit(3);
            }

            pd[3] = 2.345;
            printf("pd[2] = %.3f, pd[3] = %.3f\n", pd[2], pd[3]);


            pd1 = realloc(pd, (30 * sizeof(double)));
            if (pd1 == NULL) {
                    fprintf(stderr, "Can't allocate memory #3\n");
                    exit(4);
            }

            pd = pd1;
            printf("pd[3] = %.3f, pd[27] = %e\n", pd[3], pd[27]);
            free(pd);
    }

pc points to >abcdef<
pd[2] = 0.000, pd[3] = 2.345
pd[3] = 2.345, pd[27] = 1.03725e+34
```

The `malloc` routine takes one argument, the number of `chars`-worth of memory to allocate. If it succeeds, it returns a pointer to the beginning of the allocated space. Historically, `malloc` (and `calloc` and `realloc`) returned a pointer to `char` even though it didn't know how the allocated space was going to be used. Since ANSI C added generic pointers, the return type is now `void *`. If the space can not be allocated, a pointer with value `NULL` is returned instead. The allocated space is not initialized. By assigning the returned pointer to a pointer to a non-void type, you can access and manipulate the allocated space as if it were an array, since the space allocated is guaranteed to be contiguous.

The `free` routine releases the allocated space back to the heap manager. The return type of `free` is `void`, so you can not tell if the attempt to free failed. You must give `free` an argument that is the value of a pointer returned by one of the three allocation routines, and the pointer must not point to space that has already been freed.

The `calloc` function is only slightly different from `malloc`. It takes two arguments, the first being the number of contiguous objects for which to allocate space, and the second being the size of each object. Also, `calloc` guarantees that the space allocated is initialized to all-bits-zero. (Depending on your system, all-bits-zero might not correspond to a logical value of zero for all types. For example, floating-point zero and the null pointer value might be represented by something other than all-bits-zero.)

The `realloc` function can be used to enlarge or shrink an already allocated space. The first argument is a pointer to the existing allocated space, while the second is the new absolute size in `chars`. The contents of the smaller of the old and the new allocated space is preserved even if `realloc` has to move it to ensure the new chunk is contiguous. For this reason, `realloc` may return a non-NULL pointer value different to the one passed in, even when the space is being reduced. If the space is enlarged, the new extra space is not initialized. According to ANSI, if the first argument is the null pointer, `realloc` behaves like `malloc`. If the new size is zero, `realloc` behaves like `free`. If space can not be allocated, NULL is returned and the contents of the space at the address passed in are left intact.

The rest of the program should be self-evident and the output produced demonstrates some of the claims made above regarding preserving reallocated space and the initial contents of `calloced` and extra `realloced` space. It is up to the programmer to decide exactly when to allocate and free space. That is, the storage duration of the allocated space is programmer-defined. You can allocate the space in one function and release it in another, even after the function that allocated it has terminated.

Now, back to the linked list problem. The solution is really quite simple. First, allocate a pointer to a structure of type `link`. You can do this statically, automatically, or even dynamically. Then, whenever you need space for a new link, allocate it using `malloc`, for example, as follows:

```
struct box {
        int xpos;
        int ypos;
        unsigned xlen;
        unsigned ylen;
};


struct link {
        struct link *pfwd;
        struct link *pbwd;
        struct box abox;
};


f()
{
        struct link *pl;

        pl = malloc(sizeof(struct link));
        if (pl == NULL) {
                fprintf(stderr, "Can't allocate memory\n");
                exit(2);
        }

        pl->pfwd = NULL;          /* assuming new end link */
        /* ... */
}
```

To insert a new link in the middle of the chain, allocate space for it, initialize its contents and adjust the existing links' forward and backward pointers where the new link is to be inserted.

To traverse a linked list, simply point to its starting node, process that, and move your link pointer along the forward path to the next link, process that, and continue this process until the forward pointer is NULL. You also might find that recursive functions are elegant and efficient for certain list processing. The actual implementation of these techniques is left as a reader exercise.

A word of caution about dynamic memory allocation: While you always should check for a NULL pointer being returned, if one is, it usually spells serious trouble. In most applications, this means you can't get the resources you need to continue, yet you may not be able to terminate gracefully, particularly if you have partially updated several files, etc. You must consider the impact of running out of heap at design time. You may find that you need to allocate large amounts of dynamic memory at the start of the program and manage it yourself.

> **Exercise 9-8:** See if your compiler has a header called stdlib.h. This standard header might be missing, in which mem.h or memory.h may be provided. In any case, locate the header where malloc, calloc, realloc and free are declared and look at their declarations. Do they return the old type of char * or the new type void *? Check that your library documentation matches that in this section for these functions. Are other (non-standard) heap manipulation functions such as brk and sbrk also provided?

> **Exercise 9-9:** calloc initializes the space it allocates with all-bits-zero. Does this match the logical zero value of all of the types on your system? Specifically, are floating-point zero and the NULL pointer value stored as all-bits-zero?

> **Exercise 9-10:** On some systems, dynamic memory allocation is relatively expensive. See if your compiler and/or system documentation gives you any information about this.

> **Exercise 9-11*:** Define an array of three structures of type struct word. word contains two members called pword (a pointer to char) and length (an int). Using a for loop indexed from 0 to 2, read in three strings (maximum 20 characters each) from standard input, allocate space dynamically for them using malloc and store their addresses and lengths in the pword and length members, respectively. Don't forget to check if malloc fails to allocate space. What happens if an input word contains spaces or tabs? What happens if an input word is longer than 20 characters? How would you use pointers instead of array subscripts to access the members in the array of structures? (This would require use of the arrow operator instead of the dot operator.)

> **Exercise 9-12*:** Modify the previous solution to handle an arbitrary number of strings where the number is entered as an integer by the user each time the program begins. How could you handle an arbitrary number if that number were not known? For example, a string "end" would signify the end of input.

9.11   sizeof and Structures

It seems intuitive that the amount of space allocated to a structure is the sum of the sizes of each of its members. However, as it happens, it may be more because certain environments may require, or prefer, some member types to be aligned on specific boundaries. For example, the PDP-11 requires all word operations to be performed on word boundaries. The Intel 80x86 (but not the 80x88) family and the

VAX can benefit by doing word operations on word boundaries rather than on odd byte boundaries. The VAX also prefers larger objects to be on stricter boundaries. However, both these Intel and VAX machines do not actually require such alignment, they simply can benefit from it if it is present.

Outside of structures, a compiler has the freedom to place any object on any memory address boundary or to pack it however it pleases since C places no requirements of such alignment or the relative positioning of one object in relation to another. However, within structures, the compiler has much less freedom. For example, the members must be allocated in the order in which they are defined in the template. That is, the first member has an address lower than the second, which in turn has a lower address than the third, etc.

ANSI C states that a structure may contain *holes* for whatever reason (presumably to allow members to be aligned on the best address boundary possible) so that the size of a structure is at least as big as the sum of its member sizes. It may be more. However, holes may not exist before the start of the first member. That is, the address of the first member is the same as that of the structure itself.

It is very easy to write an experiment to see what, if any, alignment is produced with your compiler. In fact, it is even possible to determine it at run-time. By subtracting the address of member 1 from that of member 2, you can tell if the difference is more than the sizeof(member 1). (Take care to cast both addresses to char * before you do the subtraction because you want the result in the same units as sizeof and, if you are running on a word machine, you may have other considerations.)

Consider the following example:

```
/* inspecting the size of a structure */

#include <stdio.h>

struct {
        char c1;
        int i1;
        char c2;
        char *pc;
        char c3;
        float f1;
} st1;


struct {
        char c1;
        char c2;
        char c3;
        int i1;
        char *pc;
        float f1;
} st2;
```

```
        struct {
                float f1;
                char *pc;
                int i1;
                char c1;
                char c2;
                char c3;
        } st3;


        main()
        {
                printf("size of st1 = %lu\n",
                        (unsigned long)sizeof(st1));
                printf("size of st2 = %lu\n",
                        (unsigned long)sizeof(st2));
                printf("size of st3 = %lu\n",
                        (unsigned long)sizeof(st3));
        }



        size of st1 = 16        /* PC-DOS large model, word-aligned */
        size of st2 = 14
        size of st3 = 14


        size of st1 = 14        /* PC-DOS small model, word-aligned */
        size of st2 = 12
        size of st3 = 12


        size of st1 = 13        /* PC-DOS large model, byte-aligned */
        size of st2 = 13
        size of st3 = 13


        size of st1 = 11        /* PC-DOS small model, byte-aligned */
        size of st2 = 11
        size of st3 = 11
```

Some compilers provide a compile-time switch to specify the alignment criteria. (This was the case with the DOS compiler used to produce the output shown.) Others use some form of directive or extended keyword in the member definition. (VAX C uses _align for this purpose.)

Since holes may exist in structures, it is a good idea to use sizeof when referring to the whole object. Then, if you move the code or otherwise change the alignment, the correct size still will be used when the code is recompiled.

A problem can exist when different machines are networked as is the case in a public network. An object of a given structure type may compile into different sizes and alignments in different nodes; so if a message packet contains such a structure, it will be interpreted incorrectly by those systems on which the size and/or layout is different. (The problem actually may be more complex. For example, the byte ordering within words and words within longwords, etc., also may have to be changed.)

The reason that structure comparison is not permitted in the language is that structures may contain holes. And since those holes may contain arbitrary values at any time, comparing two structures may not simply be a matter of a block compare instruction. Therefore, to compare two structures, you must explicitly compare each member yourself. (Actually, if there were no holes or you could guarantee the holes in each had identical contents, you could use the memcmp library routine.)

Exercise 9-13: What are the alignment requirements (if any) of structure members with your compiler? Can you change the defaults using a compiler switch or extended keyword?

Exercise 9-14: ANSI C defines a macro called offsetof in stddef.h. This macro allows you to find the offset of a given member within a particular template. See if you have this header and macro.

9.12 Bit-Fields

In certain kinds of applications, it is useful to be able to pack objects into something less than a byte or word. For example, to record the status of a two-state condition, you only need one bit. The choice out of a palette of eight colors can be stored in three bits and the parity of an asynchronous communications port can be represented in two bits.

Most languages, including C, provide "bit-fiddling" operators to perform AND, OR and Exclusive-OR operations on integer quantities; however, this manual approach is time consuming and error-prone. It is also inflexible in that altering the size and/or ordering of such objects after programming begins has a non-trivial effect on code written that references the old bit offsets.

C provides a way for the programmer to express the size and ordering of such objects without having to worry about the masking and shifting required to set and test them. All this is achieved by using *bit-fields*, variables whose size is defined in terms of the number of bits rather than bytes or machine words.

Consider the following example:

```
#define FALSE 0
#define TRUE 1

/* possible values for color */

#define BLACK 0
#define BLUE 1
#define GREEN 2
#define CYAN 3
#define RED 4
#define MAGENTA 5
#define BROWN 6
#define WHITE 7
```

```
struct attributes {
        unsigned bordash : 1;   /* solid or dashed */
        unsigned bcolor  : 3;   /* border foreground color */
        unsigned fill    : 1;   /* fill/nofill with fcolor */
        unsigned fcolor  : 3;   /* fill color */
};


main()
{
        static struct attributes atr;

        atr.bordash = FALSE;
        atr.bcolor = RED;
        atr.fill = TRUE;
        atr.fcolor = WHITE;
        /* ... */
}
```

In previous examples, we have used the idea of a rectangular box. Such a box can have other attributes such as those shown in this example. However, there is no point using a `char` (or `unsigned char`) for each when they only need one or a few bits. Each bit-field is a "normal" structure member except it has a width specified at the end, after a colon. The width must be a compile-time integral constant expression that is between zero and the number of bits in an "ordinary" object of that type. In this case, the "ordinary" type of all bit-fields is `unsigned int` so the width is limited by the number of bits in an `unsigned int` on the host machine. (A width of zero bits will be discussed later.)

Bit-fields may be specified with only a colon and width, in which case, that (un-named) number of bit-fields is reserved in the structure object. The order in which bit-fields are packed is implementation-defined and, because C does not require that bit-fields be directly addressable, member 1 does not have to have a lower address than member 2. Typically, your implementation will pack bit-fields either left-to-right or right-to-left into some *storage unit*. And, of course, the size of that storage unit is implementation-defined (byte, word, longword, etc.) and whether bit-fields can span units or unused bits are skipped is implementation-defined. (An unnamed bit-field with width zero causes unused bits in the current unit to be wasted and the next member to begin on the next container boundary.)

When you are using bit-fields in software structures, you may not care about their order of packing, etc. However, when you are mapping into hardware ports and/or registers, you care very much.

ANSI C permits three types of bit-fields: `signed int`, `int` and `unsigned int`. Whether a "plain" `int` is signed or unsigned is implementation-defined. (Note that in all other contexts, a plain `int` is signed.) Some machines (for example, the VAX) do have signed bit instructions, so a `signed int` bit-field of three bits can represent the range -4 to +3.

In all respects, a bit-field behaves like an ordinary object of the same type, so the programmer can deal with bit-fields logically once they are satisfied with any implementation-defined behaviors that may affect them.

There are a few restrictions on bit-fields. You can not find their size using `sizeof`, not because the compiler doesn't know, but because the units `sizeof` traffics in are `chars` and it has no way to indicate a bit count. Also, you can not take the address of a bit-field because few machines are bit-addressable. As a consequence, you can not have arrays of bit-fields.

Since bit-fields are members, they can coexist in a structure with non-bit-field members. In fact, we can combine the `attributes` and the `box` templates into one big template, or at least as two members of a `boxatr` template as follows (also, the macros can be placed in a header called `atr.h`):

```
#include "atr.h"

struct boxatr1 {
        int xpos;
        int ypos;
        unsigned xlen;
        unsigned ylen;
        unsigned bordash : 1;
        unsigned bcolor  : 3;
        unsigned fill    : 1;
        unsigned fcolor  : 3;
};

struct boxatr1 b1 = {1, 1, 2, 3, FALSE, GREEN, TRUE, RED};
```

Keeping them as separate templates, we can have:

```
#include "atr.h"

struct box {
        int xpos;
        int ypos;
        unsigned xlen;
        unsigned ylen;
};


struct attributes {
        unsigned bordash : 1;
        unsigned bcolor  : 3;
        unsigned fill    : 1;
        unsigned fcolor  : 3;
};


struct boxatr2 {
        struct box abox;
        struct attributes atr;
};

struct boxatr2 b2 = {
        {1, 1, 2, 3},
        {FALSE, GREEN, TRUE, RED}
};
```

The second approach provides a nice hierarchy and permits both the `attributes` and `box` data to be manipulated as a group. However, the extra level of nesting required also makes all references longer because they include an extra dot operator and expression.

> **Exercise 9-15:** What is the maximum width of a bit-field on your system? In what order are adjacent bit-fields packed? What is the size and type of the container unit into which bit-fields are packed? Can bit-fields span unit boundaries? Are signed and unsigned bit-fields both supported or is a plain `int` bit-field unsigned?

9.13   Unions

Syntactically, a union is defined, declared and used exactly like a structure except that the keyword `union` is used instead of `struct`. Semantically, the two are subtly different. Whereas a structure allocates space for all its members concurrently, the space allocated to a union is guaranteed only to be large enough to contain the largest member.

A union is designed so that at any time it may contain one and only one of its members; it is the programmer's responsibility to keep track of which member it currently contains, if any; for example:

```
union tag {
        int i;
        double d;
        char *pc;
} u;
```

The object u has type `union tag` and it can contain either an `int`, a `double` or a pointer to `char` at any time. The behavior is implementation-defined if you store into a union through one member and read out of it through another and the two members have different types. Despite this, it is common practice to use a union as a means of interpreting one type as another; for example:

```
#include <stdio.h>

union {
        double d;
        unsigned char c[sizeof(double)];
        unsigned long l[sizeof(double)/sizeof(long)];
} u1;

main()
{
        int i;

        u1.d = 1.2345;

        for (i = 0; i < sizeof(double); ++i)
                printf("c[%d] = %02X\n", i, u1.c[i]);

        for (i = 0; i < sizeof(double)/sizeof(long); ++i)
                printf("l[%d] = %08lX\n", i, u1.l[i]);
}
```

```
c[0] = 8D
c[1] = 97
c[2] = 6E
c[3] = 12
c[4] = 83
c[5] = C0
c[6] = F3
c[7] = 3F
l[0] = 126E978D
l[1] = 3FF3C083
```

On this system, a `char` is one byte, a `double` is eight and a `long int` is four.

Another common use for a union is in defining a buffer that at any one time contains one of many transaction types, each having a different layout (and possibly, size); for example:

```
union transaction {
        struct {
                unsigned int ttype;
                /* rest of transaction type 1 data items */
        } t1;
        struct {
                unsigned int ttype;
                /* rest of transaction type 2 data items */
        } t2;
        struct {
                unsigned int ttype;
                /* rest of transaction type 3 data items */
        } t3;
};
```

```
main()
{
        union transaction buffer;
        void gettrans(union transaction *);

        gettrans(&buffer);

        if (buffer.t1.ttype == 1)
                /* ... */;
        else if (buffer.t1.ttype == 2)
                /* ... */;
        else
                /* ... */;
}
```

We define `buffer` as a union of structures, each of which represents a different transaction type. Since all members in a union start at the same address as the start of the union and the first member in each overlapping structure has the same type, the three members called `ttype` map into exactly the same space (guaranteed). Therefore, we meaningfully can access `buffer` by any of these three members to identify the transaction type contained. Once this information is known, the contents of buffer can be manipulated by the transaction-specific members in the structure corresponding to that transaction type.

Earlier in this section, we learned that, syntactically, unions are treated just like structures. Specifically, unions may be nested and initialized and union expressions are possible. You can have arrays of unions, pointers to unions and union templates without tags. With the advent of ANSI C, a union may contain bit-fields without them first being defined inside a structure. Holes do not exist in a union unless one or more of the members is a structure, and a pointer to any union member (suitably cast) points to the address of the union.

Union initialization is worth a special comment. Consider the following example:

```
static union {
        int i;
        double d;
} u2 = {1.23}, u3;
```

A union is not a scalar and it's not necessarily an aggregate. So, what is it? Well, ANSI C couldn't decide either, so it refers to scalars, aggregates and unions. That is, unions are in a category of their own. In any case, their initializer list must be enclosed in braces just as that for an aggregate. Also, there is the question of which member is used to determine how the initializer list is to be interpreted. ANSI C states that the initial type of a union's contents is that of the first member specified. In this case, then, u2 is initialized with the `int` value 1. If you want it to be the `double` value 1.23, you must swap the member definitions. Similarly, u3 is initialized as an `int` of value zero.

A union may seem like the obvious way to emulate FORTRAN's EQUIVALENCE capability. While it may achieve some of the same results, it can not do all because a union requires all its members to start at the same address. It is neither elegant nor simple to have two int arrays partially overlap, for example. For such cases, a better solution is to use pointers and subscripting as follows. Here, two five-element arrays of double have two common elements:

```
#include <stdio.h>

main()
{
        static double d[8];
        double *pd1 = &d[0];
        double *pd2 = &d[3];

        pd1[3] = 1.234;
        pd1[4] = 9.876;

        printf("pd2[0] = %f\n", pd2[0]);
        printf("pd2[1] = %f\n", pd2[1]);
}

pd2[0] = 1.234000
pd2[1] = 9.876000
```

Exercise 9-16*: Implement a union version of the overlapping object example shown above and discuss the merits of that version versus the pointer approach.

Exercise 9-17: Does your compiler permit unions to have initializer lists?

Exercise 9-18*: Define an object so that at different times, it may contain a char, an int, an unsigned int, a long int, a float or a double value. The object also must contain some sort of variable that indicates the type of the current variable stored there. What if no value is currently stored? If this object has class static and no initializer list, what is its initial type and value?

9.14 Chapter Summary

- A structure is an object that contains one or more other objects called members.

- Before a structure object can be declared, a template for that structure must be defined. This template indicates the name, type and ordering of the members within that structure.

- You can not have different structures with the same tags in the same scope.

- Structure member names can be used only in conjunction with their parent structure name so they do not conflict with other identifiers of the same name, even in other structure templates. That is, each structure has its own unique member namespace and the only requirement on member names is that there be no duplicates within a given template.

- A template definition does not cause any storage to be allocated.

- To reference a member in a particular structure, the expression must include the parent structure name, the dot operator and the member name. The expression to the left of the dot does not have to be a structure name. It must be an expression that designates a structure.

- The type of a dot expression is the type of the right-most expression, the member named.

- Structures may be nested and there is no limit on the depth of such nesting, except for your memory capacity.

- A structure can contain members of any type except functions and structures of the same type as that being defined. That is, a structure can not contain an instance of itself. (It can, however, contain a pointer to an instance of itself.)

- When an aggregate is being initialized, the braces delimiting the initializer list are required.

- Just as with arrays, when initializing structures and nested structures, you must specify the complete leading part of any initializer list. In partial initializer lists, unspecified trailing members take on the value zero cast to their respective type. (This is true even for automatic structures.)

- In the late 1970s, AT&T added structure expressions to its C compilers. Prior to that, an expression containing the name of a structure (except when used as the argument of `sizeof`) was converted to a pointer to that structure, just like array names.

- Structures may be assigned, passed by value and returned from a function by value.

- There are more ways of designating a structure than naming it.

- Arrays of and pointers to structures and unions are permitted.

- The arrow operator is provided for use specifically with structure pointers. It has the same precedence as dot, subscripting and function call.

- Dot and arrow expressions always can be rewritten in terms of each other.

- It is also possible, and sometimes necessary, to have both dot and arrow operators in the same expression.

- There are four dynamic memory manipulation routines in the standard library. `malloc`, `calloc` and `realloc` allocate space while `free` releases it. All are declared in the standard header `stdlib.h`. (Prior to ANSI C, there was wide discrepancy as to the header [if any] in which they were declared.)

- ANSI C states that a structure may contain holes for whatever reason (presumably to allow members to be aligned on the best address boundary possible) so that the size of a structure is at least as big as the sum of its member sizes. However, holes may not exist before the start of the first member. That is, the address of the first member is the same as that of the structure itself.

- C provides a way for the programmer to express the size and ordering of small objects without having to worry about the masking and shifting required to set and test them. All this is achieved by using bit-fields, variables whose size is defined in terms of the number of bits, rather than bytes or machine words.

- ANSI C permits three types of bit-fields: `signed int`, `int` and `unsigned int`. Whether a "plain" `int` is signed or unsigned is implementation-defined. (Note that in all other contexts, a plain `int` is signed.)

- In all respects, a bit-field behaves like an ordinary object of the same type so the programmer can deal with bit-fields logically once they are satisfied with any implementation-defined behaviors that may affect them.

- There are a few restrictions on bit-fields. You can not find their size using `sizeof`, not because the compiler doesn't know, but because the units `sizeof` traffics in are `char`s and it has no way to indicate a bit count. Also, you can not take the address of a bit-field because few machines are bit-addressable. As a consequence of this, you can not have arrays of bit-fields.

- Syntactically, a union is defined, declared and used exactly like a structure except that the keyword union is used instead of `struct`. However, whereas a structure allocates space for all its members concurrently, the space allocated to a union is guaranteed only to be large enough to contain the largest member. A union is designed so that at any time it may contain one and only one of its members. It is the programmer's responsibility to keep track of which member it currently contains, if any.

- Unions may be nested and initialized and union expressions are possible. You can have arrays of unions, pointers to unions and union templates without tags. With the advent of ANSI C, a union may contain bit-fields without their first being defined inside a structure. Holes do not exist in a union unless one or more of the members is a structure and a pointer to any union member (suitably cast) points to the address of the union.

- A union's initializer list must be enclosed in braces just as that for an aggregate.

Chapter 10

Miscellaneous Topics

Except perhaps for the `switch` construct, the topics in this chapter typically are used less often or are more advanced. Each section is self-contained and may be read in any order.

10.1   The `switch` Construct

C provides a computed `goto` mechanism via the *switch* construct. In a switch, a controlling expression is evaluated at run-time and, based on its value, control is passed to one of a number of *labels*. If no label matches, some default action is taken.

The general format of a switch construct is as follows:

```
switch ( expression )
        statement;
```

However, in almost all reasonable uses of `switch`, the statement is compound and contains one or more `case` labels as follows:

```
switch ( expression ) {

case 1:
        statement;

case 2:
        statement;

        /* ... */

case n:
        statement;

default:
        statement;
}
```

The controlling expression enclosed in the mandatory parentheses must have some integral type. (It is implementation-defined as to which type.) At run-time, its value

219

is determined and control is passed to the `case` label whose value matches that of
the controlling expression. If no `case` label matches, control is passed to the `default`
label, if present. If there is no `default` label, control is passed to the statement
following the switch construct. That is, the body of the switch is skipped.

A switch construct may involve the three keywords `switch`, `case` and `default`.
`case` and `default` may only appear in the context of a switch, however, a switch need
not contain `case` labels nor a `default` label. ANSI C requires that an implementation
support at least 257 `case` labels for each switch.

A `case` label consists of the keyword `case` followed by a compile-time integral
constant expression, a colon and, eventually, a statement. (All labels eventually must
be followed by a statement.) A `default` label contains just that keyword and a colon.

In order for the transfer of control to be unambiguous, each `case` within a switch
must have a unique value. Also, no `case` ranges are permitted in ANSI C. (Some
implementations have added `case` ranges as an extension.) However, multiple `case`
labels are permitted on the same statement, as follows:

```
        /* ... */
case 'A':
case 'a':
        processa();
        /* ... */
```

In Chapter 8, we wrote several versions of a character-counting program. Here is
another, except that it reads from standard input rather than a user-specified file:

```
/* wc4 - count characters, lines, pages, etc., in a file. */

#include <stdio.h>

main()
{
        int c;
        static unsigned long numlines;
        static unsigned long numchars;
        static unsigned long numpages;
        static unsigned long numspaces;
        static unsigned long numnonsp;


        while ((c = getchar()) != EOF) {
                ++numchars;
                switch (c) {

                case '\n':
                        ++numlines;
                        break;


                case '\f':
                        ++numpages;
                        break;
```

```
                    case ' ':
                    case '\t':
                    case '\v ':
                            ++numspaces;
                            break;


                    default:
                            ++numnonsp;
                            break;
                }
        }


        printf("    Char count: %5lu\n", numchars);
        printf("    Line count: %5lu\n", numlines);
        printf("    Page count: %5lu\n", numpages);
        printf("   Space count: %5lu\n", numspaces);
        printf("Nonspace count: %5lu\n", numnonsp);
}
```

The important thing to notice here is the use of the **break** statements. Earlier, it was stated that **switch** implements a computed **goto** construct. That is, control transfers to some label and does not come back or otherwise terminate at the end of that case. In fact, once you have transferred control to a **case** or **default** label, control keeps on "dropping through" into the next statement, if there is one, possibly until it reaches the brace closing the whole switch. To terminate a particular **case** gracefully, we use the **break** statement. This causes control to transfer to the statement immediately following the switch. Of course, you also could end the case using **return**, a call to **exit** or **abort**, or via a **goto**. If the **case** were within a **while**, **for** or **do-while** construct, you also could use **continue**.)

Note that the final **break** is redundant since control passes to the statement following the switch anyway. However, it is a good practice to place this **break** here because you may add a new last **case** label later.

The ordering of the **case** and **default** labels is important in only one situation—when you intend to drop through from one label to the next—as shown in the next example:

```
switch (i) {

case 10:
        f();

case 5:
        g();

case 50:
        h();
}
```

In this example, if i equals 10, control transfers to the first **case** label and drops through the other two as well. Likewise, if i equals 5, cases 5 and 50 are executed. Note, though, that an implementation has significant flexibility in how it can implement such switches. In particular, it does not have to check the controlling expression against the `case` labels in the order in which they occur in the source. The only requirement is that if no `break` (or other "abnormal" terminator) exists to change the flow of control, control must "drop" through to the next `case` or `default` label as written in the source. An implementation may implement a switch as a nested `if-else`, testing the `case` labels in the order written or in their reverse order (or any other order it pleases). Obviously, in either case, the `default` would have to be tested for last. Alternatively, the switch may be implemented using a jump table such as that used to take advantage of case instructions available in modern machines.

Because the ordering of `case` labels is not guaranteed to dictate the test order for a match, you may wish to use a nested `if-else` construct instead when you know, for example, that certain transaction types occur more often than others. Also, the `if-else` approach is not limited to integral controlling expressions.

Switch constructs may be nested with each switch having its own set of `case` and `default` labels. In such instances, a `case` or `default` label is deemed to belong to the innermost switch at the place of its occurrence.

Consider the following program and its output (or lack thereof):

```c
#include <stdio.h>

main()
{
        int i = 10;
        void f(void);

        switch (i) {
                int j = 100;
                static int k = 200;

                f();

        case 10:
                printf("j = %d, k = %d\n", j, k);
                break;
        }
}


void f(void)
{
        printf("In function f\n");
}


j = 4108, k = 200
```

C permits declarations at the beginning of any block and, as such, we have declared the automatic variable j and the static variable k. However, the value of j displayed is not 100 as you might expect. The problem is that j has automatic storage duration and, as such, is created and initialized at run-time, conceptually when its parent block is entered. The interesting thing here is that we never drop into this block—we always enter it via one of the `case` or `default` labels. What we really have is the following situation:

```
switch (i) {
        int j;

        j = 100;

case 10:

        /* ... */
}
```

And, because we can never get to the assignment statement, it is not executed. (An ANSI C Compiler is not required to diagnose this, but a conscientious implementation should warn you about "unreachable code.") The same situation exists for the call to function `f`. That function is never called because the call precedes all the `case` and `default` labels. Similar situations can occur if you use `goto` to jump into `switch` blocks that contain automatic declarations.

The reason that `k`'s value is predictable is that it has static storage duration and, as such, is initialized sometime before `main` gets control during program startup.

Exercise 10-1: The type of a switch-controlling expression is some unspecified integral type. What happens when this type is signed and one or more `case` labels have unsigned type with values that can not be represented as signed quantities? Try it with your compiler. A similar problem can occur with a negative `case` label value and an unsigned controlling expression.

Exercise 10-2: Does your implementation support `case` ranges? If so, how does it handle overlapping ranges?

Exercise 10-3: Does your compiler support at least 257 different `case` labels per `switch`?

Exercise 10-4: Write a `switch` where control always drops through from one `case` to the next. Look at the code generated by your compiler to see how it implements the construct. Vary the example by adding more `cases` and/or making the set of `case` label values contiguous (1–10, for example) and non-contiguous (1, 20, 50, 100). What if part of the set of `case` values is contiguous and part is not (1–5 and 20, 50, 100, for example)? Perhaps the compiler solves each part in a different way.

Exercise 10-5: Does your compiler warn you about "unreachable code" inside `switch` blocks as a result of automatic initializer lists and executable code before the first `case` or `default` label?

10.2   The goto Statement

Like almost all languages, C provides a goto statement that unconditionally transfers control to a statement specified by the programmer. The format of a goto statement and corresponding label are:

> goto *identifier*;

> identifier:
>   *statement*;

The scope of a goto label is function-wide and, as such, you can jump to any statement in the whole function including into and out of blocks. Note that a label eventually must be followed by a statement, before the current block ends. All of the structured programming warnings apply as they do for goto in other programming languages. However, the use of goto should not be forbidden arbitrarily because in certain situations, it may be the only elegant and/or efficient solution; for example:

```
#include <stdio.h>
#include <stdlib.h>

main()
{
        static int a[4][6] = {
                { 1,  5,  6,  8,  2,  9},
                { 3,  4,  0,  7, 11, 23},
                {43, 45, 76, 87, 32, 24},
                {54, 65, 76, 88, 99, 12}
        };
        int i;          /* row subscript */
        int j;          /* column subscript */
        int value;

        /* initialize value somehow */


        /* search for value in the table */

        for (i = 0; i < 4; ++i) {
                for (j = 0; j < 6; ++j) {
                        if (a[i][j] == value)
                                goto found;
                }
        }

        printf("Invalid value\n");
        exit(2);

found:

        printf("Match found at %d, %d\n", i, j);
}
```

To solve this problem using a structured approach, you must keep looping (without comparing) once you have found a match, until the i and j for loops expire. However, you must save the values of i and j from the match first because they will be overwritten by the next iterations of each loop. Another problem comes from the fact that you always drop into the statement following the lookup loops whether you found a match or not. Therefore, you must requalify if you found a match to determine how to continue. Not only does such an approach require less readable code, it clearly is less efficient than the unconditional branch or jump instruction that a goto would generate.

Clearly, goto can be abused, so you should avoid it when you can write readable and efficient code in other ways. You should limit goto to forward transfers only in a local scope. Jumping into or out of block statements is considered very poor style. In any case, if you jump into a block containing automatic declarations having initializers, the initialization is not guaranteed to take place, although the space will be allocated to the objects declared.

The continue and break statements were introduced in Chapter 2 and, presumably, you can see the merits of them. Of course, both are cleverly disguised versions of goto. They are not disliked and avoided as goto often is because, with continue and break, the compiler gets to choose where to jump to. This demonstrates that the problem with goto is not that it permits control to be transferred unconditionally to some statement, but that because the programmer gets to specify which statement, you run the risk of a "silly" request.

Both continue and break can be implemented using goto and, while you are unlikely to do this, the following example may help to reinforce your understanding of them. In each example, the continue statement is replaced by goto cont; and the label cont:; break is implemented using goto brk; and brk:.

```
/* --- while --- */

while (exp) {

        goto cont;

        goto brk;

cont:   ;
}

brk:
```

```
/* --- for --- */

for (exp1; exp2; exp3) {

        goto cont;

        goto brk;

cont:   ;
}

brk:


/* --- do/while --- */

do {

        goto cont;

        goto brk;

cont:   ;
} while (exp);

brk:


/* --- switch --- */

switch (exp) {

case 1:
        /* ... */
        goto brk;

case n:
        /* ... */
        goto brk;

default:
        /* ... */
        goto brk;
}

brk:
```

Labels that are the object of goto are never confused with case and default
labels. A label used with goto must be an identifier while that of a case must be an
integral constant expression. And you can not write goto default; because default
is a reserved word and, as such, can not be used as an identifier.

Since a non-switch label can be used only in conjunction with the goto keyword and in front of a colon and preceding a statement, the compiler always can determine a label from other identifiers. Therefore, such labels have their own namespace. That is, in ANSI C you can use the same identifier as a label, variable (or function), structure or union tag, and a structure or union member, all in the same scope. However, in the interests of readability, you should not take advantage of this "feature."

> **Exercise 10-6:** Can you think of other situations in which `goto` may be the most elegant and/or efficient approach?

> **Exercise 10-7:** Write a main program in which you use several `goto`s to jump into a block using different labels, Declare an automatic object with an initializer at the start of the block. Look at the code generated and you should see that the space for the automatic object is not allocated when the block is entered (because it doesn't know at compile-time which way the block will be entered), but rather at some time previously.

10.3   Enumerated Data Types

C supports the notion of an *enumerated type* in which a set of valid member names (with corresponding values) are associated with a programmer-specified type name. Consider the following declaration:

```
enum color {red, blue, green, brown};
```

Here we have invented an enumerated type called `enum color`. Just as structure and union types include the keywords `struct` and `union`, respectively, an enumerated type includes the keyword `enum`. The identifiers listed inside the braces are known as members or, more commonly, as *enumeration constants*.

Enumerated type declarations look somewhat like structure and union templates, but the similarities are few. The `enum` tagname is optional and the general format is similar, although `enum` constant lists often are written across the page rather than one per line. Also, we will not be referring to `enum` member sets by the term template because they do not specify the internal storage mapping as do structure and union templates. In fact, an `enum` is a bit like a union in that at any time, an object of `enum` type may contain only one of the specified members.

```
#include <stdio.h>

enum color {red, blue, green, brown};

main()
{
        enum color my_color = red;

        switch (my_color) {

        case brown:
                break;

        case blue:
                break;

        case red:
                break;

        case green:
                break;

        }


        printf("The value of red is %d\n", red);
        printf("The value of blue is %d\n", blue);
        printf("The value of green is %d\n", green);
        printf("The value of brown is %d\n", brown);
}

The value of red is 0
The value of blue is 1
The value of green is 2
The value of brown is 3
```

Internally, the automatic variable my_color is stored as an implementation-defined integer type, so an enumerated type is really a synonym for that integer type. Each enumeration constant is exactly that, a constant. It has type int and may be used in any context in which a compile-time integer constant expression is permitted. As shown in the above example, such constants can be used as case labels. (They also can be used in initializer lists of static objects, as the width of bit-fields, and in array dimensions, for example.)

The storage duration and linkage rules defined in Chapter 5 apply equally as well here, so the scope and life of enum types is up to the programmer.

As shown above, the internal representation of the enumeration constants starts at zero and increments by one for each successive name specified in the set. This natural ordering is quite useful because it allows the constants to be used as array subscripts. However, you can override these representations by supplying your own values as follows:

```
enum color {red = 3, blue, green = -2, brown};
```

In this declaration, the members take on the values 3, 4, -2 and -1, respectively. And, because the set of values does not need to be contiguous, the predecessor and successor operators present in PASCAL are not possible. (Is the successor to blue green or is it the non-existent value 5?) Once you specify the constants' values, you also can have duplicates; for example:

```
enum color {red = 3, blue, green = 3, brown};
```

Of course, the fact that red and green are "the same," as are blue and brown, may make no sense at all. What that means certainly is not intuitive.

We know that an automatic object takes on an undefined default value. Therefore, such an initial value may or may not be one of the valid values in the set. Also, a static object is initialized to zero, by default, and that does not need to be the value of any of the enumeration constants. Clearly, it is possible then for an enumerated type object to contain something other than the value of one of the defined members. So much so, in fact, that enumerated types are very weak synonyms of an integral type. That is, the compiler will let you assign any expression to an enumerated type object provided it is assignment-compatible. ANSI C does not require a diagnostic if you attempt to assign 12345 or -6543 to my_color, for example, when those are not defined member values. However, a "better" compiler would produce a warning. The following example demonstrates the rather loose handling of enumerated types:

```
enum flower {rose, violet, lilac, petunia};

main()
{
        enum flower my_flower = rose;
        int i = 10;
        int j;

        j = i + rose + violet;
        my_flower = violet - petunia;
        my_flower = 12345;
        ++my_flower;
}
```

Tags of structure, union and enumerated types all share the same namespace despite the fact that the tag always must be used in conjunction with the keywords struct, union, or enum. The scope of enumeration constant names extends from immediately after their use inside a set of members through the end of their parent block (or source file, as the case may be). Therefore, you can not have two enumerated types in the same scope with the same named enumeration constant, even if the two initial values of those constants are the same. Enumeration constants share the same namespace as variables and functions.

As stated above, an enumerated type need not have a tag. In such cases, you therefore must declare all identifiers having that type at the same time you declare the type itself, just as for tagless structures and unions. However, ANSI C permits a tagless enumerated type declaration to also not contain any declarators; for example:

```
enum {left, right, up, down};
```

Later, we can not declare objects of this type without a tag and, because we didn't declare them here, what use is such a declaration? Well, the four enumeration constants are `int` constants and can be used in other parts of the program, depending on their scope. We have declared an enumerated type not to declare objects of that type, but so we can get a set of useful mnemonics, each guaranteed to have a unique value. Of course, you could use `#define` to achieve the same thing as follows:

```
#define left 0
#define right 1
#define up 2
#define down 3
```

or:

```
#define left 0
#define right left + 1
#define up right + 1
#define down up + 1
```

The `enum` approach is more elegant. As a style issue, macro names typically are written using uppercase. Whether enumeration constants are written in lower- or uppercase is up to the programmer and there is little difference because they "expand" to a simple `int` constant value. The rationale for writing macros in uppercase is to alert you to the fact that they may expand to some arbitrary large and/or complex expression. However, an enumeration constant really is a synonym for an `int` constant.

A few miscellaneous points are worth noting. As you might expect, you can pass and return enumerated objects by address and value to/from functions and, therefore, specify them in prototypes. You may cast to and from enumerated object types, have arrays of them and pointers to them, and, of course, they can be members of structures and unions.

A note regarding symbolic debuggers: At the time of this writing, few symbolic debuggers deal with enumeration constants by name. That is, if `red` is represented as the value 2, then that is what is displayed, not the name "`red`". Also, there is no way in the standard library to display the name of an enumeration constant. Using `%d` with `printf` will only get you its value.

Exercise 10-8*: What would you expect to happen in the following assignment? Is it an error?

```
enum flower {rose, violet, lilac, petunia};

main()
{
        enum flower my_flower;

        my_flower = 1.23;
}
```

Exercise 10-9: What is the implementation-defined type for enumerated objects in your implementation? Is it always the same for all enumerated types?

Exercise 10-10*: Consider the following program fragment. Do you see any problems? Is it portable?

```
enum flower {rose, violet, lilac, petunia};

main()
{
        enum flower my_flower;
        int *pc;

        pc = &my_flower;
}
```

Exercise 10-11*: Invent a way to display the name of the enumerated constant that corresponds to the current value of an enumerated object so that you could display "The current value of my_flower is rose."

10.4 The Comma Operator

One of the most confusing (and consequently, least used) operators is the *comma* operator. It is the only operator we have yet to discuss and it intentionally has been relegated to the "Miscellaneous Topics" bin. It has the lowest precedence of all the operators and, because it is not used often, we have stated that "for all intents and purposes" the assignment operators have the lowest precedence.

The confusing aspect is that the comma character can be used as both a punctuator and operator in the *same* expression. However, before we explain the differences, let's see what the syntax and semantics of this unusual operator are.

The comma operator has two operands that may be expressions of any type. The expressions do not need to have the same type. A comma expression is written as:

   exp1 , exp2

The left operand, in this case exp1, is evaluated and its value is discarded. That is, it is treated as a void expression. Then the right operand, in this case exp2, is evaluated and the result of the whole comma expression has the type and value of the right operand.

Consider the following program fragment:

```
/*1*/    i = (f(), g());
/*2*/    i = f(), g();
/*3*/    i = (j++, j);
```

In case 1, function f is called and the value returned (if any) is discarded. Then function g is called and the value it returns becomes the value of the whole comma expression. This value is then assigned to i. Note that the grouping parentheses are necessary because the comma operator has lower precedence than assignment.

In the second case, function f is called and the value it returns is assigned to i. Then function g is called and the value it returns is used as that of the whole comma expression, which results in it being discarded because we never use that value.

In case 3, j++ is evaluated. The comma operator is a sequence point. That is, all side-effects occurring in its left operand actually take place before the right operand is evaluated. Therefore, the expression is quite safe and j will have been incremented before the right operand is evaluated.

There are a few situations in which a comma may occur as both an operator and punctuator and the most obvious, perhaps, is in the argument list of a function call. Consider the following example:

```
f(i, j);
g((i, j));
```

The definition of an argument list is a (possibly empty) list of expressions separated by comma punctuators. Therefore, function f is called with the two arguments i and j. Function g, on the other hand, is called with only one argument because the expression in the argument list is (i, j). The outer parentheses represent the function call operator while the inner pair represent grouping. Because the only thing that can be grouped is an expression, the comma must represent the comma operator. As a result, i is evaluated and its value discarded, and the value of j is passed to g as the only argument.

It should be fairly obvious that the comma operator can detract from a program's readability. Also, almost all uses of it can be avoided by rewriting the expression. However, there are situations in which it is very convenient. In fact, when used in macro definitions it may be the only efficient solution. For example, consider the case where you wish to create a descriptor for a variable length piece of text. (Perhaps you are writing a text editor.) The descriptor contains the address and length of some string and it may be useful to have a macro that, given an address and length, expands to the assignments needed to initialize the descriptor accordingly.

A first attempt at the macro definition might be:

```
#include <string.h>
#define SETUP(addr, len) {str.address = addr; str.length = len;}

struct {
        char *address;
        unsigned length;
} str;

main()
{
        char *pc1 = "text";
        char *pc2 = "stuff";
        int i = 10;

        if (i)
                SETUP(pc1, strlen(pc1));
        else
                SETUP(pc2, strlen(pc2));
}
```

However, you will get a compilation error saying something like "dangling or unmatched else." That is, the else is not seen to belong to an if. To see the problem we need to look at the output produced by the preprocessor. The relevant section involves the if construct as follows:

```
if (i)
        {str.address = pc1; str.length = strlen(pc1);} ;
else
        {str.address = pc2; str.length = strlen(pc2);} ;
}
```

The problem is that the true path of the if contains two statements— the block statement and a null statement. Also, we know that the body of the true (and false) path is the next one statement only. (The problem also exists with the else path, yet this causes no problem because there is no further if-else nesting and the extra null statement is always "executed.")

Two quick fixes to the problem are to leave off the semicolon from the macro call or to require the use of braces around the macro call. However, both of these are messy and subvert the idea of making macro definitions self-reliant and their use intuitive. The macro can be written to expand correctly while permitting the call to be rational, using the comma operator as follows:

```
#define SETUP(addr, len) (str.address = addr, str.length = len)
```

Now the expanded code looks like:

```
if (i)
        (str.address = pc1, str.length = strlen(pc1)) ;
else
        (str.address = pc2, str.length = strlen(pc2)) ;
}
```

where each macro expands to an expression which, when followed by a semicolon, becomes a statement. If you wish, you can include an explicit void cast at the start of the macro definition so it expands to a void expression. In this example, we are using the comma operator simply to get two expressions to be "stuck" together so that they appear as one big expression. While we could (but in this case don't) rely on the order of their evaluation being left-to-right, we are not interested in the value of the whole expression. It so happens that this use of the comma operator is sometimes seen in for loops; for example:

```
for (i = 0, j = 0, k = 0; exp2; ++i, ++j, --k)
        /* ... */
```

The syntax of the for construct is three optional expressions separated by semicolons. So, to do more than one thing at initialization and at the end of the loop (or even in the case of the second expression), we simply specify a set of expressions separated by comma operators. As shown above, each comma operator expression contains three expressions. Multiple occurrences of this operator in the same expression associate left-to-right, so the order of evaluation is quite predictable.

Because comma expressions almost always can be avoided in programs (with the possible exception of some macros), once you understand them, you also should understand their advantages and disadvantages in terms of readability and possible debugging problems. As a result, you should use them sparingly, perhaps only in for constructs and macros as shown.

Exercise 10-12*: What is the value of sizeof(c++, c) where c has type char?

Exercise 10-13*: What does your compiler do when it encounters expressions such as (4, exp) where the first expression is a constant and, clearly, can have no affect on the outcome of the operation? (The answer may depend on the vintage of your compiler; that is, whether it is pre-ANSI.)

Exercise 10-14: Consider the following program fragments. Can you find any use for such things?

```
while (f(), i)
        /* ... */

for (exp1; f(), i; exp3)
        /* ... */
```

Exercise 10-15*: If you switch to and from C on a regular basis, you may find you write multidimensional array subscripts as a[5, 6] instead of a[5][6]. What kind of message (if any) does your compiler produce in such cases? If `a` is a two-dimensional array of `char`, what is the type of `a[5, 6]`? Does the compiler behave differently if the subscripts are variables instead of constants?

10.5 Type Qualifiers

ANSI C added two *type qualifier* keywords to the language. They are `const` and `volatile`. `const` was adopted from the C++ language while `volatile` was invented by ANSI C. As the name implies, a type qualifier somehow qualifies (by restricting or controlling) the way in which an object of that type can be accessed. Both qualifiers provide an organized and very useful capability that previously either was not provided or was done so in an (incompatible) implementation-defined manner.

Qualifiers apply only to objects. A type qualifier only has meaning when an identifier so qualified is used in the context of an lvalue.

A qualifier can be included in a `typedef` typename definition.

If a declaration having a qualifier has no explicit type keyword, `int` is assumed.

10.5.1 The const Qualifier

The `const` qualifier is used to prohibit the ability to store through a designated lvalue which, in the absence of the `const` keyword, would be a modifiable lvalue. (Using `const` with such an lvalue makes it a non-modifiable lvalue.)

For example, in:

```
const int ci;

f()
{
        const double cd = 10.4;

        ci = 10;        /* error */
        ci++;           /* error */
        ci += 4;        /* error */
        cd = 1.23;      /* error */
}
```

`ci` and `cd` are global and automatic definitions, respectively, that both contain the `const` qualifier. This means that neither identifier can be used in the context where a modifiable lvalue is required. Therefore, an implementation is obliged to reject all four statements because they attempt to modify the objects designated by either `ci` or `cd`. If you can not modify a `const` object, how can it ever get initialized? The only way to set the value of a `const` object is to use an initializer list in the declaration. If no initializer is provided, the default initial value is the same as if the `const` were omitted (zero for static storage duration objects and undefined for automatic storage duration).

The value of `const` is to provide a mechanism to protect memory locations that either can not be written to (such as those residing in ROM) or to provide a "one writer/many reader" arrangement when multiple cooperating programs access objects in shared memory.

The `const` qualifier can be used with any object type including aggregates. When an array is declared to be `const`, all of its elements inherit the `const` attribute. The same is true for `const` structures and unions.

It is possible to have composite `const`/non-`const` structures and unions as follows:

```
struct {
        const i;
        int j;
} s;

union {
        const int k;
        double d;
} u;
```

Type qualifiers may be used in conjunction with pointers with some interesting results. A pointer declaration actually declares the attributes of two things: the pointer itself and the object or function being pointed to. As such, the keyword `const` can appear more than once in such a declaration as follows (here, `nc` represents the attribute non-`const` while `c` represents `const`. For example, `ncpcc` is a non-`const` pointer to a `const char`):

```
char ncc = 'A';
const char cc = 'Z';

char *ncpncc = &ncc;
const char *ncpcc = &cc;
char * const cpncc = &ncc;
const char * const cpcc = &cc;

void f()
{
        ncpncc = &ncc;          /* OK */
        ncpncc = &cc;           /* error */
        ncpncc = cpncc;         /* OK */
        *ncpncc = 'a';          /* OK */

        ncpcc = &cc;            /* OK */
        ncpcc = &ncc;           /* OK */
        *ncpcc = 'a';           /* error */

        cpncc = &ncc;           /* error */
        *cpncc = 'a';           /* OK */

        cpcc = &cc;             /* error */
        *cpcc = 'a';            /* error */
}
```

The compiler is obliged to enforce all `const` declarations throughout their scope. Therefore, it prohibits a `const` pointer from being assigned to, and it prohibits the object pointed to by a pointer to `const` from being modified via that pointer. It also prohibits a pointer to a non-`const` object from being initialized with a pointer to `const`, because if that were permitted, you would be able to modify the `const` object through the pointer to non-const. However, the compiler does permit a pointer to a const object to be initialized with a pointer to a non-const object. This is not an error because the assignment simply means that the non-const object appears as a const object when referenced via the pointer to const. That is, we safely can add the const attribute when referencing an object because that adds extra protection; however, we can not safely remove it because it really may not be writable.

The const qualifier can occur in function prototypes. The following example shows some such prototypes from the standard header string.h:

```
char *strcpy(char *dest, const char *src);
char *strchr(const char *s, int c);
int strcmp(const char *s1, const char *s2);
```

Each prototype declares at least one argument of type "pointer to const char." In this context, this does not necessarily mean that the strings so declared reside in read-only memory, but that the functions strcpy, strchr and strcmp guarantee they will not modify those strings, allowing the compiler possibly to generate more optimum code when such a function is called in the presence of the appropriate prototype. And, most important, the corresponding arguments you pass to these functions need not be pointers to const char; they also can be pointers to non-const char because the two are assignment-compatible.

10.5.2 The volatile Qualifier

Syntactically, volatile is used exactly like const. That is, you can have volatile objects including aggregates, and volatile may occur in more than one place in a pointer declaration. However, the purpose of volatile is quite different from and unrelated to const. The volatile qualifier tells the compiler that the object is not "owned" by this program and that there are severe limitations on how references to it may be optimized. For example, the object may reside in shared memory and be used as a synchronizing indicator between cooperating programs. In this case, you would want an assignment to that object to be carried out immediately because other programs may be waiting on it.

Consider the following example:

```
void f()
{
        volatile int vi;
        volatile int *pvi;

        vi = 5;
        vi = 6;

        *pvi = 3;
        *pvi = 6;
}
```

The first assignments to each of vi and *pvi are not superfluous—you might be pulsing an output port twice, if vi or *pvi designates a hardware I/O port. volatile exists purely to permit the programmer to disable the optimizer explicitly.

The ANSI C library involves volatile in only a few places. The header signal.h defines a type called `sig_atomic_t` which is an integral type of an object that can be accessed as an atomic entity, even in the presence of asynchronous interrupts. `volatile` objects also are discussed in the description of the `longjmp` function in `setjmp.h`. No standard library prototype contains the `volatile` qualifier.

At first glance, the `const` and `volatile` attributes seem to be diametrically opposed; however, they are not. `const` means that in the scope of that object declaration, you can not modify that object; however, someone else might be able to. Therefore, it is possible to have all the possible combinations of `const` and `volatile` (specified in a declarator in either order) in the same declaration. For example:

```
const int * volatile vncpnvci;
```

declares `vncpnvci` as a `volatile` non-const pointer to a non-`volatile` `const` `int`.

Exercise 10-16: Does your compiler support the `const` and `volatile` qualifiers with all their semantics? If it does support `volatile`, look at the code it generates for the following expressions:

```
extern volatile int vi;

void f()
{
        int i;

        i = 2 * vi;
        i = vi + vi;
        i = vi * 0;
}
```

Exercise 10-17*: ANSI C supports structure and union assignments. If a non-`const` structure (or union) object contains one or more `const` members, can it be assigned a structure (or union) expression's value?

Exercise 10-18: Can you think of any uses for `volatile`? How about in interrupt-handlers? Read your implementation library manual for details of `longjmp` and `signal`. How is `sig_atomic_t` defined in `signal.h`?

10.6   Creating Type Synonyms

The `typedef` keyword provides the ability to create a synonym for another type; for example:

```
typedef unsigned char bool;
```

Here, we have "invented" the type `bool` which is simply a synonym for the type `unsigned char`. It now can be used in any context in which the type `unsigned char` may occur; for example:

```
bool *f(bool);

bool abc;
bool def[10];
```

To create a synonym from a type, write a declaration for an identifier of the type and prepend the keyword **typedef**. The identifier now becomes the new typename rather than a function or variable name.

Why have **typedef** when you always can write the underlying "real" type? Certainly, **typedef** can be overused. However, there are occasions when you may not always know what the actual underlying type of something is. For example, to perform file I/O, we need to define one or more objects of type **FILE ***, yet we do not (and need not) know what that type will look like for any arbitrary implementation. In performing such I/O, all we need to do is create a **FILE *** object, assign the value returned from **fopen** to it, and pass it back to one or more other I/O routines. We never inspect, display or directly modify a **FILE** object, so we don't care much about its attributes. As long as we can find its size (so we can allocate space for it dynamically, if necessary), assign to and from it and pass it by address, we have all we need. To satisfy these requirements, the type **FILE** is almost always a structure type defined something like:

```
typedef struct {
        unsigned flags;
        unsigned char *buffer;
        /* ... */
}       FILE;
```

Then, the predefined file pointers **stdin**, **stdout** and **stderr** can be macros defined to be pointers to entries in an array of **FILE** objects.

The value of **typedef**, then, is in helping to abstract real types from a program. As such, **typedef** is a very important tool available to port projects. It also can be useful in that it allows you to assign a simpler, more meaningful name to a complex type (this capability might be particularly useful when we get to declarations involving pointers to functions); for example:

```
typedef struct node {
        struct node *fwd;
        struct node *bwd;
        unsigned count;
        char *name;
} link;

typedef link chain[100];
```

Here, we have defined a type called **link** which is a synonym for a structure containing forward and backward pointers to structures of the same type. Also, we have defined the type **chain**, to be an array of 100 **links**.

It can be quite easy to get carried away with this kind of approach and invent all sorts of interesting synonyms; however, that often is not a good idea. For example, the utility of defining **link** and **chain** is significantly impacted by the way in which objects of these types are going to be used. For example, if we ever need to get at any of the members within a **link**, we must know that a **link** is really a structure. We also must know the names of the members we wish to access. Then what is the point of disguising the structure type if we still need to know what is hidden underneath?

Similarly, if we have a declaration **chain c1;**, it is not at all intuitive that **c1** is really an array of structures and that, to get at any of those structures, **c1** must be subscripted and possibly used with the dot operator.

Note, though, that some of these problems can be overcome by using macros. For example, we could write a series of macros (or library functions) to manipulate the contents of a `link` object while letting the application programmer deal with the logical type `link`. In this way, `link` (and `chain`) now can be used much like `FILE` discussed earlier.

Using the rule for constructing a `typedef` given above, we see that the following declaration is valid:

```
typedef int Int, *PInt, A5Int[5], FRInt();
```

In this case, we have defined four typenames: `Int`, `PInt`, `A5Int` and `FRInt`.

The `typedef` keyword was added quite sometime after C was designed and, as a result, was retrofitted into the language's grammar. Syntactically, `typedef` is a storage class, even though it has nothing to do with storage duration or linkage (as do `auto`, `static`, etc.). As a result, `typedef` is treated as a declaration and may appear only at the start of a block or outside any function definition.

Another consequence of `typedef` being a class is that ANSI C permits only one storage class specifier in a declaration. Therefore, the following is disallowed because it contains two class keywords, `typedef` and `static`.

```
typedef static int SInt;
```

As it happens, this is no real disadvantage because such a concept would have severe limitations anyway. For example, you could never define such an object with class `auto` or `register`. Also, you could never have a structure or union member of that type because class keywords are not permitted inside template definitions.

While you can not cause a class keyword to "stick" to a `typedef`, you can do so with the type qualifiers `const` and `volatile` because these are not class keywords.

A `typedef` typename (or derived typename) is in the same namespace as that occupied by variables, functions and enumeration constants. In the examples above, invented typenames have been written in all uppercase, all lowercase and in mixed case. There really isn't any de facto standard because ANSI C used names like `FILE` and `size_t`. (It does, however, end all newly invented types with a suffix of `_t`.) Perhaps one guideline is to write derived typenames in lowercase because that is how all built-in types defined by the language must be written.

Exercise 10-19: ANSI C requires numerous types to be defined in one or more standard headers. The types and the corresponding headers they must be defined in, follow: `clock_t time.h`; `div_t stdlib.h`; `FILE stdio.h`; `fpos_t stdio.h`; `jmp_buf setjmp.h`; `ldiv_t stdlib.h`; `ptrdiff_t stddef.h`; `sig_atomic_t signal.h`; `size_t stddef.h`, `stdio.h`, `stdlib.h`, `string.h`, `time.h`; `time_t time.h`; `va_list stdarg.h`; `wchar_t stddef.h`, `stdlib.h`. Check the headers provided by your implementation to see if all these types are defined and in the right places. Also look at how they are defined because you can use the same approach for your own abstract type needs.

Exercise 10-20*: Consider the following declarations:

```
typedef int fri(void);

fri f;
```

The identifier **f** is declared to be a function taking no arguments and returning an **int**. How is that function to be called? Do you just write **f;**?

Exercise 10-21*: In some sense, **typedef** seems to overlap with **#define** in capability. For example:

```
typedef int Int;

Int a, b[5], c(), *d;
```

and:

```
#define Int int

Int a, b[5], c(), *d;
```

achieve exactly the same thing. Discuss the merits of either approach and see if you can define a rule as to when **typedef** and **#define** should and should not be used.

10.7 Pointers to Functions

Most languages either do not permit you to take the address of anything, or just to address objects. Some, most noticeably C and assembler, permit both objects and functions to be directly addressed.

Except for a few specialized language environments, functions are statically (and permanently) allocated space at compile-time. Any reference to a function's or object's address at compile-time involves the relative address of that function or object within the source file being compiled. At link-time, all such relative references are made absolute (or virtual, if you will) and, if you enter a debugger and inspect memory at a function's or object's address shown in the linker cross-reference map, you should find the corresponding code or data. (On systems supporting either memory- or disk-overlayed code and/or data, the situation is somewhat more complicated.)

In any case, in such implementations, every object and function has an address. Conceptually, a pointer to a function is the address of the first byte (or word) of the executable code in that function. Conceptually, because it actually could be the address of a data block containing a context block for the function instead. Whatever the actual mapping, we are assured the compiler will generate the appropriate code to get at that function.

We have seen many examples of initializing and dereferencing data pointers and the same approach is used with pointers to functions. When you dereference a data pointer, you have an expression that designates the object being pointed to. Likewise, when you dereference a function pointer you have an expression that designates the function being pointed to. To call a function, you specify an expression that designates that function, followed by the function call operator () containing an optional argument list. Up to this point, the only way we have seen to designate a function is to name it. However, now we also can do so by dereferencing a pointer that points to it.

The following example shows how to declare and initialize a function pointer, and how to call the function it points to:

```
#include <stdio.h>

main()
{
        void f(void);
        void (*fp)(void);

        f();            /* call f directly */

        fp = &f;        /* make fp point to function f */
        (*fp)();        /* call f indirectly via fp */
}


void f(void)
{
        static unsigned count = 0;

        printf("%u: Inside function f\n", count++);
}

0: Inside function f
1: Inside function f
```

The variable `fp` is a pointer to a function that has no arguments or return value. The parentheses around `*fp` are necessary because without them, `fp` would become a function with no arguments that returned a pointer to `void`, a quite different declaration indeed.

The function pointer `fp` is initialized with the address of a function having the corresponding argument list and return type; in this case, to `&f`. Note that we use `&f` not `&f()`. Such parentheses designate the function call operator and would result in `f` being called. Instead, we want `f`'s address so we use the `&` operator. (Actually, an expression that designates a function, such as the name `f`, is always converted to the address of that function so the `&` operator is superfluous and will not be used further. One exception is that `sizeof(f)` generates an error because the size of a function can not necessarily be determined at compile-time, even if it were a useful thing to know. In this case, `f` is not converted to a pointer to the function.)

When a C compiler comes across a call to a function that it has never seen declared, it assumes that function returns type `int`, but it doesn't have a prototype for that function and can do no argument list checking in calls. However, when a compiler sees something like `fp = f` (or `fp = &f`), it can not deduce that `f` is a function because it is not followed by a left parenthesis token. Therefore, to use a function name in expressions other than in function calls, you first must declare that function explicitly or by including a header containing its declaration. (This is not necessarily a disadvantage because now that ANSI C provides prototypes, you always should declare functions completely anyway.)

The expression `(*fp)()` causes `fp` to be dereferenced producing a function designator that is then used with the function call operator to call the designated function. The bottom line is that we may call a function without knowing its name, and that can be quite useful.

The next example has a slightly different twist—a function receives the address of some other function it is to call, yet it knows nothing about that function except for its return type and argument list.

```
#include <stdio.h>

main()
{
        void f1(void);
        void f2(void);
        void sub(void (*pf)(void));

        sub(f1);          /* pass &f1 to sub */
        sub(f2);          /* pass &f1 to sub */
}


void sub(void (*pf)(void))
{
        (*pf)();          /* call function pointed to */
}


void f1(void)
{
        printf("Inside function f1\n");
}


void f2(void)
{
        printf("Inside function f2\n");
}

Inside function f1
Inside function f2
```

In `main`, we call `sub` twice, each time passing it the address of a different function. Note though, that the functions `f1` and `f2` have exactly the same attributes. That is required because a pointer to a function of one type is not assignment-compatible with a pointer to a function of another type, even if the only difference between the function types is that their argument lists differ. `sub` expects to receive a function pointer of the correct type and proceeds to call the function whose address it receives. As the output shows, `sub` calls `f1` first, then `f2`.

What would we use function pointers for now that we have seen how to syntactically declare and use them? Consider the case in which you are to install software on many systems, some of which have a floating-point processor, and some of which don't. A reasonable approach would be to use the hardware where it exists and to emulate where it doesn't.

Let's take the simple case of finding a square root. We write two versions of the function, one using or generating in-line floating-point instructions, the other being an emulator. Let's call them `isqrt` and `esqrt`, respectively. When the program starts up, it determines whether a floating-point processor is present and it initializes the function pointer `fsqrt` to the address of `isqrt` or `esqrt`, as appropriate. Then, whenever a square root is needed, the corresponding function is called indirectly using:

```
(*fsqrt)( expression )
```

Except for the startup pointer initialization, the rest of the program is ignorant of which version is actually being called at run-time. There is a downside to this approach: Both versions of the code must be linked into the program just in case they are needed, even though only one will be used during any program run.

Other applications for function pointers come to mind. For example, a statistician uses four different formulas to calculate standard deviation depending on various criteria. However, he only has one function pointer and that always points to the function corresponding to the current method. By selecting a menu option, he can make the pointer point to one of the other functions (after all, the pointer is modifiable unless it has the `const` attribute). Again, the program does not have to continually determine its context to make sure it calls the correct function—it simply "sets it and forgets it."

Another situation could involve the routing of packets in a network. There may be several different algorithms for calculating the most efficient route based, say, on the local time. Rather than test for each packet, a function pointer could be made to point to the appropriate function and a manual or automatic supervisory program could change the pointer at the appropriate time(s) each day.

Function pointers also can be used to reduce down-time in certain systems. For example, if a node in a network is inoperable and logically has been removed, a function pointer that points to a function that expects that node to be there can be set to `NULL` to indicate the null function pointer, or it could be made to point to some local simulation function. (If the `NULL` approach is used, your design would have to be changed so that you check for the null pointer before each attempt to call the underlying function because C guarantees that none of its functions will have such an address.)

(As you might expect, a function pointer with static storage duration has a default value of `NULL`, a non-existent function, while one of automatic storage duration points "into the wild blue yonder" and may give surprising results if dereferenced.)

A function pointer is really just another scalar type and you can have arrays of, pointers to, and functions returning function pointers. These all can be implemented by applying the rules corresponding to each of these constructs learned to date. However, because arrays of function pointers can be very useful, an example using them follows. An array of function pointers can be used to implement what is commonly referred to as a *jump table* in some languages.

```
        main()
        {
                void trans1(void);      /* transaction type #1 */
                void trans2(void);      /* transaction type #2 */
                void trans3(void);      /* transaction type #3 */

                static void (*jtable[])(void) = {
                        trans1, trans2, trans3};

                int transtype;

        /* simulate some incoming transactions, one for each type, in
        decreasing type order. */

                for (transtype = 2; transtype >= 0; --transtype)
                        (*jtable[transtype])(); /* proc transaction */
        }


#include <stdio.h>

void trans1(void)
{
        printf("Processing transaction type trans1\n");
}


void trans2(void)
{
        printf("Processing transaction type trans2\n");
}


void trans3(void)
{
        printf("Processing transaction type trans3\n");
}

Processing transaction type trans3
Processing transaction type trans2
Processing transaction type trans1
```

We always can omit the dimension of an array when a complete initializer list is provided, as in this case. The three elements of the array are initialized with the addresses of the corresponding functions. (Again, there must be no () following the function names because we can not call them here.)

Instead of the **for** loop, you typically would have a routine that received the next transaction in a buffer (declared as a structure, most likely) and returned its type. Then, the corresponding transaction processing routine is dispatched using the expression:

```
(*jtable[transtype])()
```

At first glance, this may seem to be very cryptic, but let's walk it through. The expression has the three operators (indirection, subscripting and function call) along with a pair of grouping parentheses. Let's start with the grouping parentheses because whatever they contain designates the function to be (finally) called. Because `jtable` is an array, we first must select the element we need and, because subscripting has higher precedence than the indirection operator (see Appendix A), that is what happens. The resulting expression `jtable[transtype]` is a pointer to a function which we then dereference and, finally, call the underlying function.

Because `jtable` is not a `const` array, its elements can be changed at run-time. In fact, some (or all) of them even could be made to point to the same function. For example, consider the case in which you have transaction types ranging from zero to 10, but some are no longer in use. You could initialize the "obsolete" function pointers to `NULL` and check each time before you do an indirect function call. Another, and perhaps better, approach would be to make those pointers all point to the same function, one that handles any reception of these supposedly non-existent types. (Perhaps there was an undetected transmission error and the type got trashed.)

The same approach can be taken when implementing a menu-driven system. Each number selected from a menu is used as an index into a jump table and options not implemented could have their pointers initialized to `NULL`, or to a common function that informs the user that "this option is not yet implemented." Perhaps an even better approach is to write skeletal versions of all the options and, for those that aren't complete, have them display this message. To finish one of these options requires changes only to that one function because the jump table was correctly initialized at the beginning.

There are a few points worth mentioning. A jump table approach forces you to call an actual function—you can not have the actual code in-line. Also, for a set of function addresses to be admissible in a jump table, they all must point to functions having the same return type and argument list because all functions are called via the one expression.

ANSI C has made a dispensation regarding the use of function pointers in calls: It has made the parentheses and dereferencing operator optional. For example, the expression:

```
(*jtable[transtype])();
```

used above, also can be written as:

```
jtable[transtype]();
```

to make it look like a "regular" function call.

Prior to the addition of prototypes, function pointers have less attributes assigned to them. For example, two function pointers that pointed to functions having the same return type were considered assignment-compatible because there was no way to know or specify their respective functions' argument list. That is, in the declaration `int (*fp)();`, `fp` could (and still can) be made to point to any function that returns an `int`, regardless of the function's argument list. However, now that prototypes are available, you should use them wherever possible. To not do so reduces the amount of quality control checking your compiler can do. It also lets certain design errors go undetected.

Perhaps the only real disadvantage with function pointers (assuming, of course, you don't think their declaration and use is a problem) is that they do absolutely nothing to aid readability of the code written. All you can tell is that at a given point, one of a given set of functions was called—you don't know which. Running the source through a cross-reference tool isn't much help because each function's name only will appear where it was used to initialize a function pointer and that might be in an initializer of a static jump table.

Exercise 10-22: Look at the prototype for the `signal` function in `signal.h`. (Pre-ANSI versions may call it `ssignal`.) It should look something like:

```
void (*signal(int sig, void (*func)(int)))(int);
```

This function not only takes an argument that is a function pointer, it also returns a function pointer. That is, three functions are involved in the declaration and all three prototypes may be included. Several standard macros are defined in `signal.h` that may be used as the second argument to `signal`. They are `SIG_DFL` and `SIG_IGN`. Look at their definitions (which often involve casting an `int` into a function pointer) in your header and see if any other non-standard macros named `SIG_*` are also defined.

Exercise 10-23: The library routine `atexit`, declared in `stdlib.h`, permits one or more exit processing functions to be registered so that they are called in the reverse order of their registration when the program terminates normally, such as via a direct call to `exit`, or by dropping through the closing brace of `main`. The prototype for `atexit` is:

```
int atexit(void (*func)(void));
```

Consult your library manual for more details of this function. (Note that `atexit` is an ANSI C invention and was not widely supported earlier, although some implementations had a similar routine called `onexit`.)

Exercise 10-24*: Define and initialize a two-dimensional array (of size 2x3) of function pointers that point to different functions taking one `int` argument and returning an `unsigned long`. Call each of the functions pointed to, indirectly, using a pair of nested `for` loops to vary the subscripts. Do not hard-code the loop maximum values—use `sizeof` to deduce them instead.

Exercise 10-25*: Define `ppf` as a pointer to a pointer to a function that has no arguments and no return value. Make `ppf` point (eventually) to a corresponding function that simply displays a message. Call the function indirectly via `ppf`.

10.8   Chapter Summary

- C provides a computed `goto` mechanism via the `switch` construct.

- The controlling expression enclosed in the mandatory parentheses must have some integral type. (It is implementation-defined as to which.) At run-time, its value is determined and control is passed to the `case` label whose value matches that of the controlling expression. If no `case` label matches, control is passed to the `default` label, if present. If there is no `default` label, control is passed to the statement following the switch construct.

- A switch need not contain either `case` labels, or a `default` label. ANSI C requires that an implementation support at least 257 `case` labels for each switch.

- A `case` label consists of the keyword `case` followed by a compile-time integral constant expression, a colon and, eventually, a statement. A `default` label contains just that keyword and a colon.

- In order that the transfer of control is unambiguous, each `case` within a switch must have a unique value. Also, no `case` ranges are permitted in ANSI C.

- Once control has transferred to a `case` or `default` label, control keeps on "dropping through" into the next statement, if there is one, possibly until it reaches the brace closing the whole switch. To terminate a particular `case` gracefully, `break` can be used.

- The ordering of `case` labels is not guaranteed to dictate the test order for a match.

- `switch` constructs may be nested with each `switch` having its own set of `case` and `default` labels.

- C provides a `goto` statement that unconditionally transfers control to a programmer-specified statement.

- The scope of a `goto` label is function-wide and, as such, you can jump to any statement in the whole function including into and out of blocks. Note that a label eventually must be followed by a statement, before the current block ends.

- The use of `goto` should not be forbidden arbitrarily because in certain situations, it may be the only elegant and/or efficient solution.

- `goto` can be abused, so you should avoid it when you can write readable and efficient code in other ways. You should limit `goto` to forward transfers only in a local scope. Jumping into or out of block statements is considered very poor style.

- If you jump into a block containing automatic declarations having initializers, the initialization is not guaranteed to take place, although the space will be allocated to the objects declared.

- The `continue` and `break` statements are cleverly disguised versions of `goto`.

- C supports the notion of an enumerated type in which a set of valid member names (with corresponding values) are associated with a programmer-specified type name.

- An enumerated type name includes the keyword `enum` and the identifiers listed inside its definition are known as enumeration constants.

- An enumerated type is really a synonym for an implementation-defined integer type.

- Each enumeration constant is a constant having type `int`.

- By default, the internal representation of enumeration constants starts at zero and increments by one for each successive name specified in the set. If these constants are explicitly initialized, the set of values need not be contiguous and duplicates are permitted.

- Tags of structure, union and `enum` types all share the same namespace. The scope of enumeration constant names extends from immediately after their use inside a set of members through the end of their parent block (or source file, as the case may be).

- The comma operator has two operands which may be expressions of any type. The expressions need not have the same type. The left operator is evaluated and its value is discarded. That is, it is treated as a `void` expression. Then the right operand is evaluated and the result of the whole comma expression has the type and value of the right operand.

- The comma operator has the lowest precedence of all the operators.

- One confusing aspect is that the comma character can be used as both a punctuator and operator in the same expression.

- The comma operator is a sequence point. That is, all side-effects occurring in its left operand actually take place by that point.

- Because comma expressions almost always can be avoided in programs (with the possible exception of some macros), once you understand them, you also should understand their advantages and disadvantages in terms of readability and possible debugging problems. As a result, you should use them sparingly, perhaps only in `for` constructs and macros as shown.

- A type qualifier somehow qualifies (restricts or controls). A type qualifier can be used only with object declarations.

- A type qualifier only has meaning when an identifier so qualified is used in the context of an lvalue.

- If a declaration having a qualifier has no explicit type keyword, `int` is assumed.

- The `const` qualifier is used to prohibit the ability to store through a designated lvalue which, in the absence of the `const` keyword, would be a modifiable lvalue.

- The value of `const` is to provide a mechanism to protect memory locations which either can not be written to (such as those residing in ROM) or, to provide a "one writer/many reader" arrangement when multiple cooperating programs access objects in shared memory.

- `const` can be used with any object type including aggregates.

- A pointer declaration actually declares the attributes of two things: the pointer itself and the object or function being pointed to. As such, the keyword `const` can appear more than once in such a declaration.

- The `const` qualifier can occur in function prototypes.

- Syntactically, `volatile` is used exactly like `const`. The purpose of `volatile` is quite different from, and unrelated to, `const`. The `volatile` qualifier tells the compiler that the object is not "owned" by this program and that there are severe limitations on how references to it may be optimized.

- At first glance, the `const` and `volatile` attributes seem to be diametrically opposed, but they are not.

- The `typedef` keyword provides the ability to create a synonym for another type.

- To create a synonym from a type, write a declaration for an identifier of the type and prepend the keyword `typedef`. The identifier now becomes the new typename rather than a function or variable name.

- The value `typedef` is in helping to abstract real types from a program and, as such, `typedef` is a very important tool available to porting projects.

- Syntactically, `typedef` is a storage class, even though it has nothing to do with storage duration or linkage (as do `auto`, `static`, etc.).

- While you can not cause a class keyword to "stick" to a `typedef`, you can do so with the type qualifiers `const` and `volatile` because these are not class keywords.

- A `typedef` typename (or derived typename) is in the same namespace as that occupied by variables, functions and enumeration constants.

- C, like assembler, permits both objects and functions to be addressed directly.

- Except when used with `sizeof`, an expression that designates a function (such as the name `f`), is always converted to the address of that function, so the `&` operator is superfluous.

- To use function names in expressions other than in function calls, you first must declare that function explicitly or by including a header containing its declaration.

- A function pointer with static storage duration has a default value of `NULL`, a non-existent function pointer, while one of automatic storage duration has an undefined value.

- A function pointer is really just another scalar type, so you can have arrays of, pointers to and functions returning function pointers.

- An array of function pointers can be used to implement what is commonly referred to as a jump table in some languages.

Chapter 11

C's Typing Mechanism

Once you become reasonably familiar with the basics of the C language, you may wish to explore the limits to the types of objects you can construct in C. As it happens, there is no limit to the set of possible types. However, once you get past the basic and elementary derived types, it is no longer obvious by quick inspection just what a given declaration means, assuming, of course, it compiles without error. On the other hand, given that you want to define an object of some type, you have the problem of expressing it so that not only must it compile, but it has to do exactly what you want. And, if it contains a syntax error, you must be able to determine why without trying "all of the possibilities and looking at the generated code." That is, you must be able to read and write declarations with absolute confidence.

Clearly, you need to know how to write a declaration so you can define an object of a given type. However, type information is needed in other areas as well. Specifically, you need to understand declarations so you can use them to generate casts, define functions that have a given return type, utilize the `typedef` capability, and to use `sizeof`. All four build on the knowledge you use in generating a declaration. In this chapter, we will address each of them.

11.1 Mastering Declarations

Almost all of the declarations you will read and write in your C careers will be quite simple and you will just "know" how to read and write them. In these simple cases, you don't need to follow any rules and, sadly, most C veterans don't even know what the rules are. Perhaps this is excusable because the rules don't ever seem to have been explicitly spelled out. However, if you can not reliably read and write arbitrary complex declarations, you will never be able to fully exploit C's type capabilities. In this chapter, we open up the innermost sanctum of C and go where only the high priests have gone before.

11.1.1 The Base Types

The base types in C are those that involve only C language type keywords and only apply to objects. They are the signed and unsigned versions of the integral types `char`, `short`, `int` and `long`; the floating-point types `float`, `double` and the ANSI C addition, `long double`; structures, unions and enumerated types. (Note that pointers and arrays are not included here, because they are derived types.)

Declaring an object of one of these base types is simple—you write the type and follow it with an identifier. (For the purposes of this discussion we will ignore the fact that a declaration may include multiple declarators [as in `int i, j, k;`] since this has no impact on our discussion. For the most part, we also will ignore the trailing semicolon because this is not part of the declarator.)

Some examples of declarations involving base types are:

```
int i;
double d;
struct tag s;
enum color my_color;
```

The `void` type is not quite a base type because you can not have an object of that type. (However, ANSI C permits a pointer to `void` and functions returning `void`.) By its very nature, an object exists and can not, therefore, have type `void`. However, it can be argued that `void` is a base type, although we will not further debate it here.

11.1.2   Derived Types

There are three possible ways to derive a type *T1* from another type *T*. They are:

1. *T1* is an array of objects each having type *T*.

2. *T1* is a function having a return type *T*.

3. *T1* is a pointer to an object or function of type *T*.

Consider the following declarations:

```
int i, a[10], f(), *pi;
void g(), *pv;
```

Here we have declared `i` as an object having the base type `int`, `a` as an array of `int`, `f` as a function that returns an `int`, and `pi` as a pointer to an `int`. Also, `g` is a `void` function (that is, it has no return value), and `pv` is a pointer to `void`. (This ANSI C invention does not mean `pv` is a pointer to a non-existent object as the declaration may imply. Rather, `pv` points to an object whose type is not currently known. That is, a `void` pointer is a generic pointer.) For the purposes of this discussion, let's call the types of `a`, `f`, `pi`, `g` and `pv` *derived types* because they are derived from other types (in this case, base types).

The following declarations are illegal:

```
void v, b[10];
```

The simple rule to remember here involves the position in the declaration of the derived type punctuation. In the case of arrays and functions, the `[]` and `()` are postfix punctuators. That is, they follow immediately after the declarator they apply to. The pointer notation `*` is a prefix punctuator and thus comes immediately before the declarator it applies to.

11.1.3   Deriving from Derived Types

Because a derived type in fact is derived from another type, you can derive a type from another derived type ad infinitum. Some common and simple examples follow:

```
char **ppc, ***pppc;
long table[10][5], counts[5][4][6];
```

The identifier `ppc` is a pointer to a pointer to a `char`. It is derived from the type "pointer to `char`" which in turn is derived from the base type `char`. In fact, all derived types ultimately come down to a base type because the base types are the only ones for which we have keywords. Because `*` is a prefix punctuator, simply add an extra `*` in front of a valid type declarator until you get the desired level of indirection.

With arrays, the situation is very similar except that `[]` is a postfix punctuator and is added to the end of the type declarator we wish to modify. This gives rise to the notion of a multidimensional array being an array, each of whose elements is an array, etc., until the final dimension array contains either objects of a base type or pointers (to some level of indirection) to a base type.

In the declarations above, we have derived a type using the same punctuator only and we have omitted the `()` punctuator. This is because this punctuator can not be applied to itself. For example, `int f()();` is illegal because a function can not return another function. (It can, however, return a pointer to a function.)

Of course, we can mix and match the three punctuators giving rise to other useful (and, perhaps, not so useful) possibilities. However, not all such declarations are acceptable to the compiler. Two valid combinations follow:

```
char *keywords[10];
double *test();
```

Other combinations are possible, but we need to introduce some extra punctuation to write them. For now, let's summarize just what combinations of these punctuators are permissible:

Valid Derived Type Combinations			
Derived type	Pointer	Array	Function
Pointer to	YES	YES	YES
Array of	YES	YES	NO
Function returning	YES	NO	NO

Note that a pointer to an array is different from a pointer to the first element in that array.

11.1.4   Precedence of Punctuators

Once a declarator contains more than one occurence of the three punctuators discussed above, we become concerned about the order in which they apply to the identifier. For example, does `char *keywords[10];` declare `keywords` to be an array of 10 pointers to `char` or a pointer to an array of 10 `char`? According to our matrix, both are possible, so which is it and how do we write the other if not this way?

The three punctuator character pairs *, [] and () also happen to be used as operators and, as such, have precedence. Consider the following example:

```
main()
{
        char *keywords[10];
        char c;

        c = *keywords[0];
}
```

While `keywords` itself is being declared, we immediately can deduce that whatever `keywords` is, an expression of the form `*keywords[i]` has type `char`—the declaration tells as that immediately. Therefore, we can assign such an expression to a `char` variable such as `c`. To resolve the order of evaluation of the right-hand side of the assignment expression, we go to the operator precedence table (in Appendix A). This indicates that the [] takes precedence over the unary * indirection operator. Therefore, `keywords` is subscripted giving a pointer to `char` which is then dereferenced to give the value of the `char` it points to and that `char`'s value is assigned to `c`.

Clearly, the order of precedence of operators in the expression must be identical to that of the same characters used as punctuators in a declaration. So, we can talk about precedence of evaluation of operators in expressions and precedence of binding of punctuators in declarations. In any event, we use C's precedence table to resolve both.

Using this information, let's reconsider the declaration `char *keywords[10];`. Because [] takes precedence over *, `keywords` is first and foremost an array of 10 elements, each of which is a pointer, each of which points to a `char`.

If you return to the earlier example:

```
char **ppc, ***pppc;
long table[10][5], counts[5][4][6];
```

you'll find the same rules can be applied. In the case of `ppc`, we have two punctuators with the same precedence. However, the precedence table indicates that multiple * operators (and punctuators) associate right-to-left. In the case of multiple [] punctuators, they associate left-to-right, as would a combination of [] and ().

11.1.5   Forcing Punctuator Precedence

We have shown that `char *keywords[10];` declares `keywords` to be an array of 10 pointers to `char`, but because we also need exactly the same set of punctuators to declare a pointer to an array of 10 `char`, how do we write that? Clearly, we need some mechanism to change the default-binding of the punctuators.

If we again draw an analogy between declarations and expressions we have the answer. The way you change the precedence of operators in an expression is to use grouping parentheses. Now we have identified the fourth and final punctuator that is permitted in declarations. (Note that parentheses are used here for two purposes, representing both function call and grouping. However, it is unambiguous to the compiler as to which is being meant, and you should get comfortable with the difference.)

Consider the following declaration:

```
char (*pa)[10];
```

Here, the parentheses force the * to bind closer to `pa` than does [], causing `pa` to be first and foremost a pointer. It is then a pointer to an array of 10 elements, each of which is a `char`. (Such a type is rarely used; however, such things often exist without our thinking about them as such, in multidimensional arrays. For example, if `ary` is declared as `int ary[5][10]`, `ary` has type "pointer to array of 10 int", not "pointer to int" as many people incorrectly believe.)

Just as you can have redundant grouping parentheses in expressions, they also can exist in declarations. Therefore, some of our earlier declarations can be rewritten as follows:

```
char *(*ppc);
long (table[10])[5];
char *(keywords[10]);
double *(test());
```

In these cases, the grouping parentheses simply document the default binding—they serve no other purpose. Once you have mastered the reading of such declarations, you generally would not use the extra parentheses because they tend to clutter up the declaration.

Other examples of redundant parentheses are:

```
int (i), ((a)[10]), ((f)()), (*(pi));
```

11.1.6 Writing a Declaration

Consider the following declaration requirement. `fp` is to be a pointer to a function that returns a pointer to an `int`. The trick to converting these words into the corresponding declaration is to work top down. First and foremost, `fp` is a pointer, so let's write that.

```
(*fp)
```

Because the pointer notation uses a prefix punctuator, we write the * before the `fp`. (Note that, just like expressions, white space between punctuators and identifiers is ignored, so we could write (* fp) instead, although this doesn't add anything. In fact, it might reduce the readability.) We surround `*fp` with parentheses to ensure that the * binds tightest regardless of any other punctuators that may be added.

Next, `fp` is a pointer to a function, so we add the postfix function call punctuator and the binding parentheses giving:

```
((*fp)())
```

The function returns a pointer, so we add the prefix * and yet another pair of grouping parentheses to produce:

```
(*((*fp)()))
```

Finally, the function returns a pointer to an `int`, so we add the base type as a prefix (and the trailing semicolon) giving the syntactically complete declaration:

```
int (*((*fp)()))
```

We religiously have added grouping parentheses at every step, just in case they were needed. In this case, as often happens, one or more of the pairs is redundant and, therefore, can be removed. To determine which sets of parentheses are redundant, we work from the bottom up (or from the outside in). To make it easier, we'll number the sets of grouping parentheses.

```
int (*((*fp)()))
    | ||_3_|  ||
    | |___2___||
    |____1_____|
```

Clearly, pair 1 is redundant because no other punctuators are outside them. So is pair 2 because () has higher precedence than *. If we erase those two pairs we get:

```
int *(*fp)()
```

Now we have one pair left—pair 3. (The () are not grouping parentheses; they represent the function call punctuator.) Pair 3 ensures that * has precedence over () and, because this is not the case by default, the parentheses are needed. If they were removed, as in int **fp();, fp would become a function that returns a pointer to a pointer to an int. That's not the goal, so that's as far as you can go.

You now have sufficient knowledge to be able to write almost any declaration you can think of. Of course, if such a declaration is invalid (for example, a function returning a function) you will get the corresponding error from your compiler; but nevertheless, if such a declaration would have been valid, you would know how to write it simply by following the rules outlined above.

Exercise 11-1: To see if you are keeping up, use the rules outlined above to prove that the declarations shown below actually match their English descriptions:

- Declare funct as a function returning a pointer to a function returning a pointer to an array of 10 structures of type tag.

```
struct tag (*(*funct())())[10];
```

- Declare ptr as a pointer to a pointer to an array of five pointers to double.

```
double *(**ptr)[5];
```

- Declare ary as an array of 10 arrays each of five pointers to functions returning short.

```
short int (*ary[10][5])();
```

11.1.7 Reading a Declaration

Once you understand the rules and you can write any declaration, reading declarations is easy—you simply apply the rules in reverse. The only difference is that the declaration almost certainly does not contain redundant grouping parentheses, in which case, you will have to revert to the precedence table to determine the order of binding of the punctuators.

To demonstrate this, we'll reverse engineer one of the three declarations seen earlier. Given the following declaration, what does it mean?

```
double *(**ptr)[5];
```

Working inside out, we see (**ptr) and, because * associates right-to-left, ptr is a pointer to a pointer. Then we either apply the * or [] and, because [] binds tighter, ptr is a pointer to a pointer to an array of five elements. Finally, each of those array elements is a pointer to a double. If the declaration had contained redundant parentheses as follows, we would have no need to look at the precedence table:

```
double *((*(*ptr))[5]);
```

Exercise 11-2: Convince yourself that the following declarations mean what the narrative says:

```
long int (*(*point)())[5];
```

declares point as a pointer to a function returning a pointer to an array of five long ints.

```
enum color *(*(*(*a1[5])[3])())[6];
```

declares a1 as an array of five pointers to an array of three pointers to functions returning a pointer to an array of six pointers to enums of type color.

11.1.8 Function Prototypes

With the addition of function prototypes by ANSI C, declarations involving functions now may contain argument information as well. However, this does not change any of the rules for reading and writing declarations. It just makes the declarations more complex. For example:

```
int f1(double, char *);
```

declares f1 to be a function that takes two arguments (of type double and char *, respectively) and that returns an int. In the following, more complex case:

```
double (*f2(void))(double);
```

f2 is declared as a function that has no arguments and returns a pointer to a function, taking one double argument and returning a double value.

In these cases, you may find it easier to ignore the argument list information until you have gotten the rest of the declaration correct.

Exercise 11-3*: The standard library routines signal (in signal.h) and atexit (in stdlib.h) have the following prototypes. Explain in English, what these declarations are:

```
void (*signal(int sig, void (*func)(int)))(int);
int atexit(void (*func)(void));
```

11.1.9   Classes and Type Qualifiers

Declarations may contain class and type qualifier keywords such as `register`, `static`, `extern`, `auto`, `const` and `volatile`. (And, in the case of MS-DOS implementations, `near`, `far` and `huge`.) Again, like prototypes, these keywords have no affect on how you read or write declarations. Once you work out how to write the required declaration without these keywords, it is relatively simple to insert them in the appropriate places. Of course, the term "relative" is subjective and, depending on the combination of keywords, you may take a few tries to get exactly what you want. For example:

```
static volatile char *const p;
```

declares p to be a `static const` non-volatile pointer to a `volatile` non-const `char`.

11.2   Using Type Information

It is absolutely necessary to know how to construct a declaration if you are ever to have an identifier of that type. However, once you have mastered the reading and writing of declarations, your job is not completed, because to really exploit the language, you must learn how to apply that type information in other ways. The ways in which C uses type information are numerous. Apart from identifier declarations, types are used in casts, with `sizeof`, in defining function return types, and in defining type synonyms with `typedef`. We will look at the rules in constructing each of these and will apply them to a series of types that have a varying degree of complexity.

11.2.1   Type Usage Rules

The following five rules describe how to apply type information:

Rule 1: To extract the type information from a declaration, omit the identifier. (We will ignore the trailing semicolon in declarations because it is not part of the declarator.) The following table shows some examples of declarations and their corresponding types:

| Some Declarations and their Extracted Types ||
Declaration	*Type*
`double d`	`double`
`short int s[6]`	`short int [6]`
`struct tags *pstr`	`struct tags *`
`union tagu (*pun)[7]`	`union tagu (*)[7]`
`enum tage (*(*fp)())[3]`	`enum tage (*(*)())[3]`

Rule 2: To generate a cast for type *T*, using Rule 1, extract the type information and enclose it in parentheses and use it as a prefix operator.

Rule 3: To find the size of an object of type *T*, use Rule 1 to extract the type information, enclose it in parentheses and use it as the postfix operand of the `sizeof` operator.

Rule 4: To define a function so that it returns a value of type *T*, declare an identifier ID to have that type. Then replace the identifier ID in the declaration with the name of the function followed immediately by a pair of parentheses containing the function's formal argument list. At the end of this declaration, you then write the function body enclosed in braces.

Rule 5: To create a synonym for a type, declare an identifier ID to have that type. Add the keyword `typedef` in front of the declaration, replace ID with an identifier that is the type synonym you wish, and add a trailing semicolon.

11.2.2 Some Examples

To reinforce the five rules outlined above, let's take each of four declarations and apply the rules to them.

1. `pc` is a pointer to `char`.

Action	Result
declaration	`char *pc;`
cast	`(char *)` *expression*
sizeof	`sizeof(char *)`
function returning	`char *f(`*arg-list*`) { /* ... */ }`
type synonym	`typedef char *PTC;`

2. `ap` is an array of five pointers to `char`.

Action	Result
declaration	`char *ap[5];`
cast	`(char *[5])` *expression*
sizeof	`sizeof(char *[5])`
function returning	`char *f(`*arg-list*`)[5] { /* ... */ }`
type synonym	`typedef char *A5PTC[5];`

Note that the cast generated by the rules in this example is illegal—it it not permitted to cast anything into an array (or a structure or a union). Also, the function definition is illegal because an array can not be returned by value.

3. `pa` is a pointer to an array of five `char`.

Action	Result
declaration	`char (*pa)[5];`
cast	`(char (*)[5])` *expression*
sizeof	`sizeof(char (*)[5])`
function returning	`char (*f(`*arg-list*`))[5] { /* ... */ }`
type synonym	`typedef char (*PA5C)[5];`

The parentheses around * are not redundant; they serve to distinguish between
an array of pointers (as in example 2) and a pointer to an array. The two types
are quite different.

4. `pf` is a pointer to a function that returns an `int`.

Action	Result
declaration	`int (*pf)();`
cast	`(int (*)()) ` *expression*
`sizeof`	`sizeof(int (*)())`
function returning	`int (*f(`*arg-list*`))() { /* ...  */ }`
type synonym	`typedef int (*PTFRI)();`

As in example 3, the parentheses around * are not redundant.

Exercise 11-4: Look at the definitions of the macros `SIG_IGN` and `SIG_DFL`
in `signal.h`. They typically involve a complex cast expression.

11.2.3   The Importance of `typedef`

As types get more complex to write, the value of `typedef` becomes more obvious. In
example 4 above, the function `f` is defined using:

```
int (*f(arg-list))() { /* ... */ }
```

However, once the type synonym `PTFRI` has been defined, it can be used in place
of the long-hand declaration as follows:

```
typedef int (*PTFRI)();

PTFRI f(arg-list) { /* ... */ }
```

That looks more manageable.

11.2.4   Prototypes, Type Qualifiers and Classes

As mentioned in the first section of this chapter, types also may contain prototype
information and qualifier and class keywords. However, not all of these actually are
part of the type. Let's look at each separately.

Any declaration involving a function type can, according to ANSI C, contain
argument list type information. For example, if `f` is a function taking a `double` and
a `char` pointer as arguments, and it returns no value, its prototype is:

```
void f(double, char *);
```

The only thing we can do with such a declaration apart from declare other functions of the same type, is to `typedef` it because you can not cast into a function,
return a function or find its size.

A declaration can contain more than one reference to a function (`signal` in `signal.h` is one such example); for example:

```
long int *(*f1(int, double))(int, int)
```

Here, `f1` is a pointer to a function that takes an `int` and a `double` argument, and returns a pointer to a function that takes two `int` arguments and returns a pointer to a `long int`. This type can be used with all of the rules described above.

With the advent of prototypes, they can exist also in casts, `sizeof` operands and `typedefs`, as well as function definitions and declarations.

The type usage rules do not include class keywords because these are not part of an identifier's type specifier. That is, it makes no sense to cast into a `static` type, return a `register` type or `typedef` an `auto` declaration.

The type qualifier keywords `const` and `volatile` can be used in a limited sense with the rules. Certainly, they can be present in declarations, function definitions and `typedefs`. However, they have no effect in casts and with `sizeof`.

11.3 A Declaration Puzzle

The following puzzle was contrived by a perverted C programmer as an exercise in understanding types. And while it is a nonsensical program, it uses much of what we have learned in this chapter.

```
#include <stdio.h>

static glob1 = 1;
static glob2 = 2;
static glob3 = 3;

int *(*func(void))[3]
{
        static *ary[3] = {&glob1, &glob2, &glob3};

        return (&ary);
}

main()
{
        int *(*(*x)(void))[3] = func;

        printf("value = %d\n", *1[*(*x)()] +
                sizeof(glob3++) + glob3);
}
```

The `glob1`, `glob2` and `glob3` objects are static internal objects; that is, they have static storage duration and internal linkage. As such, they are allocated space and initialized prior to `main` beginning execution. (On most hosted implementations, this would be done at compile-time.) No type is specified, although the class is, in which case, the type `int` is implied. `ary` is an array of three pointers to `int`. (Again, the `int` type is implied by the absence of type information.) `ary` also has static storage duration; however, it has no linkage. It is local to the function `func`. It is initialized with the addresses of the three static `int`s defined earlier.

The value returned from `func` is `&ary` and, to the uninitiated, the `&` operator may seem superfluous; however, it is not. The address of an array is different from the address of its first element. When an array designator (such as an array name) is used in an expression (other than with `sizeof` or with `&`), it is converted to a pointer to its first element. Therefore, the expression `ary` has type array of three pointers to `int`s and its value is a pointer to a pointer to an `int`. On the other hand, `&ary` has type "pointer to array of three pointers to `int`." This type is written as follows:

```
int *(*p)[3];
```

As we learned in Rule 4 above, the rule for declaring a function to return a type is to replace the identifier in the above declaration with the function name and argument list as follows:

```
int *(*f())[3] { /*...*/ }
```

In this puzzle, the function name is `func` and it has no arguments. So, using the function prototype method of defining a function, we finish with the following:

```
int *(*func(void))[3] { /*...*/ }
```

In `main` an automatic variable `x` is defined using:

```
int *(*(*x)(void))[3] = func;
```

If we remove the function argument list and the initializer, the declaration becomes a little simpler:

```
int *(*(*x)())[3]
```

Reading this declaration we see that `x` is a pointer to a function that returns a pointer to an array of three pointers to `int`. If we add all of the redundant grouping parentheses to the declaration we get:

```
int *((*((*x)())))[3])
```

When a function designator (such as a function name) is used in an expression, it is treated as the address of that function. Therefore, `x` is initialized with the address of a function which returns a pointer to an array of three pointers to `int`.

The next part of the program to solve is the expression `*1[*(*x)()]`. Clearly, we have a subscript operator enclosing an expression. Because `x` is a pointer to a function, `*x` designates the function being pointed to and `(*x)()` is a call to that function (in this case, to function `func`). `func` returns the address of the array `ary` and, indirecting on that return value, we have an array designator; that is, `*(*x)()` designates the array `ary`. So, we effectively have `*1[ary]`, a rather unusual-looking expression.

Almost all languages require you to write array subscripts in a particular way, with the name of the array followed by a pair of `()` or `[]` (or similar) punctuators which enclose an integral expression, representing the subscript. While C also permits this approach, it is far more liberal. First, the name of an array does not need to be present. What is needed is an array designator expression of which an array name is but one example. This is possible because [] is an operator in C, not a punctuator and, as such, it takes operands which themselves are expressions.

Second, K&R (and ANSI C) specify that one of the operands of the [] operator must be a pointer expression and the other must be an integral expression. It is not required that the integral expression be inside the [] and in this puzzle it is not. (Despite the fact that the [] operator is commutative, you should write the integral expression inside the brackets. Not only is this preferred style, many implementations [incorrectly] won't accept it otherwise.) To make it simpler, let's swap the operands around giving *ary[1]. The [] has higher precedence than indirection, so we subscript ary resulting in a pointer to its second element, glob2. If we indirect on that pointer, we get the actual value of glob2, 2.

So, the type of the whole expression is int with value 2. To this we add two other integer values and display the answer using printf with a mask of %d. The answer, therefore, is 2 + sizeof(glob3++) + 3 and will vary depending on your machine. For example, under VAX/VMS, the result is 9; on a PDP- 11 or MS-DOS machine, the result is 7; and for the 64-bit word Cray-2, the result is 13.

You may find the expression sizeof(glob3++) a bit tricky. What is the significance of the ++ operator? None whatsoever. sizeof is only interested in the type of its operand, and the type of glob3++ is the same as the type of glob3. sizeof evaluates its operand purely from the point of ascertaining what the type of the result is. It does not actually evaluate the expression, so no code is generated for the ++ operator.

Actually, it is possible the result produced by printf will be garbage depending on your implementation. In any case, the call to printf is not portable for the following reasons. First, the type of a sizeof expression is unsigned, so the second argument passed to printf is unsigned and the display mask should be at least %u. This in itself should never be a problem, though, because signed and unsigned ints always have the same size and sizeof(int) should never result in a value so big that when printed using %d, the sign bit will be set. However, there is a more subtle and real problem.

The type of a sizeof expression is implementation-defined. It may be either unsigned int or unsigned long at the implementer's pleasure. Whatever type is chosen, it is typedefed as size_t in stddef.h (and other standard headers). Therefore, the printf mask needed could be either %u or %lu.

To make the call to printf totally portable, we could use the following code:

```
main()
{
        int *(*(*x)(void))[3] = func;
        unsigned long int ul;

        ul = *1[*(*x)()] + sizeof(glob3++) + glob3;
        printf("value = %lu\n", ul);
}
```

Of course, the temporary variable ul could be avoided simply by casting the addition expression to unsigned long before passing it to printf.

This works fine for the given data; however, the order of evaluation of the addition expression is undefined. If glob2 had been initialized to the largest possible int value

(INT_MAX in limits.h) and that had been added to glob3 first, overflow would have
occurred because int + int produces an int. On the other hand, if one of the int
values were added to sizeof first, that int would have been promoted to unsigned
(or unsigned long) as necessary. To completely "bulletproof" the code, we explicitly
could cast the first and/or third expression on the right side of the assignment to type
size_t. That way, we ensure no overflow can occur. This trivial example gives you
some indication of what you have to worry about if you are *REALLY* interested in
portability.

11.4   Chapter Summary

- You need to understand declarations so you can use them to generate casts,
  define functions that have a given return type, to utilize the typedef capability
  and to use sizeof.

- The base types in C are those involving only C language type keywords and
  only apply to objects. They are the signed and unsigned versions of the integral
  types char, short, int and long; the floating-point types float, double and
  the ANSI C addition, long double; structures, unions and enumerated types.
  (Pointers and arrays are not included here, because they are derived types.)

- The void type is not quite a base type because you can not have an object of
  that type. (However, ANSI C permits a pointer to void and functions returning
  void.) By its very nature, an object exists and can not, therefore, have type
  void. However, it can be argued that void is a base type.

- There are three possible ways to derive a type *T1* from another type *T*. They
  are: *T1* is an array of objects each having type *T*, *T1* is a function having a
  return type *T*, and *T1* is a pointer to an object or function of type *T*.

- In the case of arrays and functions, the [] and () are postfix punctuators. That
  is, they follow immediately after the declarator they apply to. The pointer notation * is a prefix punctuator and thus comes immediately before the declarator
  it applies to.

- Because a derived type is in fact derived from another type, you can derive a
  type from another derived type ad infinitum.

- A pointer to an array is different from a pointer to the first element in that
  array.

- The order of precedence of operators in the expression is identical to that of the
  same characters used as punctuators in a declaration. So, we can talk about
  precedence of evaluation of operators in expressions and precedence of binding
  of punctuators in declarations. In any event, we use C's precedence table to
  resolve both.

- The way to change the precedence of punctuators in a declaration is to use
  grouping parentheses.

- Just as you can have redundant grouping parentheses in expressions, they also
  can exist in declarations.

- The trick to converting an English description of a type into the corresponding declaration is to work top down starting with the identifier and applying one type modifying punctuator at a time.

- Once you understand the rules for writing any declaration, reading declarations is easy. You simply apply the rules in reverse. The only difference is that the declaration almost certainly does not contain redundant grouping parentheses, in which case, you will have to revert to the precedence table to determine the order of binding of the punctuators.

- With the addition of function prototypes by ANSI C, declarations involving functions now may contain argument information as well. However, this does not change any of the rules for reading and writing declarations. It just makes the declarations more complex.

- In declarations involving functions, you may find it easier to ignore the argument list information until you have gotten the rest of the declaration correct.

- Declarations may contain class and type qualifier keywords such as `register`, `static`, `extern`, `auto`, `const` and `volatile`. Like prototypes, these keywords have no affect on how you read or write declarations. Once you work out how to write the required declaration without these keywords, it is relatively simple to insert them in the appropriate places.

- The following five rules describe how to apply type information: Rule 1 explains how to extract type information from a declaration while Rules 2–5 explain how to build a cast, use `sizeof`, define a function return type and use `typedef`, respectively.

  Rule 1: To extract the type information from a declaration, omit the identifier.

  Rule 2: To generate a cast for type T, using Rule 1, extract the type information and enclose it in parentheses and use it as a prefix operator.

  Rule 3: To find the size of an object of type T, use Rule 1 to extract the type information, enclose it in parentheses and use it as the postfix operand of the `sizeof` operator.

  Rule 4: To define a function so that it returns a value of type T, declare an identifier ID to have that type. Then replace the identifier ID in the declaration with the name of the function followed immediately by a pair of parentheses containing the function's formal argument list. At the end of this declaration, you write the function body enclosed in braces.

  Rule 5: To create a synonym for a type, declare an identifier ID to have that type. Add the keyword `typedef` in front of the declaration, replace ID with an identifier that is the type synonym you wish, and add a trailing semicolon.

- As types get more complex to write, the value of `typedef` becomes more obvious.

- With the advent of prototypes, they can exist also in casts, `sizeof` operands and `typedef`s as well as function definitions and declarations.

Appendix A

Precedence Table

Each of C's operators has a given precedence. Expressions involving more than one operator are evaluated according to the precedence of the operators involved. However, such precedence can be overridden by using grouping parentheses.

Operators listed higher in the precedence table shown below have higher precedence. If an expression involves multiple operators of the same precedence (such as in *pc++), the associativity column entry determines the evaluation order.

Note that some characters are used for more than one operator; for example, & is used as the "address-of" operator and as the bit-wise OR operator.

<table>
<tr><td colspan="2" align="center">C Language Operator Precedence</td></tr>
<tr><td>Operator</td><td>Associativity</td></tr>
<tr><td>() [] -> .</td><td>Left to Right</td></tr>
<tr><td>! ~ ++ -- - + * & sizeof (type)</td><td>Right to Left</td></tr>
<tr><td>* / %</td><td>Left to Right</td></tr>
<tr><td>+ -</td><td>Left to Right</td></tr>
<tr><td><< >></td><td>Left to Right</td></tr>
<tr><td>< <= > >=</td><td>Left to Right</td></tr>
<tr><td>== !=</td><td>Left to Right</td></tr>
<tr><td>&</td><td>Left to Right</td></tr>
<tr><td>^</td><td>Left to Right</td></tr>
<tr><td>|</td><td>Left to Right</td></tr>
<tr><td>&&</td><td>Left to Right</td></tr>
<tr><td>||</td><td>Left to Right</td></tr>
<tr><td>?:</td><td>Right to Left</td></tr>
<tr><td>= += -= *= /= %= >>= <<= &= ^= |=</td><td>Right to Left</td></tr>
<tr><td>,</td><td>Left to Right</td></tr>
</table>

Appendix B

Solutions to Selected Exercises

B.1   Chapter 1 Solutions

Solution 1-3: On many systems, attempting to link this program will produce an error indicating that no `main` entry point was found. On some others (including VAX C), the program will link and run without error; that is, the program's entry point will be the first function seen by the linker.

Solution 1-7: The following names are not legal identifiers, because they contain characters other than alphanumerics and underscores. Also, two of them begin with digits. `Todays'date`, `TOTAL$COST`, `first-name`, `3WiseMen` and `Oxabcd`. (Note that some implementations do accept dollar signs in identifiers.)

Solution 1-8: At this stage in the book, we haven't discussed external declarations. One way to write one is to declare a variable outside of a function as shown in the following example:

```
int e2345678;            /* check external identifier significance */
        int e23456789;
        int e234567890;
        int e2345678901;
        int e23456789012;
        /* ... */


        int abc = 6;             /* check external identifier casing */
        int ABC = 8;
        int Abc = 12;
```

269

```
f()
{
        int i2345678;     /* check internal ident significance */
        int i23456789;
        int i234567890;
        int i2345678901;
        int i23456789012;
        /* ... */
}
```

Solution 1-10:

```
/* use ANSI terminal escape sequences to manipulate screen/cursor */

        #include <stdio.h>

        main()
        {
                printf("\33[2J");                /* clear screen */
                printf("\33[10;5H");             /* position cursor */
                printf("HELLO!\n");              /* print text */

                printf("\33[2J\33[10;5HHELLO!\n");/* do it all */
        }
```

Solution 1-11:

```
        #include <stdio.h>

        main()
        {
                printf("|\A|\B|\C|\D|\E|\F|\G|\H|\I|\J|\K|\L|\M|\n");
                printf("|\n|\O|\P|\Q|\R|\S|\T|\U|\V|\W|\X|\Y|\Z|\n");
                printf("|\a|\b|\c|\d|\e|\f|\g|\h|\i|\j|\k|\l|\m|\n");
                printf("|\n|\o|\p|\q|\r|\s|\t|\u|\v|\w|\x|\y|\z|\n");
                printf("|\!|\@|\#|\%|\^|\&|\*|\(|\)|\_|\-|\+|\=|\n");
                printf("|\\|\||\{|\[|\}|\]|\;|\:|\'|\"|\`|\~|\/|\n");
                printf("|\?|\.|\>|\,|\<|\n");
        }
```

Solution 1-14: The following output was produced by VAX C. On the VAX, an int is four bytes and a double is eight.

```
12345
654 38584
-206159715 -893303391
16896
```

In the first case, one int is expected by printf, so it takes four bytes from the stack and displays them giving 12345. The other four bytes pushed during the call to printf are ignored.

In the second case, two ints are expected, yet only one was supplied, so printf merrily takes the next four bytes from the stack where the second int should have been, resulting in some undefined result; however, we do get the 654 as well.

A floating point constant such as 1.234 has type double, so in the third case, 12 bytes are passed—eight for the double and four for the int; however, printf is expecting two ints and picks off two lots of four bytes instead, resulting in undefined output.

Similarly, in case four, printf misinterprets the stack expecting to find one int yet being passed a double. Consequently, it takes the first four bytes of the eight-byte double and uses that as a signed int, producing undefined results.

Solution 1-15:

```
#include <stdio.h>

main()
{
        int cost = 20;
        int markup = 2;
        int quantity = 123;

        printf("value = $%d\n", (cost + markup) * quantity);
}

value = $2706
```

Solution 1-16: Because the initial value of i is undefined, the result of j + i is also undefined.

Solution 1-18:

```
#include <stdio.h>

main()
{
        long int value = 123456;

        printf("(dec)\t(oct)\t(hex)\n");
        printf("%ld\t%lo\t%lx\n", value, value, value);
}

(dec)   (oct)   (hex)
123456  361100  1e240
```

On 32-bit machines, int and long int likely will have the same representation.

If this is so, an edit mask of "%d\t%o\t%x\n" also would work; however, the program would not be portable to 16-bit systems, for example.

B.2   Chapter 2 Solutions

Solution 2-1:

```
#include <stdio.h>

main()
{
        double d = 10.0;

        while (d >= -10.0) {
                printf("%5.1f      %9.1f\n", d, d * d);
                d -= 2.5;
        }
}
```

```
  10.0          100.0
   7.5           56.2
   5.0           25.0
   2.5            6.2
   0.0            0.0
  -2.5            6.2
  -5.0           25.0
  -7.5           56.2
 -10.0          100.0
```

Solution 2-2:

```
#include <stdio.h>

main()
{
        double d = 1.0;
        unsigned long count = 0;

        while (d <= 1.000001) {
                ++count;
                printf("count = %6lu,  %10.8f\n", count, d);
                d += 0.0000005;
        }
}
```

```
count =      1,  1.00000000
count =      2,  1.00000050
```

When dealing with floating-point comparisons, you must allow for approximate representations of specific mathematic quantities. For example, in the above program, you should not have a loop-controlling expression such as (d != 1.000001), because d may never be exactly equal to that value no matter how close it does get. As such, the loop will never test false and will be infinite.

d should be at least of type double, because that is adequate for the precision required. However, float may not be. long double is overkill, because it has at least as big a range and precision as has double.

Solution 2-4: The following program was run on a 16-bit machine:

```
#include <stdio.h>

main()
{
        char c;          /* note c is a char NOT an int */

        printf("EOF = %d (dec), %o (oct), %x (hex)\n\n",
                EOF, EOF, EOF);

        c = getchar();
        while (c != EOF) {
                putchar(c);
                c = getchar();
        }
}


EOF = -1 (dec), 177777 (oct), ffff (hex)

abcdefgh<new-line>
<CTRL/Z>
```

Solution 2-7:

```
#include <stdio.h>

main()
{
        int i = 5;

        if (i = 10)
                printf("i equals 10\n");
        else
                printf("i equals %d\n", i);
}

i equals 10
```

The = operator is for assignment not comparison. Therefore, i is being assigned the value 10, which tests true because 10 is non-zero. A common problem for programmers new to C, or who frequently move to and from C, is to use = when they really want ==.

Solution 2-8:

```
#include <stdio.h>

main()
{
        int c;

        while ((c = getchar()) != EOF) {
                if (c >= 'a' && c <= 'z')
                        putchar(c - 32);
                else if (c >= 'A' && c <= 'Z')
                        putchar(c + 32);
                else
                        putchar(c);
        }
}


UPPER-CASE /// lower-case<new-line>
upper-case /// LOWER-CASE<new-line>
<CTRL/Z>
```

This is an ASCII-specific solution because it relies on the internal representation of upper- and lowercase letters. Some character sets have disjoint representation ranges for upper- and/or lowercase letter groups. There is no portable solution for all character sets using this approach.

Solution 2-9:

```
#include <stdio.h>

main()
{
        int i;
        int odd = 0;
        int even = 0;

        for (i = -10; i <= 10; ++i) {
                printf("%3d\t%3d\t", i, i * i);
                if (i/2 == i/2.0) {
                        ++even;
                        printf("EVEN\n");
                }
                else {
                        ++odd;
                        printf("ODD\n");
                }
        }

        printf("\n# odd numbers = %d\n", odd);
        printf("# even numbers = %d\n", even);
}


-10     100     EVEN
 -9      81     ODD
 -8      64     EVEN
...     ...     ...
  8      64     EVEN
  9      81     ODD
 10     100     EVEN

# odd numbers = 10
# even numbers = 11
```

To see if we have an odd or even number, we perform both integer and floating-point versions of the division. The denominator 2.0 forces that division to be done in **double** precision while i/2 truncates as necessary. The result of the first **int** division is promoted to **double** and then compared with the result of the second division. They will compare equal only if i is even.

Solution 2-10:

```
#include <stdio.h>

main()
{
        int i;

        for (i = 'Z'; i >= 'A'; --i)
                printf("%c    %3d\n", i, i);
}
```

```
Z     90
Y     89
X     88
..    ..
C     67
B     66
A     65
```

i could be either a **char**, **short** or **int** because both **char** and **short** are large enough to represent the characters A–Z, and they are both widened to **int** when passed to a function (in this case, **printf**). However, if i had type **long int**, display masks of %lc and %ld would be needed instead.

Solution 2-11:

```
#include <stdio.h>

main()
{
        int i;

        i = printf("Test Data");
        printf("\ni = %d\n", i);

        i = printf("%2d", 1234);
        printf("\ni = %d\n", i);
}
```

```
Test Data
i = 9
1234
i = 4
```

printf returns either a non-negative value indicating the number of characters it wrote out, or a negative value of an output error occurred.

Solution 2-12:

```
#include <stdio.h>

main()
{
        printf("true = %d, false = %d\n", 5 > 4, 5 < 4);
}

true = 1, false = 0
```

B.3   Chapter 3 Solutions

Solution 3-1:

```
#include <stdio.h>

main()
{
        int ia[1];       /* array of 1 element */

        ia[0] = 100;

        printf("ia[0] = %d\n", ia[0]);
}

ia[0] = 100
```

Solution 3-2:

```
#include <stdio.h>

main()
{
        int da[10];

        printf("%d, %d, %d, %d\n", da[10], da[15],
                da[100], da[-5]);
}

-26, -24, 1010, -6
```

C provides no array bounds checking at compile- or run-time. The subscript used with the [] operator is simply required to be an integral type—it may be signed or unsigned.

This program should compile without error, but it may fail at run-time depending on your system. On systems where each executing task is protected from other executing tasks, attempts to access memory locations outside of your task's address space may cause that task to abort.

Solution 3-3:

```
#include <stdio.h>

main()
{
        char ca[20];
        int i = 0;

        printf("Please enter 5 characters: ");

        while (i < 5)
                ca[i++] = getchar();

        printf("ca => |%s|\n", ca);
}

Please enter 5 characters: ab123
ca => |ab123<garbage>|
```

Because we have not appended a terminating null character, the %s mask causes printf to keep displaying characters until one is found. If none is found, printf will attempt to access a memory location outside the program's address space, which may cause the program to abort.

Solution 3-4: Whenever the compiler encounters a string literal, it allocates storage for that string, allowing for one more char than is represented in the string. The space allocated is then initialized with the contents of the string and the extra trailing char allocated is initialized with the null character. Therefore, the amount of space allocated to the strings "Europe", "", "\0" and "\0abc\0" is 7, 1, 2 and 6 chars, respectively. As shown, a string may contain any valid escape sequence representation, including that for the null character. Regardless of the string's contents, a null character is always appended.

Solution 3-5:

```
#include <stdio.h>

main()
{
        printf("%d\0%d", 10, 20);
}

10
```

The first argument to printf is a null-terminated string that contains text and/or display edit masks. `printf` knows it has completed processing this string when it reaches the null character terminator. However, if you explicitly embed a null character in that string, `printf` will terminate prematurely at that point, believing it has reached the end of the string.

Solution 3-6: The program was given its own source file as input.

```
#include <stdio.h>
#include <ctype.h>

main()
{
        int c;
        unsigned alpha = 0;
        unsigned digit = 0;
        unsigned space = 0;
        unsigned other = 0;


        while ((c = getchar()) != EOF) {
                if (isalpha(c))
                        ++alpha;
                else if (isdigit(c))
                        ++digit;
                else if (isspace(c))
                        ++space;
                else
                        ++other;
        }


        printf("\n# alpha = %u\n", alpha);
        printf("# digit = %u\n", digit);
        printf("# space = %u\n", space);
        printf("# other = %u\n", other);
}


# alpha = 237
# digit = 4
# space = 100
# other = 97
```

Solution 3-7:

```
#include <stdio.h>

main()
{
        int i;
        char ca[5][30] = {
                {"John Smith III"},
                {"Mary Jane O'conner"},
                {"Thomas Dickens"},
                {"Alice Thompson"},
                {'J', 'o', 'e', ' ', 'J', 'o', 'n', 'e', 's'}
        };

        for (i = 0; i < (sizeof(ca)/sizeof(ca[0])); ++i)
                printf("row %d ==> |%s|\n", i, ca[i]);
}
```

```
row 0 ==> |John Smith III|
row 1 ==> |Mary Jane O'conner|
row 2 ==> |Thomas Dickens|
row 3 ==> |Alice Thompson|
row 4 ==> |Joe Jones|
```

You can always use `sizeof` to determine the number of elements in an array, in this case 5. Note that `ca[i]` represents the *i*th complete row. The last initializer shows how cumbersome it is to write string initializers out in longhand. The double quoted form is easier to read and write.

Your implementation may produce a compilation error if it does not yet support automatic arrays with initializer lists. If this is the case, you can get it to work either by placing the keyword `static` in front of `char ca`, or by moving the whole array declaration outside of the function before `main` is defined. (These are discussed in Chapter 5.)

Solution 3-8:

```
#include <stdio.h>

main()
{
        int i;
        char ca[5][30];

        for (i = 0; i < (sizeof(ca)/sizeof(ca[0])); ++i) {
                printf("Enter name %d (29 chars max): ", i + 1);
                gets(ca[i]);
        }

        for (i = 0; i < (sizeof(ca)/sizeof(ca[0])); ++i)
                printf("name %d ==> |%s|\n", i + 1, ca[i]);
}
```

```
Enter name 1 (29 chars max): Allan Miller
Enter name 2 (29 chars max): James Hightower
Enter name 3 (29 chars max): William Jones
Enter name 4 (29 chars max): Mary Elizabeth Small
Enter name 5 (29 chars max): Annie Potts
name 1 ==> |Allan Miller|
name 2 ==> |James Hightower|
name 3 ==> |William Jones|
name 4 ==> |Mary Elizabeth Small|
name 5 ==> |Annie Potts|
```

Beware when using **gets** because it does not place a limit on the number of characters read. Run this program and give it more than 29 characters for one or more of the names and see if anything important gets overwritten.

Solution 3-9:

```
#include <stdio.h>

main()
{
        int ia[] = {-20, 52, 33, 0, -5, 74, -6, 1, 9, -4};
        int i;
        int sum = 0;

        for (i = 0; i < sizeof(ia)/sizeof(ia[0]); ++i)
                sum += ia[i];

        printf("The sum = %d. The average = %6.2f\n",
                sum, ((double) sum)/(sizeof(ia)/sizeof(ia[0])));
}

The sum = 134. The average =  13.40
```

Because the sum only can be integral, there is no need to use floating-point until the average is calculated. By casting either (or both) of the numerator and denominator to `double`, we force the division to be done in floating point. Note that if i and j are both type `int`, `(double) (i/j)` is quite different from `(double) i/j`. In the latter case, the cast operator has higher precedence than division.

B.4   Chapter 4 Solutions

Solution 4-5:

```
#include <stdio.h>

main()
{
        void copy(char dest[], char source[]);

        char array[80];
        char source[] = "A sunny day";

        copy(array, "This is a test.");
        printf("array contains |%s|\n", array);

        copy(array, "");
        printf("array contains |%s|\n", array);

        copy(array, source);
        printf("array contains |%s|\n", array);
}
```

```
void copy(char dest[], char source[])
{
        unsigned long i = 0;

        while (source[i] != '\0') {
                dest[i] = source[i];
                ++i;
        }

        dest[i] = '\0';
}
```

```
array contains |This is a test.|
array contains ||
array contains |A sunny day|
```

You may be tempted to put the ++ inside the assignment expression using one of the following forms. Note that both forms produce undefined behavior (one of which probably gives you the correct answer), because the order of evaluation of operands across the assignment operator is undefined.

```
while ((dest[i] = source[i++]) != '\0')
while ((dest[i++] = source[i]) != '\0')
```

Solution 4-6:

```
#include <stdio.h>

int power(int a, int b)
{
        int i;                  /* loop counter */
        int retval = 1;         /* function return value */

        for (i = 1; i <= b; ++i)
                retval *= a;

        return (retval);
}
```

```
main()
{
        int power(int a, int b);
        int i;
        int j;

        printf("value\tpow 0\tpow 1\tpow 2\tpow 3\n");
        printf("-----------------------------------\n");

        for (i = 5; i >= -5; --i) {
                printf("%3d", i);
                for (j = 0; j <= 3; ++j) {
                        printf("\t%4d", power(i, j));
                }
                putchar('\n');
        }
}
```

value	pow 0	pow 1	pow 2	pow 3
5	1	5	25	125
4	1	4	16	64
3	1	3	9	27
2	1	2	4	8
1	1	1	1	1
0	1	0	0	0
-1	1	-1	1	-1
-2	1	-2	4	-8
-3	1	-3	9	-27
-4	1	-4	16	-64
-5	1	-5	25	-125

Solution 4-7:

```
#include <stdio.h>

main()
{
        unsigned long int fact(unsigned int);
        int i;

        for (i = 0; i <= 10; ++i)
                printf(" %2d! = %lu\n", i, fact(i));
}
```

```
unsigned long int fact(unsigned int u)
{
        if (u > 1)
                return (u * fact(u - 1));
        else
                return (u);
}
```

```
 0! = 0
 1! = 1
 2! = 2
 3! = 6
 4! = 24
 5! = 120
 6! = 720
 7! = 5040
 8! = 40320
 9! = 362880
10! = 3628800
```

Solution 4-9:

```
#include <stdio.h>

main()
{
        unsigned long int word = 0xF;

        printf("word in hex = %16lx\n", word);
        word &= ~5;
        printf("word in hex = %16lx\n", word);
        word |= 0x50;
        printf("word in hex = %16lx\n", word);
        word ^= 060704;
        printf("word in hex = %16lx\n", word);
        word = ~word;
        printf("word in hex = %16lx\n", word);
}
```

```
word in hex =                f
word in hex =                a
word in hex =               5a
word in hex =             619e
word in hex =         ffff9e61
```

B.5   Chapter 5 Solutions

Solution 5-4:

```
#include <stdio.h>

main()
{
        void f(void);

        f();
        f();
        f();
}


void f(void)
{
        static int si = 100;    /* initialized once only */
        auto int ai = 123;      /* initialized each entry */

        printf("si = %d, ai = %d\n", si++, ai++);
}


si = 100, ai = 123
si = 101, ai = 123
si = 102, ai = 123
```

Solution 5-5:

```
/* file a.c */

#include <stdio.h>

main()
{
        extern void f(void);
        extern int ei;

        f();
        printf("ei = %d\n", ei);
}
```

```
/* file b.c */

#include <stdio.h>

static int ei = 123;

static void f(void)
{
        printf("ei = %d\n", ei);
}
```

This example should generate linker errors something like "unresolved externals **ei** and **f**", because it can not find external definitions for these names referenced in **main**. It is conceivable that on some implementations, the declaration **extern int ei** actually would cause space to be allocated for that object. This space would not be the same space allocated to the private copy of **ei** defined inside function **f**. In any case, the private copy of **ei** in **f** is not accessible from outside the source file **b.c**.

Solution 5-6:

```
/* file f.c */

#include <stdio.h>

char gc = 'a';

void f(void)
{
        extern int gi[5];

        printf("f: gc = %c, gi[4] = %d\n", gc, gi[4]);
}


/* file g.c */

#include <stdio.h>

int gi[5] = {1, 2, 3, 4, 5};

void g(void)
{
        extern char gc;

        printf("g: gc = %c, gi[4] = %d\n", gc, gi[4]);
}
```

```
/* file main.c */

main()
{
        void f(void);
        void g(void);

        f();
        g();
}

f: gc = a, gi[4] = 5
g: gc = a, gi[4] = 5
```

B.6   Chapter 6 Solutions

Solution 6-6:

```
#include <stdio.h>

/* ASCII-specific versions of the macros */

#define isupper(c) ((c) >= 'A' && (c) <= 'Z')
#define tolower(c) (isupper(c) ? ((c) | 0x20) : (c))

/* an alternative macro definition could be
#define tolower(c) (isupper(c) ? ((c) - 'A' + 'a') : (c))
*/


main()
{
        int i;

        printf("char     new char\n");
        for (i = 'A'; i <= 'z'; ++i)
                printf("  %c        %c\n", i, tolower(i));

        i = 'A';
        printf("\n++ version %c\n", tolower(i++));
}
```

```
char     new char
 A          a
...        ...
 Z          z
 [          [
 \          \
 ]          ]
 ^          ^

 _          _
 `          `
 a          a
...        ...
 z          z


++ version c
```

When defining macros that expand to expressions containing operators, always enclose the whole macro definition inside parentheses to preserve the intended order of evaluation when the macro is expanded. Also, always enclose each occurrence of the formal argument names with parentheses so that if an actual argument is a more complex expression than a simple identifier, the precedence of any operator present in the actual argument will be preserved.

As written, the two macros are not completely "safe" because they do not correctly handle actual arguments involving side effects (such as the ++ and -- operators and function calls). In these cases, the actual argument is evaluated more than once. In fact, it may be evaluated a total of three times. As we see in the final line of output, the lowercase version of 'A' is reported as being 'c'.

Solution 6-8:

```
main()
{
        int i;

        printf("char     new char\n");
        for (i = 'A'; i <= 'z'; ++i)
                printf("  %c          %c\n", i,
                        (((i) >= 'A' && (i) <= 'Z')
                                ? ((i) | 0x20) : (i)));

        i = 'Z';
        printf("\n++ version %c\n",
                (((i++) >= 'A' && (i++) <= 'Z')
                        ? ((i++) | 0x20) : (i++)));
}
```

Solution 6-17:

```
#include <stdio.h>

main()
{
#ifdef TEST
        printf("TEST is defined with a value of %d\n", TEST);
#    if TEST >= 100
        printf("TEST is >= 100\n");
#    else
        printf("TEST is < 100\n");
#    endif
#else
        printf("The macro TEST is not defined\n");
#endif
}
```

If TEST is not defined, the following output is produced:

```
The macro TEST is not defined
```

When TEST is defined on the compile-line using something like –DTEST=56, the output produced is:

```
TEST is defined with a value of 56
TEST is < 100
```

When TEST is defined on the compile-line using something like –DTEST, implementations may behave differently. Some assign the macro the value 1 as if –DTEST=1 had been used instead, yet others will define the macro as requested, but give it no value so that it is replaced with nothing. This produces several errors because the first call to print has no second argument and #if >= 100 is a malformed #if expression.

B.7   Chapter 7 Solutions

Solution 7-4:

a) With *pc++, the ++ takes precedence over *. By definition, the value of pc++ is the value of pc before it is incremented. pc points to the letter a, so when we dereference the pointer we get a char with value a. In the process, pc gets incremented and points to x.

b) In (*pc)++, the parentheses force the * to take precedence over ++. Because pc points to the letter a, *pc has type char and value a. The operand of ++ is *pc, so the char pointed to by pc is the object being incremented; that is, the letter a is changed to a b and the pointer pc is not changed. The type of the whole expression is char and the value is a because the value of (*pc)++ is the value of (*pc) before it is incremented.

c) In *++pc, the ++ takes precedence over the *. By definition, the value of ++pc is the value of pc after it is incremented; that is, ++pc is a pointer that points to the letter x. When we dereference that pointer, we finish up with the type char and value x.

d) With ++*pc, the * takes precedence over the ++, so pc is dereferenced first given the char a. The char is then incremented to a b. The whole expression has type char and value b. The pointer pc is not changed.

e) In the case of ++(*pc), this is exactly the same as d) because the parentheses indicate the default precedence.

f) With ++(*pc++), the expression (*pc++) is the same as that in a). The char with value a is then incremented to b. Both the pointer and the object being pointed to are modified. The whole expression has type char and value b.

g) With ++(*++pc), the expression (*pc++) is the same as that in c). The char with value x is then incremented to y. Both the pointer and the object being pointed to are modified. The whole expression has type char and value y.

Solution 7-5:

```
#include <stdio.h>

main()
{
        static char str1[] = "Even";
        static char str2[] = "Odd";
        static char str3[] = "";
        static char str4[] = "Test data";
        char *reverse(char *);

        printf("str1           is >%s<\n", str1);
        printf("str1 reversed is >%s<\n", reverse(str1));

        printf("str2           is >%s<\n", str2);
        printf("str2 reversed is >%s<\n", reverse(str2));

        printf("str3           is >%s<\n", str3);
        printf("str3 reversed is >%s<\n", reverse(str3));

        printf("\nstr4 >%s<, reversed >%s<\n",
                str4, reverse(str4));
}
```

```
#include <string.h>

char *reverse(char *str)
{
        char *start = str;
        char *end = start + strlen(start) - 1;
        char temp;

        while (end > start) {
                temp = *end;
                *end = *start;
                *start = temp;
                ++start;
                --end;
        }

        return (str);
}
```

```
str1          is >Even<
str1 reversed is >nevE<
str2          is >Odd<
str2 reversed is >ddO<
str3          is ><
str3 reversed is ><

str4 >atad tseT<, reversed >atad tseT<
```

Because **reverse** modifies the contents of the array passed to it, the pointer passed must point to a location to which you have write permission. Whether a literal string is a constant or is stored in a read-write area of memory, is implementation-defined.

Note the last line of output. It is common to attempt to display the original string and the reversed string in the same call to **printf**. However, the order of evaluation of arguments in a function call is undefined. In this case, they were evaluated right-to-left so that the string was first reversed. Consequently, we get the same contents printed twice.

Solution 7-7:

```
#include <stdio.h>
#include <string.h>
#include <ctype.h>
#include <stdlib.h>

main()
{
        char str[11];
        int flag;
        char *stoupper(char *);
        int search_table(char *str);
```

```c
        while (1) {
                printf("Enter a string (10 chars max): ");
                scanf("%10s", str);
                stoupper(str);
                if (strcmp(str, "END") == 0) {
                        printf("Program done\n");
                        exit(0);
                }

                flag = search_table(str);
                if (flag == -1)
                        printf("String %s not found\n\n", str);
                else
                        printf("String %s found at sub %d\n\n",
                                str, flag);
        }
}


int search_table(char *str)
{
        static char *table[] =
                {"ADD", "DELETE", "LIST", "REPLACE"};

        int i;

        for (i = 0; i < sizeof(table)/sizeof(table[0]); ++i) {
                if (strcmp(str, table[i]) == 0)
                        return (i);
        }

        return (-1);    /* didn't find a match */
}


char *stoupper(char *string)
{
        char *str = string;

        while ((*string = toupper(*string)) != '\0')
                string++;

        return (str);
}
```

```
Enter a string (10 chars max): Test
String TEST not found

Enter a string (10 chars max): Add
String ADD found at sub 0

Enter a string (10 chars max): DelEtE
String DELETE found at sub 1


Enter a string (10 chars max): Averylongpieceofinputdata
String AVERYLONGP not found

Enter a string (10 chars max):
String IECEOFINPU not found

Enter a string (10 chars max):
String TDATA not found

Enter a string (10 chars max): ENd
Program done
```

scanf limits the input read to 10 characters maximum, so when a very long string is entered, scanf takes the first 10 characters only. When the loop next iterates, more data is waiting in the input buffer, so scanf takes another 10. Finally, it takes the remaining five and stops because it reaches the white space (the new-line).

Solution 7-8:

```
#include <stdio.h>

char *list[] = {"abc", "defghijkl", "wxyz"};

main()
{
        printf("list[1][5]          = %c\n", list[1][5]);
        printf("*(list[1] + 5)      = %c\n", *(list[1] + 5));
        printf("*(*(list + 1) + 5) = %c\n", *(*(list + 1) + 5));
}

list[1][5]          = i
*(list[1] + 5)    = i
*(*(list + 1) + 5) = i
```

list[1][5] is a well-formed expression and because list[1] is, by definition, a pointer, we can subscript it to one level giving list[1][5]. Now list[1] points to the first character in the string "defghijkl" and list[1] + 5 points to the letter i in that string. Therefore, *(list[1] + 5) is the contents of that location and has type char and value i. And by the array/pointer conversion identity, *(list[1] + 5) can be rewritten as list[1][5].

Multidimensional arrays and arrays of pointers each have their good and bad aspects. Arrays of pointers are generally more efficient than two-dimensional arrays of chars when each string of characters has a non-uniform length, such as a list of peoples' names or addresses. By saving the otherwise wasted trailing blanks that would exist in a 2D array, using an array of pointers (sometimes) can save considerable space, even though they require the overhead to store the array of pointers as well. Also, an array requires contiguous memory allocated to it while in an array of pointers, each pointer can point to a contiguous row that is not required to be stored in memory contiguously with any other row. With an array of pointers, it is very easy to make a pointer point to a new row without having to move data. With a 2D array, you have to save the data somewhere and copy a new row in.

Note that whichever approach you choose, you still can use multiple subscripts given the very close relationship between pointers and arrays.

B.8 Chapter 8 Solutions

Solution 8-5:

```
#include <stdio.h>

sub()
{
        FILE *fp;

#ifdef SYSTEM == 1
        fp = fopen("\data\master.dat", "r");
#else
#ifdef SYSTEM == 2
        fp = fopen("/data/master.dat", "r");
#else
#ifdef SYSTEM == 3
        fp = fopen("DBA:[data]master.dat", "r");
#endif
#endif
#endif
        /* ... */
}
```

```
/* files.h */

#ifdef SYSTEM == 1
#define MASTER "\data\master.dat"
#else
#ifdef SYSTEM == 2
#define MASTER  "/data/master.dat"
#else
#ifdef SYSTEM == 3
#define MASTER  "DBA:[data]master.dat"
#endif
#endif
#endif


/* user source file */

#include <stdio.h>
#include "files.h"

sub()
{
        FILE *fp;

        fp = fopen(MASTER, "r");

        /* ... */
}
```

Solution 8-11:

```
#include <stdio.h>
#include <stdlib.h>

main()
{
        int i, j1, j2, j3;
        FILE *fp;

        fp = fopen("test.dat", "w");
        if (fp == NULL) {
                printf("Open file for write failed\n");
                exit(0);
        }


        for (i = -5; i <= 5; ++i)
                fprintf(fp, "%d\t%d\t%d\n", i, i*i, i*i*i);

        fclose(fp);
```

```
        fp = fopen("test.dat", "r");
        if (fp == NULL) {
                printf("Open file for read failed\n");
                exit(0);
        }


        for (i = -5; i <= 5; ++i) {
                fscanf(fp, "%d\t%d\t%d\n", &j1, &j2, &j3);
                printf("record contains the values %4d %4d %4d\n",
                        j1, j2, j3);
        }

        fclose(fp);
}
```

```
record contains the values   -5   25 -125
record contains the values   -4   16  -64
record contains the values   -3    9  -27
record contains the values   -2    4   -8
record contains the values   -1    1   -1
record contains the values    0    0    0
record contains the values    1    1    1
record contains the values    2    4    8
record contains the values    3    9   27
record contains the values    4   16   64
record contains the values    5   25  125
```

Rather than count the number of records read in, you could continue reading records until end-of-file is detected by scanf.

```
while (fscanf(fp, "%d\t%d\t%d\n", &j1, &j2, &j3) != EOF) {
        printf("record contains the values %4d %4d %4d\n",
                j1, j2, j3);
}
```

B.9   Chapter 9 Solutions

Solution 9-1: The advantages of the structure approach is that the member names only need to be unique within that structure, whereas in the individual global approach, each variable name must be unique among all global names. This also may be important if the length of significance of external identifiers is shorter than that for internal names. The structure approach lets you use long variable names without their being external.

Solution 9-5:

```
/* string pattern matcher using array of structures */

#include <stdio.h>
#include <stdlib.h>
#include <ctype.h>
#include <string.h>

main()
{
        char str[11];
        int flag;
        char *stoupper(char *string);
        int search_table(char *str);


        while (1) {
                printf("Enter a string (10 chars max): ");
                scanf("%10s", str);
                stoupper(str);
                if (strcmp(str, "END") == 0) {
                        printf("Program done\n");
                        exit(0);
                }

                flag = search_table(str);
                if (flag == -1)
                    printf("String %s not found\n\n", str);
                else
                    printf("String %s found with value %d\n\n",
                               str, flag);
        }
}


struct anentry {
        char *keyword;
        int value;
};


int search_table(char *str)
{

        static struct anentry table[] = {
                {"ADD", 73},
                {"DELETE", -7},
                {"LIST", 256},
                {"REPLACE", -100}
        };
```

```
        static int i;

        for (i = 0; i < (sizeof(table)/sizeof(table[0])); ++i) {
                if (strcmp(str, table[i].keyword) == 0)
                        return (table[i].value);
        }

        return (-1);    /* didn't find */
}



/* stoupper - converts string argument to its upper case equivalent.
        Returns a pointer to that argument */

        char *stoupper(char *string)
        {
                char *str;

                str = string;
                while (*string = toupper(*string))
                        string++;
                return (str);    /* return ptr to uppercase string */
        }
```

```
Enter a string (10 chars max): Add
String ADD found with value 73

Enter a string (10 chars max): DEletE
String DELETE found with value -7

Enter a string (10 chars max): replace
String REPLACE found with value -100


Enter a string (10 chars max): LiSt
String LIST found with value 256

Enter a string (10 chars max): SiLLy
String SILLY not found

Enter a string (10 chars max): END
Program done
```

Solution 9-11:

```
/* string storage allocator (. version)*/

#include <stdio.h>
#include <stdlib.h>
#include <string.h>

struct word {
        char *pword;
        int length;
};


main()
{
        static struct word words[3];
        static char text[21];
        char *pw;
        int i;
        int str_length;


        for (i = 0; i < 3; ++i) {
                printf("Please enter a word (20 chars max): ");
                scanf("%20s", text);
                str_length = strlen(text);

                pw = malloc(str_length + 1);
                if (pw == NULL) {
                        printf("Unable to allocate space");
                        printf(" for string %s\n", text);
                        exit(1);
                }

                words[i].pword = pw;
                strcpy(pw, text);
                words[i].length = str_length;
        }


/* dump out the table to show we got it right */

        for (i = 0; i < 3; ++i) {
                printf("Word %d: length is %2d\t",
                        i, words[i].length);
                printf("Text: >%s<\n", words[i].pword);
        }
}
```

```
        Please enter a word (20 chars max): yellow
        Please enter a word (20 chars max): brown
        Please enter a word (20 chars max): lavender
        Word 0: length is  6    Text: >yellow<
        Word 1: length is  5    Text: >brown<
        Word 2: length is  8    Text: >lavender<
```

```
Please enter a word (20 chars max): Hello there. My name is Fred.
        Please enter a word (20 chars max):
        Please enter a word (20 chars max):
        Word 0: length is  5    Text: >Hello<
        Word 1: length is  6    Text: >there.<
        Word 2: length is  2    Text: >My<
```

```
Please enter a word (20 chars max): AVeryVeryVeryVeryLongName indeed
        Please enter a word (20 chars max):
        Please enter a word (20 chars max):
        Word 0: length is 20    Text: >AVeryVeryVeryVeryLon<
        Word 1: length is  5    Text: >gName<
        Word 2: length is  6    Text: >indeed<
```

scanf terminates the %s conversion when it gets either 20 characters or it reads a white space character. If you enter multiple words separated by spaces as shown above, scanf won't wait for you to answer a prompt until the input buffer is empty.

The structure pointer version requires only minor modifications and follows. (Actually, we could have dispensed with the loop counter i altogether by using a pointer expression instead.)

```
        /* string storage allocator (-> version) */

        #include <stdio.h>
        #include <stdlib.h>
        #include <string.h>

        struct word {
                char *pword;
                int length;
        };


        main()
        {
                static struct word words[3];
                static char text[21];
                char *pw;
                int i;
                int str_length;
                static struct word *pword = &words[0];
```

```
            for (i = 0; i < 3; ++i) {
                    printf("Please enter a word (20 chars max): ");
                    scanf("%20s", text);
                    str_length = strlen(text);

                    pw = malloc(str_length + 1);
                    if (pw == NULL) {
                            printf("Unable to allocate space");
                            printf(" string %s\n", text);
                            exit(1);
                    }


                    pword->pword = pw;
                    strcpy(pw, text);
                    pword->length = str_length;
                    ++pword;          /* next element in array */
            }


    /* dump out the table to show we got it right */

            pword = words;
            for (i = 0; i < 3; ++i) {
                    printf("Word %d: length is %2d\t",
                            i, pword->length);
                    printf("Text: >%s<\n", pword->pword);
                    ++pword;
            }
    }
```

Solution 9-12: The solution requires relatively simple modifications to that for 9-11. Rather than statically allocate the words table, we dynamically must allocate using malloc once we know the number of entries in it. From that point, the code is the same because we can subscript a pointer to one level; that is, whether words is a pointer to a structure of type word or an array of that type is irrelevant. They both can be accessed the same way as shown below. The beauty of this is that you can change the storage allocation method once a program is written without necessarily having to change the code that accesses the data structure.

```
    #include <stdio.h>
    #include <stdlib.h>
    #include <string.h>

    struct word {
            char *pword;
            int length;
    };
```

```
main()
{
        static char text[21];
        char *pw;
        int i;
        int str_length;
        int count = 0;
        struct word *words;


        while (count < 1) {
                printf("How many strings? ");
                scanf("%d", &count);
        }


        words = malloc(sizeof(struct word) * count);
        if (words == NULL) {
                printf("Unable to allocate space for table\n");
                exit(1);
        }


        for (i = 0; i < count; ++i) {
                printf("Please enter a word (20 chars max): ");
                scanf("%20s", text);
                str_length = strlen(text);

                pw = malloc(str_length + 1);
                if (pw == NULL) {
                        printf("Unable to allocate space");
                        printf(" for string %s\n", text);
                        exit(1);
                }

                words[i].pword = pw;
                strcpy(pw, text);
                words[i].length = str_length;
        }


/* dump out the table to show we got it right */

        for (i = 0; i < count; ++i) {
                printf("Word %d: length is %2d\t",
                        i, words[i].length);
                printf("Text: >%s<\n", words[i].pword);
        }
}
```

```
How many strings? -4
How many strings? 4
Please enter a word (20 chars max): Hello
Please enter a word (20 chars max): How
Please enter a word (20 chars max): Anybody
Please enter a word (20 chars max): Red
Word 0: length is  5      Text: >Hello<
Word 1: length is  3      Text: >How<
Word 2: length is  7      Text: >Anybody<
Word 3: length is  3      Text: >Red<
```

To solve the case where the number of strings is not known, you would need to build a linked list allocating memory for each new structure of type word as a new string arrived. The structure template needed for a doubly-linked list is as follows:

```
struct word {
        struct word *fwdp;        /* forward pointer */
        struct word *bwdp;        /* backward pointer */
        char *pword;
        int length;
};
```

You also might need to keep a pointer to the root (or first) element in the list. With a little extra work, you could maintain the list in sorted order, and by using the %[mask for scanf you could accept strings containing embedded white space.

Solution 9-16: You probably will agree that the pointer solution is more elegant, particularly because it doesn't require a structure or a union and their accompanying dot operators.

```
        #include <stdio.h>

        main()
        {
                union {
                        double d1[5];
                        struct {
                                double filler[3];
                                double d2[5];
                        } s;
                } u;

                u.d1[3] = 1.234;
                u.d1[4] = 9.876;

                printf("u.s.d2[0] = %f\n", u.s.d2[0]);
                printf("u.s.d2[1] = %f\n", u.s.d2[1]);
        }

u.s.d2[0] = 1.234000
u.s.d2[1] = 9.876000
```

Solution 9-18:

```
        #include <stdio.h>

        /* possible vales for type */

        #define CHAR 0
        #define INT 1
        #define UNSIGNED 2
        #define LONG 3
        #define FLOAT 4
        #define DOUBLE 5


        struct object {
                unsigned int type;
                union {
                        char c;
                        int i;
                        unsigned int ui;
                        long int li;
                        float f;
                        double d;
                } value;
        };
```

```
main()
{
        static struct object obj;

        printf("Default type = %u\n\n", obj.type);

        obj.value.d = 1.2345e56;
        obj.type = DOUBLE;
        printf("double value = %e\n", obj.value.d);

        obj.value.i = 100;
        obj.type = INT;
        printf("int value = %d\n", obj.value.i);
}

Default type = 0

double value = 1.23450e+56
int value = 100
```

An object with static storage duration has a default initial value of zero (cast to its type or, if it is an aggregate, cast to each of its elements/members). Therefore, obj starts out with obj.type being zero and its union member being initialized as a char (the type of its first member) with the value zero, representing the null character. By design, the macro CHAR has a value of zero and the first member of the union also has type char. If the first member were double, the union would contain floating-point zero initially and that would not reflect the value of obj.type.

B.10 Chapter 10 Solutions

Solution 10-8: An enumerated object has some implementation-defined integer type. As such, it is assignment-compatible with all arithmetic types, including double, which is the type of the floating-point constant 1.23. Therefore, 1.23 can be assigned to my_flower and, as you would expect, the fractional part of the value is discarded. Enumerated data types are very weak synonyms for integer types and a compiler is not required to warn of attempts to store "invalid" numbers in them.

Solution 10-10: The program is not portable because it assumes the type of enum flower is really int. If my_flower has type unsigned int instead, the assignment of the address of an unsigned int to a pointer to a signed int is not permitted under ANSI C rules.

Solution 10-11:

```
#include <stdio.h>

enum flower {rose, violet, lilac, petunia};
char *names[] = {"rose", "violet", "lilac", "petunia"};

main()
{
        enum flower my_flower;

        my_flower = rose;
        printf("my_flower contains the value '%s'\n",
                names[my_flower]);

        my_flower = petunia;
        printf("my_flower contains the value '%s'\n",
                names[my_flower]);
}

my_flower contains the value 'rose'
my_flower contains the value 'petunia'
```

Solution 10-12:

```
#include <stdio.h>

main()
{
        char c = 'a';

        printf("sizeof(c++, c) = %lu\n",
                (unsigned long) sizeof(c++, c));
}

sizeof(c++, c) = 1
```

The left-hand expression is evaluated and its value is discarded. The increment side effect is guaranteed to be done before the right side is evaluated. The type of the right side is `char` and `sizeof(char)` is 1 by definition.

Solution 10-13:

```
#include <stdio.h>

main()
{
        int i = 10;
        int j = (4, i);
        int k = (i, j);
        static int l = 10;
        static int m = (4, 5);
        void f(int);

        (4, f((10, 5)));
}
```

ANSI C states "Constant expressions shall not contain ... comma operators, except where they are contained within the operand of a **sizeof** operator."

In this example, the initializer of **m** must be a compile-time constant expression. As such, it can not contain a comma operator. However, prior to ANSI C, this rule was not widely followed. (10, 5) is also a constant expression containing a comma operator.

Solution 10-15:

```
#include <stdio.h>

main()
{
        char a[10][12];
        int i = 5;

        printf("sizeof(a[5, 6]) = %lu\n",
                (unsigned long) sizeof(a[5, 6]));

        printf("sizeof(a[i, 6]) = %lu\n",
                (unsigned long) sizeof(a[i, 6]));
}

sizeof(a[5, 6]) = 12
sizeof(a[i, 6]) = 12
```

Refer to Solution 10-13 for a discussion of comma operators in constant expressions.

Because a[5, 6] is really the same as a[6] and a[6] is a whole row in the two-dimensional array a, its type is "array of 12 char", and this is demonstrated by the result produced by **sizeof**. Note, though, that except when used with **sizeof** and **&**, the expression a[6] is converted to a pointer to the first element in that row.

In strict ANSI-mode, a[5, 6] is not permitted as discussed above. If, however, the 5 were replaced with a non-constant expression, such as a[i, 6], it would be acceptable to the compiler (but still be rather strange in terms of utility).

Solution 10-17: The following program tests the problem:

```
struct tag {
        int i;
        const int ci;
};

main()
{
        struct tag s, f(void);

        s = f();
}
```

Although the type of the structure **s** itself is not **const**-qualified, one of its members is. Therefore, the structure as a whole can not be modified. However, expressions such as **s.i = 5** are still permitted.

Solution 10-20:

```
#include <stdio.h>

typedef int fri(void);

main()
{
        fri f;

        f;
        f();
}

int f(void)
{
        printf("In f\n");
}

In f
```

The expression **f** does nothing. Because **f** is an expression that designates a function, it is converted to the address of that function (as you will learn in the next section of this chapter). However, because it is not followed by the function call operator (), its value is discarded. As shown above, the function **f** is only called once—by using **f()**.

Solution 10-21: For most non-trivial uses, the **#define** directive and the **typedef**

keyword can not be used to achieve the same end. The confusing aspect is that both approaches can be used interchangeably in simple cases, and this has led to a belief that "you never need typedef."

The #define directive is recognized by the C preprocessor, a simple-minded (and possibly standalone) program whose forte lies in substituting strings. Simply put, it is nothing more than a macro processing language that requires no knowledge of C. It conditionally pulls in strings, it replaces strings in macro expansions and it includes files of strings—everything it does is string-oriented. The only requirement placed on the preprocessor is that when it has finished manipulating strings, its output must be acceptable to a C compiler so that no syntax errors are generated.

On the other hand, typedef is part of the C language proper. typedef is a keyword and the compiler assigns special meaning to it. The C compiler knows about typedef whereas it doesn't know about #define. The purpose of typedef is to define a new type in terms of an existing type. typedef is only concerned about types; it knows nothing about strings. Whereas #define can be used to generate a string that is not a complete C construct, typedef is obliged to deal with syntactically complete types.

Given that there seems to be some overlap between #define and typedef, how should you decide when to use each one? Clearly, when only one of them will do the job, that is the one to use. When either will do the job, choose #define when creating a synonym for an arbitrary string and choose typedef when deriving a new type.

Solution 10-24: The tricky parts of this problem are the use of sizeof to determine the array dimension sizes, and the declaration of the array itself.

```c
#include <stdio.h>

unsigned long fun00(int), fun01(int), fun02(int);
unsigned long fun10(int), fun11(int), fun12(int);

unsigned long (*ptrs[2][3])(int) = {
        {fun00, fun01, fun02},
        {fun10, fun11, fun12}
};

#define NUM_ROWS (sizeof(ptrs)/sizeof(ptrs[0]))
#define NUM_COLS (sizeof(ptrs[0])/sizeof(ptrs[0][0]))


main()
{
        int i, j;

        for (i = 0; i < NUM_ROWS; ++i)
                for (j = 0; j < NUM_COLS; ++j)
                        (*ptrs[i][j])(i + j);
}
```

```
unsigned long fun00(int i)
{
        printf("fun00 -- %d\n", i);
}


unsigned long fun01(int i)
{
        printf("fun01 -- %d\n", i);
}


unsigned long fun02(int i)
{
        printf("fun02 -- %d\n", i);
}


unsigned long fun10(int i)
{
        printf("fun10 -- %d\n", i);
}


unsigned long fun11(int i)
{
        printf("fun11 -- %d\n", i);
}


unsigned long fun12(int i)
{
        printf("fun12 -- %d\n", i);
}


fun00 -- 0
fun01 -- 1
fun02 -- 2
fun10 -- 1
fun11 -- 2
fun12 -- 3
```

Solution 10-25:

```
#include <stdio.h>

main()
{
        void (**ppf)(void);
        void (*pf)(void);
        void f(void);

        pf = &f;        /* get address of function f */
        ppf = &pf;      /* get address of pointer pf */

        (**ppf)();      /* call the underlying function f */
}


void f(void)
{
        printf("Inside f\n");
}

Inside f
```

B.11   Chapter 11 Solutions

Solution 11-3: signal is a function that takes two arguments whose types are int and a pointer to a function taking one int argument and returning no value. The return type of signal is a pointer to a function taking one int argument and returning no value. signal's return type is the same as that of its second argument. atexit is a function that takes one argument (of type pointer to function taking no arguments and having no return value) and returns an int value.

Appendix C

Standard Run-Time Library

C.1   The ANSI Standard Headers

Standard C Library Headers	
Header	*Purpose*
assert.h	Program diagnostic purposes
ctype.h	Character-testing and conversion
errno.h	Various error-checking facilities
float.h	Floating type characteristics
limits.h	Integral type sizes
locale.h	Internationalization support
math.h	Math functions
setjmp.h	Nonlocal jump facility
signal.h	Signal handling
stdarg.h	Variable argument support
stddef.h	Miscellaneous
stdio.h	Input/output functions
stdlib.h	General utilities
string.h	String functions
time.h	Date and time functions

C.1.1   The assert Library Header

assert.h Library Header	
Name	*Purpose*
assert	Put diagnostics into programs

```
void assert(int expression);
```

C.1.2   The ctype Library Header

ctype.h **Library Header**	
Name	*Purpose*
isalnum	Alphabetic or numeric
isalpha	Alphabetic
iscntrl	Control
isdigit	Digit 0–9
isgraph	Graphic (printable)
islower	Lowercase
isprint	Printable
ispunct	Punctuation
isspace	White space
isupper	Uppercase
isxdigit	Hexadecimal
tolower	Convert to lowercase
toupper	Convert to uppercase

```
int isalnum(int c);
int isalpha(int c);
int iscntrl(int c);
int isdigit(int c);
int isgraph(int c);
int islower(int c);
int isprint(int c);
int ispunct(int c);
int isspace(int c);
int isupper(int c);
int isxdigit(int c);
int tolower(int c);
int toupper(int c);
```

C.1.3   The errno Library Header

errno.h **Library Header**	
Name	*Purpose*
EDOM	errno macro value for domain errors
ERANGE	errno macro value for range errors
errno	Error indicator used by standard library

C.1.4 The float Library Header

float.h **Library Header**	
Name	*Purpose*
DBL_DIG	Number of decimal digits of precision
DBL_EPSILON	Special minimum positive number
DBL_MANT_DIG	Number of digits in mantissa
DBL_MAX	Maximum representable finite number
DBL_MAX_10_EXP	Finite number maximum integer
DBL_MAX_EXP	Finite number maximum integer
DBL_MIN	Minimum normalized positive number
DBL_MIN_10_EXP	Normalized number minimum integer
DBL_MIN_EXP	Normalized number minimum integer
FLT_DIG	Number of decimal digits of precision
FLT_EPSILON	Special minimum positive number
FLT_MANT_DIG	Number of digits in mantissa
FLT_MAX	Maximum representable finite number
FLT_MAX_10_EXP	Finite number maximum integer
FLT_MAX_EXP	Finite number maximum integer
FLT_MIN	Minimum normalized positive number
FLT_MIN_10_EXP	Normalized number minimum integer
FLT_MIN_EXP	Normalized number minimum integer
FLT_RADIX	Radix of exponent representation
FLT_ROUNDS	Rounding behavior indicator
LDBL_DIG	Number of decimal digits of precision
LDBL_EPSILON	Special minimum positive number
LDBL_MANT_DIG	Number of digits in mantissa
LDBL_MAX	Maximum representable finite number
LDBL_MAX_10_EXP	Finite number maximum integer
LDBL_MAX_EXP	Finite number maximum integer
LDBL_MIN	Minimum normalized positive number
LDBL_MIN_10_EXP	Normalized number minimum integer
LDBL_MIN_EXP	Normalized number minimum integer

C.1.5   The `limits` Library Header

limits.h Library Header	
Name	*Purpose*
CHAR_BIT	Number of bits in a char
CHAR_MAX	Maximum value of a plain char
CHAR_MIN	Minimum value of a plain char
INT_MAX	Maximum value of an int
INT_MIN	Minimum value of an int
LONG_MAX	Maximum value of a long int
LONG_MIN	Minimum value of a long int
MB_LEN_MAX	Maximum number of bytes in a multibyte character
SCHAR_MAX	Maximum value of a signed char
SCHAR_MIN	Minimum value of a signed char
SHRT_MAX	Maximum value of a short int
SHRT_MIN	Minimum value of a short int
UCHAR_MAX	Maximum value of an unsigned char
UINT_MAX	Maximum value of an unsigned int
ULONG_MAX	Maximum value of an unsigned long int
USHRT_MAX	Maximum value of an unsigned short int

C.1.6   The `locale` Library Header

locale.h Library Header	
Name	*Purpose*
lconv	A structure containing formatting information
LC_ALL	All categories macro for setlocale
LC_COLLATE	Collating sequence category macro for setlocale
LC_CTYPE	ctype header category macro for setlocale
LC_MONETARY	Currency category macro for setlocale
LC_NUMERIC	Numeric category macro for setlocale
LC_TIME	Date and time category macro for setlocale
localeconv	Initialize an lconv object with current locale
NULL	The null pointer constant
setlocale	Set to requested locale and category

```
struct lconv *localeconv(void);
char *setlocale(int category, const char *locale);
```

C.1.7   The math Library Header

<table>
<tr><th colspan="2" align="center">math.h Library Header</th></tr>
<tr><th align="center">Name</th><th align="center">Purpose</th></tr>
<tr><td align="right">acos</td><td>Arc cosine</td></tr>
<tr><td align="right">asin</td><td>Arc sine</td></tr>
<tr><td align="right">atan</td><td>Arc tangent</td></tr>
<tr><td align="right">atan2</td><td>Arc tangent of y/x</td></tr>
<tr><td align="right">ceil</td><td>Smallest integral value not less than x</td></tr>
<tr><td align="right">cos</td><td>Cosine</td></tr>
<tr><td align="right">cosh</td><td>Hyperbolic cosine</td></tr>
<tr><td align="right">exp</td><td>Exponential</td></tr>
<tr><td align="right">fabs</td><td>Absolute value</td></tr>
<tr><td align="right">floor</td><td>Largest integral value not greater than x</td></tr>
<tr><td align="right">fmod</td><td>Compute a floating-point remainder</td></tr>
<tr><td align="right">frexp</td><td>Break a number into integer and fraction</td></tr>
<tr><td align="right">HUGE_VAL</td><td>Positive double value returned by several functions</td></tr>
<tr><td align="right">ldexp</td><td>Multiplies a number by a integral power of 2</td></tr>
<tr><td align="right">log</td><td>Natural logarithm</td></tr>
<tr><td align="right">log10</td><td>Base-10 logarithm</td></tr>
<tr><td align="right">modf</td><td>Break an fp number into integer and fraction</td></tr>
<tr><td align="right">pow</td><td>Power</td></tr>
<tr><td align="right">sin</td><td>Sine</td></tr>
<tr><td align="right">sinh</td><td>Hyperbolic sine</td></tr>
<tr><td align="right">sqrt</td><td>Square root</td></tr>
<tr><td align="right">tan</td><td>Tangent</td></tr>
<tr><td align="right">tanh</td><td>Hyperbolic tangent</td></tr>
</table>

```
double acos(double x);
double asin(double x);
double atan(double x);
double atan2(double y, double x);
double ceil(double x);
double cos(double x);
double cosh(double x);
double exp(double x);
double fabs(double x);
double floor(double x);
double fmod(double x, double y);
double frexp(double value, int *exp);
double ldexp(double x, int exp);
double log(double x);
double log10(double x);
double modf(double value, double *iptr);
double pow(double x, double y);
double sin(double x);
double sinh(double x);
double sqrt(double x);
```

```
double tan(double x);
double tanh(double x);
```

C.1.8   The setjmp Library Header

setjmp.h **Library Header**	
Name	*Purpose*
jmp_buf	Type for buffer to save a program's environment
longjmp	Restores a program's environment
setjmp	Saves a program's environment

```
void longjmp(jmp_buf env, int val);
int setjmp(jmp_buf env);
```

C.1.9   The signal Library Header

signal.h **Library Header**	
Name	*Purpose*
raise	Raise a specific signal
SIGABRT	Abort signal type macro
SIGFPE	Floating-point exception signal type macro
SIGILL	Illegal instruction signal type macro
SIGINT	Interrupt signal type macro
signal	Specify signal handling method
SIGSEGV	Segment violation signal type macro
SIGTERM	Termination signal type macro
sig_atomic_t	Type of atomic entity that can be accessed
SIG_DFL	Default signal handling macro
SIG_ERR	signal error indicator macro
SIG_IGN	Ignore signal macro

```
int raise(int sig);
void (*signal(int sig, void (*func)(int)))(int);
```

C.1.10   The stdarg Library Header

stdarg.h **Library Header**	
Name	*Purpose*
va_arg	Macro to get next argument in list
va_end	Macro to terminate variable argument processing
va_list	Type for storing variable argument list information
va_start	Macro to prepare for variable argument processing

```
type va_arg(va_list ap, type);
void va_end(va_list ap);
void va_start(va_list ap, parmN);
```

C.1.11   The stddef Library Header

stddef.h Library Header	
Name	*Purpose*
NULL	The null pointer constant
offsetof	Macro to find offset of a structure's member
ptrdiff_t	Type of difference between pointers
size_t	Type of sizeof operator
wchar_t	Type of a wide character

C.1.12   The stdio Library Header

stdio.h Library Header	
Name	*Purpose*
BUFSIZ	Macro, specifying the size of the setbuf buffer
clearerr	Clears both error and end-of-file flags
EOF	Macro representing end-of-file
fclose	Closes an open stream
feof	Test if end-of-file flag set
ferror	Test if error flag set
fflush	Flush output stream buffer
fgetc	Read character from a stream
fgetpos	Read stream's current character position
fgets	Read a string from a stream
FILE	The (derived) type of a file object
FILENAME_MAX	Maximum length of a filename for this system
fopen	Opens a stream
FOPEN_MAX	The number of streams that can be open simultaneously
fpos_t	A (derived) type used by fgetpos and fsetpos
fprintf	Formatted write to a stream
fputc	Write a character to a stream
fputs	Write a string to a stream
fread	Read binary data from a stream
freopen	Recycles an open stream's FILE pointer

stdio.h **Library Header** (continued)	
Name	*Purpose*
fscanf	Formatted input from a stream
fseek	Position stream to a specific character position
fsetpos	Position stream to a specific character position
ftell	Read stream's current character position
fwrite	Write binary data to a stream
getc	Macro, to read a character from a stream
getchar	Reads a character from stdin
gets	Reads a string from stdin
_IOFBF	Buffer type macros used with setvbuf
_IOLBF	Buffer type macros used with setvbuf
_IONBF	Buffer type macros used with setvbuf
L_tmpnam	Macro, the size of a temporary filename
NULL	The null pointer constant
perror	Maps an errno error number to a message
printf	Formatted write to stdout
putc	Macro, writes a character to a stream
putchar	Writes a character to stdout
puts	Writes a string to stdout
remove	Removes (deletes) a file
rename	Renames a file
rewind	Resets a file to its start character position
scanf	Formatted input from stdin
SEEK_CUR	Macro, for positioning with fseek
SEEK_END	Macro, for positioning with fseek
SEEK_SET	Macro, for positioning with fseek
setbuf	Sets a stream's buffering type
setvbuf	Sets a stream's buffering type
size_t	Type of sizeof operator
sprintf	Formatted write to a character array
sscanf	Formatted input from a character array
stderr	Standard error stream
stdin	Standard input stream
stdout	Standard output stream
tmpfile	Create and open a temporary file
tmpnam	Construct a unique temporary filename
TMP_MAX	Number of unique temporary filenames available
ungetc	Pushback (unread) a character to an input stream
vfprintf	Special formatted write to a stream
vprintf	Special formatted write to stdout
vsprintf	Special formatted write to a string

```
void clearerr(FILE *stream);
int fclose(FILE *stream);
int feof(FILE *stream);
int ferror(FILE *stream);
int fflush(FILE *stream);
int fgetc(FILE *stream);
```

```
int fgetpos(FILE *stream, fpos_t *pos);
char *fgets(char *s, int n, FILE *stream);
FILE *fopen(const char *filename, const char *mode);
int fprintf(FILE *stream, const char *format, ...);
int fputc(int c, FILE *stream);
int fputs(const char *s, FILE *stream);
size_t fread(void *ptr, size_t size, size_t nmemb,
        FILE *stream);
FILE *freopen(const char *filename, const char *mode,
        FILE *stream);
int fscanf(FILE *stream, const char *format, ...);
int fseek(FILE *stream, long int offset, int whence);
int fsetpos(FILE *stream, const fpos_t *pos);
size_t fwrite(const void *ptr, size_t size, size_t nmemb,
        FILE *stream);
int getc(FILE *stream);
int getchar(void);
char *gets(char *s);
long int ftell(FILE *stream);
void perror(const char *s);
int printf(const char *format, ...);
int putc(int c, FILE *stream);
int putchar(int c);
int puts(const char *s);
int remove(const char *filename);
int rename(const char *old, const char *new);
void rewind(FILE *stream);
int scanf(const char *format, ...);
void setbuf(FILE *stream, char *buf);
int setvbuf(FILE *stream, char *buf, int mode, size_t size);
int sprintf(char *s, const char *format, ...);
int sscanf(const char *s, const char *format, ...);
FILE *tmpfile(void);
char *tmpnam(char *s);
int ungetc(int c, FILE *stream);
int vfprintf(FILE *stream, const char *format, va_list arg);
int vprintf(const char *format, va_list arg);
int vsprintf(char *s, const char *format, va_list arg);
```

C.1.13   The stdlib Library Header

stdlib.h **Library Header**	
Name	*Purpose*
abort	Abnormally terminate program
abs	Absolute value of an int
atexit	Register an exit processing function
atof	String to double conversion
atoi	String to int conversion
atol	String to long int conversion
bsearch	Search a table for given value
calloc	Allocate and initialize dynamic memory
div	Quotient and remainder of int division
div_t	Structure type returned by div
exit	Normally terminate program
EXIT_FAILURE	Failure macro value for use with exit
EXIT_SUCCESS	Success macro value for use with exit
free	Free dynamic memory
getenv	Get environment string
labs	Absolute value of a long int
ldiv	Quotient and remainder of long int division
ldiv_t	Structure type returned by ldiv
malloc	Allocate dynamic memory
MB_CUR_MAX	Maximum number of bytes in a multibyte character
mblen	Number of bytes in a multibyte character
mbstowcs	Multibyte string to wide character string
mbtowc	Multibyte character to wide character character
NULL	The null pointer constant
qsort	Sort an array of values
rand	Generate a random number
RAND_MAX	Macro with maximum value returned by rand
realloc	Change size of allocated dynamic memory
size_t	Type of sizeof operator
srand	Set the seed for random number generator
strtod	Convert a string of digits to double
strtol	Convert a string of digits to long int
strtoul	Convert a string of digits to unsigned long int
system	Pass a command-line to the operating system
wchar_t	Type of a wide character
wcstombs	Wide character string to multibyte string
wctomb	Wide character to multibyte character

```
void abort(void);
int abs(int j);
int atexit(void (*func)(void));
double atof(const char *nptr);
int atoi(const char *nptr);
long int atol(const char *nptr);
```

```
void *bsearch(const void *key, const void *base, size_t nmemb,
        size_t size, int (*compar)(const void *,
        const void *));
void *calloc(size_t nmemb, size_t size);
div_t div(int numer, int denom);
void exit(int status);
void free(void *ptr);
char *getenv(const char *name);
long int labs(long int j);
ldiv_t ldiv(long int numer, long int denom);
void *malloc(size_t size);
int mblen(const char *s, size_t n);
size_t mbstowcs(wchar_t *pwcs, const char *s, size_t n);
int mbtowc(wchar_t *pwc, const char *s, size_t n);
void qsort(void *base, size_t nmemb, size_t size,
        int (*compar)(const void *, const void *));
int rand(void);
void *realloc(void *ptr, size_t size);
void srand(unsigned int seed);
double strtod(const char *nptr, char **endptr);
long int strtol(const char *nptr, char **endptr, int base);
unsigned long int strtoul(const char *nptr, char **endptr,
        int base);
int system(const char *string);
size_t wcstombs(char *s, const wchar_t *pwcs, size_t n);
int wctomb(char *s, wchar_t wchar);
```

C.1.14   The string Library Header

string.h Library Header	
Name	*Purpose*
memchr	Locate a character in a block of memory
memcmp	Compare two blocks of memory
memcpy	Copy a block of memory
memmove	Copy a block of memory and handle overlap
memset	Initialize a block of memory
NULL	The null pointer constant
size_t	Type of sizeof operator
strcpy	Copy whole of one string to another
strncpy	Copy part of one string to another
strcat	Concatenate two whole strings
strncat	Concatenate part of one string to another
strcmp	Compare two whole strings
strncmp	Compare leading part of two strings
strcoll	Locale-specific string compare
strchr	Search for a character in a string
strerror	Maps an error number to a message string
strrchr	Reverse search for a character in a string
strstr	Search a string for a substring
strcspn	Find match with one of a set of characters
strpbrk	Find match with one of a set of characters
strspn	Find match with one of a set of characters
strtok	Parse a string into specified tokens
strlen	Find the length of a string
strxfrm	String transformation

```
void *memchr(const void *s, int c, size_t n);
int memcmp(const void *s1, const void *s2, size_t n);
void *memcpy(void *s1, const void *s2, size_t n);
void *memmove(void *s1, const void *s2, size_t n);
void *memset(void *s, int c, size_t n);
char *strcat(char *s1, const char *s2);
char *strchr(const char *s, int c);
int strcmp(const char *s1, const char *s2);
int strcoll(const char *s1, const char *s2);
char *strcpy(char *s1, const char *s2);
size_t strcspn(const char *s1, const char *s2);
char *strerror(int errnum);
size_t strlen(const char *s);
char *strncat(char *s1, const char *s2, size_t n);
int strncmp(const char *s1, const char *s2, size_t n);
char *strncpy(char *s1, const char *s2, size_t n);
char *strpbrk(const char *s1, const char *s2);
char *strrchr(const char *s, int c);
size_t strspn(const char *s1, const char *s2);
```

```
char *strstr(const char *s1, const char *s2);
char *strtok(char *s1, const char *s2);
size_t strxfrm(char *s1, const char *s2, size_t n);
```

C.1.15   The time Library Header

time.h Library Header	
Name	*Purpose*
asctime	Convert broken-down time to a string
clock	Determine the processor time used
clock_t	Type capable of representing a time
CLOCKS_PER_SEC	Number/second of value returned by clock
ctime	Convert calendar time to a string
difftime	Difference between two calendar times
gmtime	Convert calendar time to UTC (GMT) time
localtime	Convert calendar time to broken-down time
mktime	Convert broken-down time to calendar time
NULL	The null pointer constant
size_t	Type of sizeof operator
strftime	Format a time into a string
time	Determine current calendar time
time_t	Type capable of representing a time
tm	Structure type capable of holding a broken-down time

```
char *asctime(const struct tm *timeptr);
clock_t clock(void);
char *ctime(const time_t *timer);
double difftime(time_t time1, time_t time0);
struct tm *gmtime(const time_t *timer);
struct tm *localtime(const time_t *timer);
time_t mktime(struct tm *timeptr);
size_t strftime(char *s, size_t maxsize, const char *format,
        const struct tm *timeptr);
time_t time(time_t *timer);
```

C.1.16   Pre-Defined Standard Macros

Pre-Defined Standard Macros	
Name	*Purpose*
__DATE__	Date of compilation in the form "Mmm dd yyyy"
__FILE__	Name of source file as a string
__LINE__	Current source line number as a decimal constant
__STDC__	Set to 1 for Standard-conforming implementations
__TIME__	Time of compilation in the form "hh:mm:ss"

C.2   Identifiers in Alphabetical Order

The following list contains all identifiers in alphabetical order. This list may be used
as the basis for a project's reserved identifier list. (Those in `<math.h>` marked with a
† are not required to be present in an ANSI-conforming implementation. They have
a suffix of `f` or `l` and represent `float` and `long double` versions, respectively, of the
math library. If an implementation chooses to provide functions with this capability,
they must use the names as shown.)

Reserved Identifier List			
Identifier	*Header*	*Identifier*	*Header*
abort	`<stdlib.h>`	cos	`<math.h>`
abs	`<stdlib.h>`	cosf †	`<math.h>`
acos	`<math.h>`	cosl †	`<math.h>`
acosf †	`<math.h>`	cosh	`<math.h>`
acosl †	`<math.h>`	coshf †	`<math.h>`
asctime	`<time.h>`	coshl †	`<math.h>`
asin	`<math.h>`	ctime	`<time.h>`
asinf †	`<math.h>`	__DATE__	predefined macro
asinl †	`<math.h>`	DBL_DIG	`<float.h>`
assert	`<assert.h>`	DBL_EPSILON	`<float.h>`
atan	`<math.h>`	DBL_MANT_DIG	`<float.h>`
atanf †	`<math.h>`	DBL_MAX	`<float.h>`
atanl †	`<math.h>`	DBL_MAX_10_EXP	`<float.h>`
atan2	`<math.h>`	DBL_MAX_EXP	`<float.h>`
atan2f †	`<math.h>`	DBL_MIN	`<float.h>`
atan2l †	`<math.h>`	DBL_MIN_10_EXP	`<float.h>`
atexit	`<stdlib.h>`	DBL_MIN_EXP	`<float.h>`
atof	`<stdlib.h>`	default	C keyword
atoi	`<stdlib.h>`	difftime	`<time.h>`
atol	`<stdlib.h>`	div	`<stdlib.h>`
auto	C keyword	div_t	`<stdlib.h>`
break	C keyword	do	C keyword
bsearch	`<stdlib.h>`	double	C keyword
BUFSIZ	`<stdio.h>`	EDOM	`<errno.h>`
calloc	`<stdlib.h>`	else	C keyword
case	C keyword	entry	C keyword
ceil	`<math.h>`	enum	C keyword
ceilf †	`<math.h>`	EOF	`<stdio.h>`
ceill †	`<math.h>`	ERANGE	`<errno.h>`
char	C keyword	errno	`<errno.h>`
CHAR_BIT	`<limits.h>`	exit	`<stdlib.h>`
CHAR_MAX	`<limits.h>`	EXIT_FAILURE	`<stdlib.h>`
CHAR_MIN	`<limits.h>`	EXIT_SUCCESS	`<stdlib.h>`
clearerr	`<stdio.h>`	exp	`<math.h>`
clock	`<time.h>`	expf †	`<math.h>`
clock_t	`<time.h>`	expl †	`<math.h>`
CLOCKS_PER_SEC	`<time.h>`	extern	C keyword
const	C keyword	fabs	`<math.h>`
continue	C keyword	fabsf †	`<math.h>`
		fabsl †	`<math.h>`

Reserved Identifier List (continued)			
Identifier	*Header*	*Identifier*	*Header*
fclose	`<stdio.h>`	ftell	`<stdio.h>`
feof	`<stdio.h>`	fwrite	`<stdio.h>`
ferror	`<stdio.h>`	getc	`<stdio.h>`
fflush	`<stdio.h>`	getchar	`<stdio.h>`
fgetc	`<stdio.h>`	getenv	`<stdlib.h>`
fgetpos	`<stdio.h>`	gets	`<stdio.h>`
fgets	`<stdio.h>`	gmtime	`<time.h>`
FILE	`<stdio.h>`	goto	C keyword
__FILE__	predefined macro	HUGE_VAL	`<math.h>`
FILENAME_MAX	`<stdio.h>`	INT_MAX	`<limits.h>`
float	C keyword	INT_MIN	`<limits.h>`
floor	`<math.h>`	if	C keyword
floorf †	`<math.h>`	int	C keyword
floorl †	`<math.h>`	_IOFBF	`<stdio.h>`
FLT_DIG	`<float.h>`	_IOLBF	`<stdio.h>`
FLT_EPSILON	`<float.h>`	_IONBF	`<stdio.h>`
FLT_MANT_DIG	`<float.h>`	isalnum	`<ctype.h>`
FLT_MAX	`<float.h>`	isalpha	`<ctype.h>`
FLT_MAX_10_EXP	`<float.h>`	iscntrl	`<ctype.h>`
FLT_MAX_EXP	`<float.h>`	isdigit	`<ctype.h>`
FLT_MIN	`<float.h>`	isgraph	`<ctype.h>`
FLT_MIN_10_EXP	`<float.h>`	islower	`<ctype.h>`
FLT_MIN_EXP	`<float.h>`	isprint	`<ctype.h>`
FLT_RADIX	`<float.h>`	ispunct	`<ctype.h>`
FLT_ROUNDS	`<float.h>`	isspace	`<ctype.h>`
fmod	`<math.h>`	isupper	`<ctype.h>`
fmodf †	`<math.h>`	isxdigit	`<ctype.h>`
fmodl †	`<math.h>`	jmp_buf	`<setjmp.h>`
fopen	`<stdio.h>`	labs	`<stdlib.h>`
FOPEN_MAX	`<stdio.h>`	lconv	`<locale.h>`
for	C keyword	LC_ALL	`<locale.h>`
fortran	extended keyword	LC_COLLATE	`<locale.h>`
fpos_t	`<stdio.h>`	LC_CTYPE	`<locale.h>`
fprintf	`<stdio.h>`	LC_MONETARY	`<locale.h>`
fputc	`<stdio.h>`	LC_NUMERIC	`<locale.h>`
fputs	`<stdio.h>`	LC_TIME	`<locale.h>`
fread	`<stdio.h>`	LDBL_DIG	`<float.h>`
free	`<stdlib.h>`	LDBL_EPSILON	`<float.h>`
freopen	`<stdio.h>`	LDBL_MANT_DIG	`<float.h>`
frexp	`<math.h>`	LDBL_MAX	`<float.h>`
frexpf †	`<math.h>`	LDBL_MAX_10_EXP	`<float.h>`
frexpl †	`<math.h>`	LDBL_MAX_EXP	`<float.h>`
fscanf	`<stdio.h>`	LDBL_MIN	`<float.h>`
fseek	`<stdio.h>`	LDBL_MIN_10_EXP	`<float.h>`
fsetpos	`<stdio.h>`	LDBL_MIN_EXP	`<float.h>`

Reserved Identifier List (continued)			
Identifier	*Header*	*Identifier*	*Header*
ldexp	<math.h>	printf	<stdio.h>
ldexpf †	<math.h>	ptrdiff_t	<stddef.h>
ldexpl †	<math.h>	putc	<stdio.h>
ldiv	<stdlib.h>	putchar	<stdio.h>
ldiv_t	<stdlib.h>	puts	<stdio.h>
__LINE__	predefined macro	qsort	<stdlib.h>
localeconv	<locale.h>	raise	<signal.h>
localtime	<time.h>	rand	<stdlib.h>
log	<math.h>	RAND_MAX	<stdlib.h>
logf †	<math.h>	realloc	<stdlib.h>
logl †	<math.h>	register	C keyword
log10	<math.h>	remove	<stdio.h>
log10f †	<math.h>	rename	<stdio.h>
log10l †	<math.h>	return	C keyword
long	C keyword	rewind	<stdio.h>
longjmp	<setjmp.h>	scanf	<stdio.h>
LONG_MAX	<limits.h>	SCHAR_MAX	<limits.h>
LONG_MIN	<limits.h>	SCHAR_MIN	<limits.h>
L_tmpnam	<stdio.h>	SEEK_CUR	<stdio.h>
malloc	<stdlib.h>	SEEK_END	<stdio.h>
MB_CUR_MAX	<stdlib.h>	SEEK_SET	<stdio.h>
MB_LEN_MAX	<limits.h>	setbuf	<stdio.h>
mblen	<stdlib.h>	setjmp	<setjmp.h>
mbstowcs	<stdlib.h>	setlocale	<locale.h>
mbtowc	<stdlib.h>	setvbuf	<stdio.h>
memchr	<string.h>	short	C keyword
memcmp	<string.h>	SHRT_MAX	<limits.h>
memcpy	<string.h>	SHRT_MIN	<limits.h>
memmove	<string.h>	SIGABRT	<signal.h>
memset	<string.h>	SIGFPE	<signal.h>
mktime	<time.h>	SIGILL	<signal.h>
modf	<math.h>	SIGINT	<signal.h>
modff †	<math.h>	signal	<signal.h>
modfl †	<math.h>	signed	C keyword
NULL	<locale.h>	SIGSEGV	<signal.h>
NULL	<stddef.h>	SIGTERM	<signal.h>
NULL	<stdio.h>	sig_atomic_t	<signal.h>
NULL	<stdlib.h>	SIG_DFL	<signal.h>
NULL	<string.h>	SIG_ERR	<signal.h>
NULL	<time.h>	SIG_IGN	<signal.h>
offsetof	<stddef.h>	sin	<math.h>
perror	<stdio.h>	sinf †	<math.h>
pow	<math.h>	sinl †	<math.h>
powf †	<math.h>	sinh	<math.h>
powl †	<math.h>	sinhf †	<math.h>

Reserved Identifier List (continued)			
Identifier	*Header*	*Identifier*	*Header*
sinhl †	<math.h>	switch	C keyword
size_t	<stddef.h>	system	<stdlib.h>
size_t	<stdio.h>	tan	<math.h>
size_t	<stdlib.h>	tanf †	<math.h>
size_t	<string.h>	tanl †	<math.h>
size_t	<time.h>	tanh	<math.h>
sizeof	C keyword	tanhf †	<math.h>
sprintf	<stdio.h>	tanhl †	<math.h>
sqrt	<math.h>	time	<time.h>
sqrtf †	<math.h>	__TIME__	predefined macro
sqrtl †	<math.h>	time_t	<time.h>
srand	<stdlib.h>	tm	<time.h>
sscanf	<stdio.h>	tmpfile	<stdio.h>
__STDC__	predefined macro	tmpnam	<stdio.h>
static	C keyword	TMP_MAX	<stdio.h>
stderr	<stdio.h>	tolower	<ctype.h>
stdin	<stdio.h>	toupper	<ctype.h>
stdout	<stdio.h>	typedef	C keyword
strcat	<string.h>	UCHAR_MAX	<limits.h>
strchr	<string.h>	UINT_MAX	<limits.h>
strcmp	<string.h>	ULONG_MAX	<limits.h>
strcoll	<string.h>	ungetc	<stdio.h>
strcpy	<string.h>	union	C keyword
strcspn	<string.h>	unsigned	C keyword
strerror	<string.h>	USHRT_MAX	<limits.h>
strftime	<time.h>	va_arg	<stdarg.h>
strlen	<string.h>	va_end	<stdarg.h>
strncat	<string.h>	va_list	<stdarg.h>
strncmp	<string.h>	va_start	<stdarg.h>
strncpy	<string.h>	vfprintf	<stdio.h>
strpbrk	<string.h>	void	C keyword
strrchr	<string.h>	volatile	C keyword
strspn	<string.h>	vprintf	<stdio.h>
strstr	<string.h>	vsprintf	<stdio.h>
strtod	<stdlib.h>	wchar_t	<stddef.h>
strtok	<string.h>	wchar_t	<stdlib.h>
strtol	<stdlib.h>	wcstombs	<stdlib.h>
strtoul	<stdlib.h>	wctomb	<stdlib.h>
struct	C keyword	while	C keyword
strxfrm	<string.h>		

C.3 Identifiers Reserved for Future Use

The following families of identifiers are reserved for future use by standards-making bodies such as ANSI and ISO. In the table, $ represents an uppercase letter optionally followed by any combination of letters, digits and underscores. # represents a lower-case letter optionally followed by any combination of letters, digits and underscores. % represents an uppercase letter or digit optionally followed by any combination of letters, digits and underscores.

Identifiers Reserved for Future Use	
Name	*Purpose*
E%	`errno.h` macros
is#	`ctype.h` macros and functions
LC_$	`locale.h` macros
mem#	`string.h` macros and functions
SIG$	`signal.h` macros
SIG_$	`signal.h` macros
str#	`string.h` and `stdlib.h` macros and functions
to#	`ctype.h` macros and functions
wcs#	`string.h` macros and functions

As indicated in the previous sections, the function names in the Standard math library together with a suffix of `f` or `l` are reserved for implementations that wish to provide `float` and/or `long double` versions as well as `double`.

All external identifiers that begin with an underscore are reserved. All other identifiers that begin with an underscore followed by another underscore or an uppercase letter are reserved. This name space is reserved for implementers so they may add macros and library functions to the Standard headers. Users should not use such names except to map into those provided by the implementer.

Appendix D

Language Syntax Summary

This chapter contains only part of the whole C language syntax. For a detailed look at the formal grammar, refer to the ANSI C Standard.

D.1 C Keywords

The following tokens are defined as keywords by ANSI C:

Standard C Language Keywords			
Name	*Purpose*	*Name*	*Purpose*
auto	Declaration class	int	Type specifier
break	Jump statement	long	Type modifier
case	Label (in switch only)	register	Declaration class
char	Type specifier	return	Jump statement
const	Type qualifier	short	Type modifier
continue	Jump statement	signed	Type modifier
default	Label (in switch only)	sizeof	A compile-time operator
double	Type specifier	static	Declaration class
do	Iteration statement	struct	Type specifier
else	Optional path in if	switch	Selection statement
enum	Type specifier	typedef	Declare a type synonym
extern	Declaration class	union	Type specifier
float	Type specifier	unsigned	Type modifier
for	Iteration statement	void	Type specifier
goto	Jump statement	volatile	Type qualifier
if	Selection statement	while	Iteration statement

The **entry** keyword reserved in the original definition of C is not reserved by ANSI C.

D.2   Statements

D.2.1   Jump Statements

```
        goto identifier;

identifier:
        statement;

continue;
break;
return [ expression ];
```

D.2.2   Selection Statements

```
if ( expression )
        statement;
[else
        statement;]


switch ( expression ) {

case 1:
        statement;
        [break;]

case 2:
        statement;
        [break;]

        . . .

case n:
        statement;
        [break;]

default:
        statement;
        [break;]
}
```

D.2.3   Iteration Statements

```
while ( expression )
        statement;
```

```
for ([ expression ]; [ expression ]; [ expression ])
        statement;



do
        statement;
while ( expression );
```

D.3   The C Preprocessor

Standard C Preprocessor Directives	
Name	*Purpose*
`#define`	Define a macro
`#undef`	Remove a macro definition
`#include`	Include a header
`#if`	Compile based on expression
`#ifdef`	Compile based on macro defined
`#ifndef`	Compile based on macro not defined
`#else`	Conditional compilation false path
`#elif`	Compound if/else
`#endif`	End conditional compilation path
`#line`	Override line number and/or source file name
`#error`	Generate a translation error
`#pragma`	Implementation-defined action
`#`	Null directive
Standard C Preprocessor Operators	
Name	*Purpose*
`#`	Stringize
`##`	Token pasting
`defined`	Shorthand for multiple `#ifdef`s

Appendix E

Recommended Reading and References

The following books and documents should prove useful in providing other C-related information.

- *American National Standard X3.159-198x, Programming Language C.* ANSI X3J11 Committee.

  This two-volume document comprises the ANSI C Language Standard and Rationale. It is the first formal and official definition of the C language, its preprocessor and run-time library. It is expected that the final version of the Standard will be completed in mid-1989. A copy of the Standard is available from Global Engineering Documents, Inc., in Santa Ana, California. Telephone (800) 854-7179 or (714) 540-9870, telex 692373 callback globaldoc sna. Price US$65 (US$84.50 for international orders), prepaid.

- *POSIX Standard P1003.1 – Portable Operating System Interface for Computer Environments.* Institute of Electrical and Electronics Engineers, Inc. (IEEE), New York.

  This Standard defines an operating system interface and environment based on the UNIX operating system. It is designed to support applications portability at the source level. While X3J11 ANSI C has responsibility for operating system-independent library routines, POSIX has adopted the UNIX-specific routines from the *de facto* Standard C library provided by AT&T.

- *System V Interface Definition* (SVID). AT&T. 1986. ISBN 0-932764-10-X.

  This three-volume set defines the interface mechanisms for the UNIX System V operating system. Both operating system-specific and general-purpose library routines are defined, many of which are included (possibly in a modified or expanded form) as part of either the IEEE POSIX or the ANSI C X3J11 standards.

- *The X/OPEN Portability Guide.* Elsevier Science Publishers. ISBN 0-444-70179-6. (Five-volume set.)

  X/OPEN is a consortium of computer vendors that is defining a common software interface for operating systems, languages and access methods. Originally comprising European vendors such as Bull, ICL, Nixdorf, Philips and Siemens, it now includes major U.S. vendors such as DEC, Hewlett-Packard and Unisys. This standard, for the most part, is based on existing and emerging standards, such as those from ANSI C and IEEE POSIX.

- *Standard C: Programmers Quick Reference Guide.* Plauger, P.J., and Brodie, Jim. Microsoft Press. 1989. ISBN 1556151586.

I believe this book will be one of the very best distillations of the ANSI C Standard. This is especially so because Plauger not only served as the Standard committee's secretary, he was instrumental in crafting much of the new terminology. Brodie served as the Committee's chairman.

- *The C Programming Language.* Kernighan, Brian W., and Ritchie, Dennis M. Prentice-Hall, Inc. 1978. ISBN 0-13-110163-3.

This classic text, affectionately referred to as K&R, was the definitive C reference when it was published in 1978. Since then, Appendix A has formed the basis for the grammar handled by the vast majority of C language translators. However, the language definition was incomplete and the book contains little information regarding the C library. In April 1988, the second edition was released. This version is essentially the same book as the earlier one, with the new language and preprocessor capabilities retrofitted. In particular, function prototypes are used throughout. A summary of almost the complete library is included.

- *The C Answer Book.* Tondo, Clovis L., and Gimpel, Scott E. Prentice-Hall. 1985 and 1988. ISBN 0-13-109877-2.

This book contains worked solutions for the problems provided in K&R. Each solution uses only the information learned up to that point in the book. Make sure you buy the edition corresponding to that of your K&R.

- *A C Reference Manual,* second edition. Harbison, Samuel P., and Steele, Guy L. Prentice-Hall, Inc. 1987. ISBN 0-13-109810-1. ISBN 0-13-109802-0 (pbk.)

Although the first edition was an excellent book, the second edition additionally contains a considerable amount of information about the ANSI C Standard as well as common language extensions. It also contains one of the few complete treatments of the run-time library. Harbison is a respected member of the ANSI C Committee.

- *The C Puzzle Book.* Feuer, Alan R. Prentice-Hall. 1982. ISBN 0-13-109926-4.

This book of puzzles is well-written and well-organized. Not only is it very useful to the beginning C programmer, it provides a valuable refresher course to advanced C programmers as well. Note that some puzzles (in particular those involving replacement of macro arguments within strings) are based on the UNIX pcc compiler and will not work as written, under ANSI C. Where machine architectures may affect a puzzle's answer, solutions are provided for both a 16-bit DEC PDP-11 and a DEC VAX.

- *Portability and the C Language.* Jaeschke, Rex. Hayden. 1989. ISBN 672-48428-5.

This is the first text dedicated to the topic of C and portability. It contains some 375 pages of information and recommendations regarding the preprocessor, language and library and addresses issues related to both ANSI and non-ANSI C. The chapters are organized in the same manner as the ANSI C Standard so the two can be used as companion volumes. Appendix C describes the optional portability software suite.

- *Notes on the Draft C Standard*. Plum, Thomas. Plum Hall, Inc. 1987. ISBN 0-911537-06-6.

  This 90-page booklet contains an overview of the differences between ANSI C and K&R C. Presumably, it is a forerunner to a full-length ANSI C text once the Standard is completed.

- *Portable C and UNIX System Programming*. Lapin, J E. Rabbit Software. Prentice-Hall, Inc. 1987. ISBN 0-13-686494-5.

  This book is aimed specifically at those porting code between UNIX and its derivative systems. It describes a port philosophy, briefly covers C language issues and concentrates on the operating system and library issues.

- C *Programming Guidelines*. Plum, Thomas. Plum Hall, Inc. 1984. ISBN 0-911537-03-1.

  Programming style is most important when writing code that is to be ported and Tom Plum is one of the masters in this area. He is also the vice chairman of the ANSI C Standards Committee.

- *Efficient C*. Plum, Thomas., and Brodie, Jim. Plum Hall, Inc. 1985. ISBN 0-911537-05-8.

  There is little point in having code that is portable yet fails to perform in a time- and space-efficient manner on any of the target environments. This text provides considerable insight into defining and measuring efficiency. Brodie and Plum are the chairman and vice chairman, respectively, of the ANSI C Standards Committee. All of the source code in the book is available on DOS diskettes and is in the public domain.

- *Reliable Data Structures in C*. Plum, Thomas. Plum Hall, Inc. 1985. ISBN 0-911537-04-X.

  Plum discusses approaches to coding in a reliable manner. All the source code in the book is available on DOS diskettes and is in the public domain.

- *C Standard Library*. Purdum, Jack, and Leslie, Timothy C. Que. 1987. ISBN 0-88022-279-4.

  This book contains a thorough definition and tutorial on almost all the library routines defined by ANSI C. It also contains discussion of numerous SVID-specific routines and indicates whether or not a particular routine is supported by ANSI C and SVID.

- *Advanced C Programming for Displays*. Rochkind, Marc J. Prentice-Hall, Inc. 1988. ISBN 0-13-010240-7.

  This book is a great aid to those writing programs that are to interact with character displays and keyboards on various UNIX and DOS systems.

- *Crafting C Tools for the IBM PCs*. Campbell, Joe. Prentice-Hall. 1986. ISBN 0-13-188418-2.

  This is one of the best texts that is specific to C on IBM-PC-class systems. It is intended for serious C and DOS users.

- *Solutions in C.* Jaeschke, Rex. Addison-Wesley. 1986. ISBN 0-201-15042-5.

  This is a 200-page book (seven chapters) of advanced C language tips.

- *The C++ Programming Language.* Stroustrup, Bjarne. Addison-Wesley. 1986. ISBN 0-201-12078-X.

  This definitive reference on C++ was written by that language's author. It is to C++ what K&R was (originally) to C. This book is useful should you consider moving from C to C++. Note, though, that C++ is evolving and other documents have been written about its evolution. Sources of more recent information include the *Bell Laboratories Technical Journal* and Usenix C++ conference proceedings from 1987 and 1988.

- *The C Users Journal.* Edited by Robert Ward. R&D Publications, 2120 West 25th St., Suite B, Lawrence, Kansas 66046.

  This publication was formerly *The C Journal*, cofounded and edited by Rex Jaeschke as a quarterly. Since that publication was sold, it has been combined with *The C Users Group Newsletter* to become *The C Users Journal* and is now published eight times per year. While it is primarily aimed at micro-based systems, occasional articles address other environments. Contributing editors include P J. Plauger and Rex Jaeschke.

- *The C Gazette.* Edited by Andrew Binstock. Pacific Data Works, 1341 Ocean Ave., #257, Snata Monica, CA 90401-1016.

  This quarterly started life as *The DeSmet Gazette* and covered only those issues relevant to the DeSmet C Language development system distributed by C Ware. The owners eventually acquired *The Lattice and Microsoft C User Group* and newsletter from Bill Hunt and the two are now combined to cover C issues under DOS. The publication is code-oriented and contains a large amount of source.

- "Let's C Now." *DEC PROFESSIONAL*. Professional Press, Spring House, PA.

  Rex Jaeschke, the C Language editor, has been writing this monthly column since January 1984. The first 26 installments were published as a two-volume workbook. Although the publication is aimed at DEC-specific hardware and software, much of the C material is generic in nature. There are occasional references to VAX/VMS, UNIX, DOS and other environments, as appropriate.

- *The Programmers Journal.* Edited by Steve Baker. Oakley Publications, Springfield, Oregon.

  This PC-related technical journal is published eight times per year. In each issue Rex Jaeschke writes a column about ANSI C. He also reviews DOS C compilers (and other tools) with regard to their support for the ANSI C Standard.

- Other publications that regularly contain C language columns and/or articles, include: *Dr. Dobbs Journal of Software Tools*, *Computer Language*, and *UNIX Review*. Those interested in C++ and other object-oriented languages may be interested in *The Journal of Object-Oriented Programming*.

Appendix F

Glossary of C Terms

This appendix contains a brief description of the C language keywords and operators, the preprocessor and other terms used throughout this book. Entries containing the text "(X3J11)" have been invented or adopted by the ANSI C Standard.

!   Logical negation (unary) operator.

!=   Inequality (binary) operator.

\#   Stringize preprocessor (unary) operator (X3J11).

\#\#   Token pasting preprocessor (binary) operator (X3J11).

%   Modulus (binary) operator. Also used as a prefix to the `printf` and `scanf` function family edit masks.

%=   Remainder (binary) operator, compound assignment.

&   Bit-wise AND (binary) operator. Also address-of (unary) operator.

&&   Logical AND (binary) operator.

&=   Bit-wise AND (binary) operator, compound assignment.

()   Cast (unary) operator. Also function call operator and evaluation order punctuator.

*   Multiplication (binary) operator. Also pointer indirection (unary) operator.

*=   Multiplication (binary) operator, compound assignment.

+   Addition (binary) operator. Also unary plus operator (X3J11).

++   Increment operator, unary prefix or postfix.

+=   Addition (binary) operator, compound assignment.

,   Comma (binary) operator. Also a punctuator.

-      Subtraction (binary) operator. Also the unary minus operator.

--   Decrement operator, unary prefix or postfix.

-=   Subtraction (binary) operator, compound assignment.

->   Structure/union pointer (arrow) operator.

.   Structure/union member (dot) operator. Also decimal point character in floating-point constants.

...   Ellipsis notation. Used in function prototypes (X3J11).

/   Division (binary) operator.

/* */   Comment delimiters.

/=   Division (binary) operator, compound assignment.

:   Label terminator.

;   Statement terminator.

<   Less-than (binary) operator.

<<   Left-shift (binary) operator.

<<=   Left-shift (binary) operator, compound assignment.

<=   Less-than-or-equal-to (binary) operator.

=   Assignment (binary) operator (different from equality ==). Also used in declaration and enumeration constant initializer lists.

==   Equality (binary) operator (different from assignment =).

>   Greater-than (binary) operator.

>=   Greater-than-or-equal-to (binary) operator.

>>   Right shift (binary) operator.

>>=   Right shift (binary) operator, compound assignment.

?:   Conditional (ternary) operator.

??x Trigraph sequence used to input characters not available on a keyboard or machine character set (X3J11). The valid sequences and their meaning are:

Standard C Trigraph Sequences	
Sequence	*Meaning*
??!	|
??'	^
??(	[
??)	]
??-	~
??/	\
??<	{
??=	#
??>	}

[]   Array subscript operator.

\   Backslash character; prefixes the following character constants:

Standard C Escape Sequences	
Sequence	*Meaning*
\"	Double quote
\'	Single quote
\0	Null character
\?	Question mark (X3J11)
\a	Terminal alert (X3J11)
\b	Backspace
\ddd	Octal value ddd
\f	Form-feed
\n	New-line
\r	Carriage return
\t	Horizontal tab
\v	Vertical tab (X3J11)
\x$hh$	Hexadecimal value hh (X3J11)
\	Backslash

^   Exclusive OR (binary) operator.

^=   Exclusive OR (binary) operator, compound assignment.

_   Underscore. May be used in identifier names. Identifiers with leading underscores are reserved for system and Standard use.

{}   Opening and closing brace. Delimits a compound statement or initializer list.

| Bit-wise inclusive OR (binary) operator.

|=   Bit-wise inclusive OR (binary) operator, compound assignment.

|| Logical OR (binary) operator.

~   Bit-wise (one's) complement (unary) operator.

abort A standard library function that causes a program to terminate abnormally and to return control back to the calling environment. See `exit`.

aggregate One of the types structure, union and array. Opposite to a scalar type such as `int`, `char` and `float`.

alignment Some machines, such as the PDP-11 series, require certain object types to begin on specific address boundaries; that is, to be aligned. And, while other machines such as the VAX and Intel 8086 can manipulate objects on any boundary, it is more efficient if words are aligned on word boundaries, longwords on longword boundaries, etc.

ANSI C The formal definition of the C language, preprocessor and run-time library. See **X3J11**.

argc The first argument passed to **main** (the second is **argv**). It contains the number of arguments found on the command-line. It typically is at least one, although the actual string used on the command-line to invoke the program itself may not be preserved by the task loader. Note that different loaders/compilers may treat quoted arguments and arguments with embedded white space differently.

argument Any expression passed to a function in a function call. A comma-separated list of arguments comprises an argument list. Also used in the context of a command-line argument as with **argv** and with a call to a function-like macro. An argument is sometimes called an "actual argument" and is not to be confused with a "formal argument" or parameter.

argv The second argument passed to **main** (the first is **argc**). **argv** is an array of pointers to the strings specified as command-line arguments. The number of elements in the array is **argc** + 1 where **argv[argc]** contains NULL. **argv[0]** might not always point to a meaningful string.

array An aggregate type consisting of one or more elements, each of which has exactly the same attributes and occupies consecutively higher memory locations.

arrow operator See ->.

assignment The operation of assigning the value of an expression to the memory location designated by another expression (which is typically a variable name).

assignment, simple Implemented using the = operator. Not to be confused with the equality operator ==.

assignment, compound One of the family of *op=* operators which are abbreviated versions of the constructs = exp1 *op* exp2. For example, i += 6 is equivalent to i = i + 6. The complete family is +=, -=, *=, /=, %=, <<=, >>=, &=, ^= and |=.

auto A class keyword used in the declaration of an object inside a function definition to designate automatic storage duration. If such a declaration contains no class keyword, **auto** is assumed.

backslash Used as an escape character prefix to indicate that the character following is to be given special treatment. See the table of escape sequences in the entry for \ at the beginning of this glossary.

bit-field A special structure or union member whose size is specified in bits. Bit-fields usually are declared as **unsigned int**, although some implementations may support signed bit-fields as well. It is implementation-defined as to whether a plain **int** bit-field is signed. You can not take the address of a bit-field or find its size using **sizeof**.

block That part of a function definition delimited by a matching pair of braces (not those braces delimiting initializer lists). It defines the scope and life of locally declared identifiers and it can be used to delimit the scope of a statement such as **if-else**, **while** and **for**. Blocks may be nested and optionally may contain declarations followed, optionally, by statements. Also referred to as a compound statement.

break This statement causes termination of the innermost current `while`, `for` or `do` loop, or `switch` statement. Control is transferred to the statement immediately following that being terminated. It is subtly different from `continue`.

case This keyword is used only in the context of a `switch` statement to designate a switch value label.

case label See **label, case**.

case sensitivity C is a case-sensitive language; that is, the identifiers `ABC`, `abc`, `Abc` and `AbC` all represent different names. Note that an implementation is permitted to ignore case in handling external names (i.e., function and global variables) because many linkers are not case-sensitive. C language keywords must be written in lowercase to be recognized as such.

cast The operation of converting an expression from one type to another. It is performed using a cast operator of the form (*type*) where *type* is any scalar type. A cast expression is not an lvalue.

char An integer type keyword. A `char` is big enough to hold any character in the target system's character set. ANSI C requires it to be at least eight bits. It is implementation-defined as to whether a plain `char` is signed or unsigned. `char` expressions typically are widened to `int` when used as subexpressions and as arguments to functions.

character constant A token of the form `'x'` where `x` is either a printable graphic character or an escape sequence. By definition, its type is `int` not `char`. (There is no such thing as a constant with type `char`.) Some implementations permit multicharacter character constants such as `'ab'` and `'abcd'`. Note that `'x'` is different from `"x"`.

class Indicated in a declaration by one of the keywords `auto`, `static`, `extern` and `register`. Inside a function definition, an object declaration containing no class keyword has class `auto`. The particular class keyword used and the location of the declaration in a source file (relative to being inside or outside a function definition) dictate the identifier's storage duration and linkage. Technically, `typedef` is also a class keyword; however, it implies neither storage duration nor linkage.

comma operator If two expressions are separated by a comma, they are evaluated left-to-right, and the type and value of the whole expression is the type and value of the right operand. When a comma operator is used so that it may be misinterpreted as a comma punctuator (such as in a function argument list), the comma operator expression must be enclosed in grouping parentheses. It typically is used only in the first and third expressions in a `for` loop, and in macro definitions.

command-line The set of arguments specified when a program is invoked at the operating system level. They are typically made available to `main` via `argc` and `argv`. The existence of a command-line processor can be determined via the library routine `system`.

comment Any character sequence delimited by `/*` and `*/`. A comment can occur anywhere white space is permitted. That is, between any two adjacent source tokens. During tokenizing, a comment is replaced by one space character. ANSI C does not permit comments to nest. Except where they separate source tokens, comments are ignored by a translator.

compiler Usually used to mean a C language translator and includes such tools as interpreters and incremental compilers as well.

compound statement See **block**.

conditional operator An expression containing the conditional operator has the form `exp1 ? exp2 : exp3` where, if `exp1` is true, then `exp2` is evaluated, otherwise `exp3` is evaluated; while, like an `if-else` statement, `?:` results in an expression.

conforming implementation A C translation environment that conforms to the ANSI Standard specification for C. Specifically, a conforming hosted implementation must contain all of the library functions.

`const` This keyword is used as a type qualifier. It indicates that the object being declared can not be stored into in the scope of this declaration. Specifically, it causes the identifier to become a non-modifiable lvalue. `const` was adopted by ANSI C from C++.

`continue` This statement causes the current innermost iteration of a `for`, `while` or `do` loop to be terminated and a new iteration (if any) to be started. It is subtly different from `break`.

`_DATE_` ANSI C predefined macro. A string containing the date of compilation in the form `"Mmm dd yyyy"`.

declaration Declares the attributes of one or more identifiers. A definition (such as `static int i;`) is always a declaration, but a declaration (such as `extern int j;`) is not necessarily a definition. Declarations optionally may occur at the start of any block, prior to any statements. They also may occur outside of function definitions.

`default` This keyword is used as a special label and only then in the context of a `switch` statement. A `switch` passes control to the `default` label if the controlling expression does not match any of the specified case label values.

`#define` A preprocessor directive used to define a macro.

definition A declaration that causes storage to be reserved for an object or function named by an identifier. A definition (such as `static int i;`) is always a declaration, but a declaration (such as `extern int j;`) is not necessarily a definition.

dereferencing See **indirection**.

derived type A type synonym created via `typedef`.

`do-while` Two keywords used to implement a loop that executes at least once (a `for` or `while` loop does not need to execute at all).

dot operator See the . operator above.

double A keyword used for one of the three floating-point types (the other two are `float` and `long double`). Traditionally, `double` meant "double precision," while `float` implied "single precision." Some compilers use the synonym `long float` instead of or as well as `double`; however, this is not permitted by ANSI C. See **floating-point type**.

edit masks Character sequences of the form %x where x may be more than one character. Used by the `printf` and `scanf` function family in interpreting formatted output and input argument lists, respectively.

#elif A preprocessor directive used as a short form of a nested `#if` (X3J11).

#else A preprocessor directive used to indicate the false path of a conditional compilation directive set. Used with `#if`, `#ifdef` and `#ifndef`.

#endif A preprocessor directive used to indicate the end of a conditional compilation directive set. Used with `#if`, `#ifdef` and `#ifndef`.

enum The keyword used to define an enumerated type and to declare identifiers of that type.

enumerated type A set of related integer values, each of which is referred to as an enumeration constant. The type optionally may have a tag. An object of an enumerated type maps to an implementation-defined integer type.

enumeration constant An identifier used inside the definition of an enumerated type. It represents a compile-time constant expression of type `int` and may have an explicit initializer.

envp Commonly used as the third argument passed to `main`. `envp` is an array of pointers to the strings specified as environment variables. `envp` is not defined by ANSI C, but is a permitted extension. It is generally provided in UNIX environments and in compilers modelled on UNIX's `pcc` compiler.

EOF An object-like macro defined in `stdio.h`. It represents the end-of-file value returned from numerous standard I/O routines.

equality The testing of two expressions to see if they are equal. Requires the `==` operator and is not to be confused with the assignment operator `=` as used in most other languages (including C).

errno An lvalue expression that designates a place in which various library routines can store a failure indicator. ANSI C permits `errno` to be either a macro or an external object. It is declared in `errno.h` along with the two standard value macros `ERANGE` and `EDOM`. Numerous other (non-standard) value macros typically are provided based on the UNIX model.

#error A preprocessor directive used to display a message on `stderr` and to terminate translation (X3J11).

exit A standard library function that causes a program to terminate normally and to return a programmer-specified `int` value back to the calling environment. Dropping through the outermost closing brace of `main` is an implied call to `exit` with an undefined `int` value. See **abort**.

exit code The `int` value returned by a user program to its calling environment via a `return exp;` from `main`, or from a call to `exit`. The code's meaning is implementation-defined except that zero and the object-like macro `EXIT_SUCCESS` signify success while `EXIT_FAILURE` indicates failure. The exit code is undefined if you drop through the outermost closing brace of `main`.

expression A valid sequence of operators and operands that specifies how to compute a value (e.g., `a + b`) or how to generate side effects (e.g., `f()`, `++i`, or `j--`) or both (e.g., `a + g() + ++k`).

extern A keyword used to indicate a storage class that signifies an identifier is defined elsewhere, either later on in the same source file or in a separate source file. If a function definition does not include a class keyword, `extern` is assumed.

field See **bit-field**.

FILE A derived type defined in `stdio.h`. It contains context information about a currently open file. Many of the standard I/O routines traffic in pointers to `FILE` objects. A programmer does not need to know the details of such a type to perform correct file I/O.

__FILE__ ANSI C predefined macro. The name of the source file as a string.

float A keyword used for one of the three floating-point types. (The other two are `double` and `long double`.) Traditionally, `double` meant "double precision" while `float` implied "single precision." Some compilers use the synonym `long float` instead of or as well as `double`; however, this is not permitted by ANSI C. See **floating-point type**.

floating-point type There are three types: `float`, `double` and `long double` (the last one being an ANSI C invention). An object of type `long double` must have as least as much range and precision as that of type `double` which, in turn, must have at least as much as `float`. As such, one or more of the three types could map to the same representation. The header `float.h` can be used to determine the attributes of an implementation's floating-point types.

for A looping construct that evaluates its criteria before each iteration of the loop like `while` and unlike `do-while` which always executes at least once. All three expressions in a `for` are optional. If the first is missing, there is no initialization. If the second is missing, it is as if a true expression were present. If the third is missing, there is nothing to do at the end of each iteration. A `for` construct always can be rewritten as a `while` construct and vice versa.

formatted I/O The `printf` family of routines provides formatted output capabilities to the screen, to disk files and to memory. Likewise, the `scanf` family handles formatted input conversions.

fprintf A library function that writes formatted output to a specified file. See `printf` and `sprintf`.

freestanding environment An environment in which a program does not run under the control of an operating system. Typically, freestanding programs do not have access to a command-line processor or a file system. (An operating system is a special case of such an environment.)

fscanf A library function that reads formatted input from a specified file. See `scanf` and `sscanf`.

function The basic executable module in a C program. It is synonymous with a subroutine in other languages. All C functions look and behave identically, including `main`. A function may have arguments, a return value, both or neither.

function prototype A declaration of a function that includes a parameter type list. Each parameter optionally may include an identifier, which has no effect. It was adapted by ANSI C from the C++ language.

getchar A library function that reads a character from standard input. The read may or may not be buffered.

gets A library function that reads a character string from standard input. Any trailing new-line found is discarded and a null character is appended to the string read. The read may or may not be buffered.

goto A keyword used to implement an unconditional branch statement to a label.

header An object whose contents are made available via the `#include` preprocessor directive. A header does not need to exist as a text file—it can be stored as a binary file, or defined internally within the translator. Typically, a header contains function declarations and macro definitions. It also may contain **typedefs**, and structure, union and enumeration declarations. Headers can be nested up to some implementation-specific depth. Standard headers are accessed using `#include <header>` and programmer-defined headers using `#include "header"`.

heap Memory that may be dynamically allocated and released by a user program using the library functions `calloc`, `malloc`, `realloc` and `free`.

hosted environment An environment in which a program runs under the control of an operating system. Typically, hosted programs have access to a command-line processor. A conforming hosted C translator must implement all of, or none of, the Standard run-time library.

identifier A name consisting of a sequence of characters that can be used to name a variable, function, enumeration constant, derived typename, structure, union or enumerated type tag or member, label or macro. An identifier must begin with a letter or an underscore and may contain alphanumeric and underscore characters. While K&R stated that the first eight characters were significant, X3J11 and many current translators recognize the first 31. (Note that due to linker and other restrictions, the length of significance of external names may be less than 31.)

if—else A construct that allows control to be directed based on the truth value of a scalar expression. The `if—else` construct may be nested.

#if A preprocessor directive used to begin a conditional compilation "block" based on the truth of an integer expression.

#ifdef A preprocessor directive used to begin a conditional compilation "block" based on the existence of a macro definition.

#ifndef A preprocessor directive used to begin a conditional compilation "block" based on the non-existence of a macro definition.

implementation A C translation environment. Collectively refers to the preprocessor, compiler and run-time library for a given host system.

implementation-defined behavior Behavior for a correct program construct and correct data that depends on the characteristics of the implementation and that each implementation shall document. For example, whether or not a `char` is sign extended on conversion to `int` is implementation-defined.

#include A preprocessor directive used to include a standard or programmer-defined header.

indirection The act of getting at an object or function via a pointer to that object or function. It is achieved using the unary * operator. This process is also known as dereferencing.

int An integer type keyword. ANSI C requires it to be at least 16 bits. Typically, it maps onto the native data type for a given machine's architecture (its word or register size, for example). A plain `int` is signed. See **integer type**.

integer type There are four kinds: `char`, `short int`, `int` and `long int`. These types are listed in nondecreasing order of their precision. As such, one or more of the types could map to the same representation. Both signed and unsigned versions are available. The header `limits.h` can be used to determine the attributes of an implementation's integer types.

jump table An array of function pointers.

K&R The book *The C Programming Language* by Brian W. Kernighan and Dennis M. Ritchie. When the first edition was written in 1978, it was the definitive reference book for C. Although the second edition was published in 1988, the name K&R normally implies the first edition.

keyword One of a set of identifier tokens that has a predefined meaning and is reserved by the language. As such, it can not be used as an identifier.

label An identifier, followed by a colon, that appears before a statement. Such a label can be used only in conjunction with a matching `goto` statement. The two other label formats, `case` and `default`, are used only with the `switch` construct and can not be the object of a `goto`.

label, case This label is used only in the context of a `switch` statement, along with the `case` keyword. It must be a compile-time integer constant expression. A `switch` passes control to a case label if the controlling expression matches its label value.

label, default See `default`.

LINE ANSI C predefined macro. The current source line number as a decimal constant.

#line A preprocessor directive used to override the current source filename and/or line number during translation.

linkage The form of coupling (if any) between occurrences of the same identifier when used as an object name. ANSI C defines three forms of linkage: none, internal and external. See **scope**.

local A term pertaining to the scope of an identifier in that it is not visible outside its parent and subordinate blocks. See **global**.

long A permitted abbreviation for `long int`.

long int An integer type keyword. ANSI C requires it to be at least 32 bits. A plain `long int` is signed. See **integer type**.

long float An archaic alternative to `double`.

long double A keyword used for one of the three floating-point types. It was invented by ANSI C. (The other two are `float` and `double`.) See **floating-point type**.

lvalue An expression that designates an object. That is, an expression must be usable with the & address-of operator to be an lvalue (except for bit-fields and `register` class objects which are lvalues, but can not be used with &). Every lvalue is an rvalue, but not every rvalue is an lvalue. The most common forms of lvalue are the name of a variable and the expression `*p` where `p` is a pointer to an object. See **lvalue, modifiable** and **lvalue, non-modifiable**.

lvalue, modifiable An lvalue that can be stored through. See **lvalue** and **lvalue, non-modifiable**.

lvalue, non-modifiable An lvalue that can not be stored through. Examples include the name of an array and any expression designating a `const` object. See **lvalue** and **lvalue, modifiable**.

macro An identifier assigned a string value by the preprocessor directive `#define`. See **macro, object-like** and **macro, function-like**.

macro, function-like A macro defined with a (possibly empty) argument list. See **macro** and **macro, object-like**.

macro, object-like A macro defined without an argument list. This form of macro often is called a symbolic constant. See **macro** and **macro, function-like.**

macro, predefined A macro automatically defined by the compiler. ANSI C defines five such macros called `__FILE__`, `__LINE__`, `__DATE__`, `__TIME__` and `__STDC__`. They can not be the subject of `#undef` and they can not be redefined.

main Each hosted program must contain a function called `main` which marks the program's logical entry point. `main` does not need to be the first function in any source file. Freestanding C programs do not need to have a `main` function. Although `main` is equivalent to FORTRAN's `PROGRAM` and PASCAL's `program`, it is just another function and, as such, has arguments passed to it. See `argc`, `argv` and `envp`.

math.h A standard header that contains macros and declarations for the math library routines.

member An identifier declared as part of a structure or union template. Such members are references using the dot or arrow operator. The term is less often used with regard to the enumeration constant "members" in an enumerated data type definition.

new-line The logical end-of-line character represented as '\n'. It is often mapped into a carriage-return and line-feed pair.

null character The character constant '\0' used to terminate character strings.

NULL The null pointer constant macro. This expression typically is defined as 0, 0L or (void *)0. When a pointer is assigned the value zero or is compared to such an integer value, the zero is first converted to the null pointer constant. C guarantees it will never allocate an object or function at an address that corresponds to the null pointer value. Therefore, NULL can be used to indicate a pointer value that does not point to an object or function. (For example, fopen returns NULL if it can not open the specified file.)

null statement A statement consisting only of a semicolon. It is equivalent to an empty block.

object A region of storage, the contents of which can represent values corresponding to a given type.

obsolescent A term applied to a practice or approach declaring it to be "outdated." Labelling something as obsolescent in a standard paves the way for it to be dropped from future versions of that standard. For example, ANSI C has declared obsolescent the declaring and defining of functions using the non-prototype approach.

parameter An expression expected by a function in a function definition. Each parameter is designated by a corresponding identifier and declaration. A function prototype also contains a comma-separated list of parameter declarations; also used in the context of a function-like macro definition. Sometimes it is called a "formal" argument. Not to be confused with an argument (or "actual argument").

pointer An expression that designates an object that contains the address of an object or function. A pointer is dereferenced using the unary operator. A pointer can be initialized by using the unary & operator (among other ways). A function can be called by dereferencing a pointer to it.

POSIX One ANSI standards group is IEEE, the Institute for Electrical and Electronic Engineers. One of its committees, P1003, is chartered and forming a standard for a portable operating system definition based on UNIX. This system is known as POSIX.

#pragma An implementation-defined preprocessor directive (X3J11).

preprocessor A program that scans a C source file, looking for lines beginning with a # which it assumes to be directives that indicate some action to be taken before subsequent source code lines are handed off to the compiler. In its strictest sense, the preprocessor understands nothing about the syntax of C.

precedence The hierarchy and associativity of operators. See Appendix A.

printf This library function writes formatted output to standard output. See `fprintf` and `sprintf`.

program One or more (possibly separately compiled) functions of which only one must be called `main`. Together they make up an execution unit. A program may include functions from an external library.

prototype See **function prototype**.

ptrdiff_t This derived typename is defined in `stddef.h`. It is an implementation-defined signed integer type corresponding to the difference between two pointers of the same type.

putchar A library function that writes a character to standard output. The write may or may not be buffered.

puts A library function that writes a character string to standard output. A new-line is appended. The write may or may not be buffered.

recursion A recursive function is one that invokes itself directly or indirectly. For each invocation, a new set of automatic objects (if any) is created. See **recursion**.

redirection characters UNIX and MS-DOS (and other operating systems) allow `stdin` and `stdout` to be redirected using the command-line symbols <, > and >>. They also may provide a way to redirect `stderr`.

register A class keyword used in the declaration of an object inside a function definition to designate automatic storage duration. `register` is a hint to the compiler to place the object in some "fast" location of memory, such as a machine register. If the compiler can not or chooses not to do so, the keyword is treated as if it were `auto`.

return A statement that causes control to be returned to the calling function. `return exp;` from `main` is equivalent to `exit(exp);`. A non-void function may return a value using the syntax `return exp;`. Falling through the end of the outermost closing brace in a function is an implied `return` without an expression.

rvalue Originally used to define those expressions permitted on the right side of an assignment. Because every expression (except a `void` expression) is an rvalue, the term hardly ever is used any more. Every lvalue is an rvalue but not every rvalue is an lvalue.

scalar A simple type like `int`, `char` or `float`. Opposite to the aggregate types structure, union and array.

scanf A library function that reads formatted input from standard input. See `fscanf` and `sscanf`.

scope That region of a program within which an identifier is visible (i.e., can be accessed by name). The kinds of scope are function, file, block and function prototype. ANSI C refers to identifier scope as linkage.

short A permitted abbreviation for `short int`.

short int An integer type keyword. ANSI C requires it to be at least 16 bits. A
plain short int is signed. short int expressions are typically widened to int
when used as subexpressions and as arguments to function. See **integer type**.

signed A keyword used as a signed integer data type prefix. It may be applied
to char, short int, int and long int. It allows signed arithmetic to be
performed. When used on its own, it implies signed int. The use of signed
with short, int and long is redundant because these types are signed anyway.
The reason for ANSI C's inventing this modifier was to permit an explicitly
signed char. Prior to that, you only had unsigned and plain chars and it was
implementation-defined as to the signedness of a plain char. See **integer type**.

size_t A derived typename defined in several of the standard headers. It is the
unsigned integer type of a sizeof expression. It is used by all library routines
dealing with arguments and/or return values that represent sizes.

sizeof A keyword used to represent a compile-time operator. It returns the size in
bytes of its operand. It can be used with expressions or types of other than
function and void type. It can not be used with bit-fields.

sprintf A library function that writes formatted output to memory. See printf and
fprintf.

sscanf A library function that reads formatted input from memory. See scanf and
fscanf.

stack An area of memory in which automatic objects and function argument lists
often are stored depending on the machine's architecture. Depending on the
amount of space required by these (and the existence of recursion), you may
need to specify a stack size to your linker or compiler.

statement A C statement consists of either one of the constructs defined by the
language (such as if–else, for and while) or an expression statement. An
expression statement is any expression followed by a semicolon. See **null statement** and **block**.

static A class keyword used in the declaration of an object to designate static storage
duration. Also used with functions. A static function is callable only from
functions defined in the same source code file. See extern.

__STDC__ ANSI C predefined macro. Set to 1 for Standard-conforming implementations.

stderr A FILE pointer representing the standard error device. On hosted systems,
stderr is always open. It is usually mapped to the user's terminal screen or
printer, but may be redirected to another device or file on some systems. See
stdin and stdout.

stdin A FILE pointer representing the standard input device. On hosted systems,
stdin is always open. It is usually mapped to the user's terminal keyboard but
may be redirected to another device or file on some systems. See stderr and
stdout.

stdio.h A standard header that contains macros and declarations for the I/O library
routines.

`stdout` A FILE pointer representing the standard output device. On hosted systems, stdout is always open. It is usually mapped to the user's terminal screen or printer, but may be redirected to another device or file on some systems. See `stdin` and `stderr`.

storage duration The life of an identifier is applicable only to data objects and it refers to the time during which an object is guaranteed to actually exist. (An implementation may make it live longer.) ANSI C refers to an identifier's life as its storage duration. There are two kinds of storage duration: static and automatic.

storage duration, automatic The life of an object declared with the class keyword `auto` or `register`, or inside a function definition and having no class keyword. Such objects are created each time their parent block is entered at run-time and are destroyed when that block is exited. Automatic variables typically are maintained on a stack and their initial value (if none is provided) is undefined.

storage duration, static The life of an object declared inside a function definition with the class keyword `static`, or outside a function definition either with or without a class keyword. Such objects are created prior to `main` beginning execution. They retain their values across function calls. Their initial value (if none is provided) is zero, cast to their type.

stream The logical channel on which I/O is performed. The three standard streams `stdin`, `stdout` and `stderr` refer to standard input, standard output and standard error, respectively. They are opened for you at the start of each program and closed when the program terminates.

string, literal A source token having the form `"..."`. It is stored by the compiler as a `static` array of `char` with a trailing null character appended. It is implementation-defined as to whether strings are stored in a writable memory location and whether identical strings are distinct.

`struct` The keyword used to define a structure type and to declare identifiers of that type.

structure An aggregate type that contains one or more members which typically are related. Sufficient storage is allocated to a structure so that at any time one occurrence of each member can be stored. The size of a structure is at least the sum of the sizes of its members.

SVID The base documents used by X3J11 and P1003 came from AT&T which has developed this de facto standard, known as the System V Interface Definition.

`switch` A construct that allows control to be passed to one of a given set of `case` (or `default`) labels based on the value of a controlling integer expression.

symbolic constant See **macro, object-like**.

`tag` An optional naming identifier permitted when a structure, union or enumerated type is defined. If no tag is specified, the type becomes a `struct`, `union` or `enum` of unknown type and there are severe limits on how that type can be used.

template The data-mapping declared in a structure or union type definition; not to be confused with an actual instance of a structure or union object.

__TIME__ ANSI C predefined macro; a string containing the time of compilation in the form `"hh:mm:ss"`.

token The fundamental unit of source code in a program. ANSI C defines six token types: keywords, identifiers, constants, string literals, punctuators and operators. A token can not contain another token. Tokens may be separated by an arbitrary amount of white space.

truth value Any scalar expression can be tested for a truth value. By definition, a value of zero designates false while any non-zero value designates true. However, when the compiler generates a truth value (as in `4 > 3` and `10 == 10`), it uses the value one.

type qualifier ANSI C added two of these: `const` and `volatile`. When used in an object declaration, they constrain the way in which that identifier can be used as an lvalue.

typedef A keyword used to create a synonym for a (typically complex) declaration. Technically, it is a class keyword, even though it has nothing to do with storage duration or linkage. A type synonym is often called a derived type.

translation unit ANSI C term for a source file.

translator See **compiler**.

#undef A preprocessor directive used to remove a macro definition. It is not an error to `#undef` a non-existent macro.

undefined behavior Behavior for an erroneous program construct or erroneous data for which the Standard imposes no requirements. Examples include the passing of an argument of the incorrect type to a function and using the value of a function that does not return one.

union The keyword used to define a union type and to declare identifiers of that type. This aggregate type contains one or more members which may or may not be related. Sufficient storage is allocated to a union so that at any time one occurrence of only one member can be stored. The size of a union is at least the size of its largest member.

unsigned A keyword used as an unsigned integer data type prefix. It may be applied to `char`, `short int`, `int` and `long int`. It allows unsigned arithmetic to be performed. When used on its own, it implies `unsigned int`. See **integer type**.

unspecified behavior Behavior for a correct program construct and correct data for which the Standard imposes no requirements. For example, the order of evaluation of expressions (except those involving `&&`, `||`, `?:` and the comma operator) is unspecified.

void The type of an expression that has no value. Obtained by calling a `void` function or via a `void` cast.

void pointer ANSI C invented this pointer type to help implementers on systems where pointers are not all the same size and/or representation (such as with word architectures) and to provide a generic pointer type. All standard library routines that used to use char * for such pointers, now use `void *` (for example, `malloc`, `calloc` and `memcpy`). A `void` pointer can not be directly dereferenced.

volatile A keyword used as a type qualifier. It indicates that the object being declared is not owned entirely by this program. That is, it might be being read or written asynchronously by some other program as well (it may reside in shared memory, for example) and that the optimizer had better not eliminate various accesses to this object. `volatile` was invented by ANSI C.

while This looping construct evaluates its criteria before each iteration of the loop like `for` and unlike `do-while` which always executes at least once. A `while` construct always can be rewritten as a `for` construct and vice versa.

white space One or more adjacent space, horizontal tab, vertical tab, form-feed and new-line characters that separate adjacent source tokens. A comment may occur any place white space is permitted and is replaced by a single-space character.

widening The conversion of an expression from a narrower to a wider type. For example, `char` and `short` expressions typically are promoted to type `int`, and `float` to `double`, when used in expressions such as function call arguments. (ANSI C permits narrow types to be kept as such via the appropriate use of prototypes, although an implementation is not obliged to do so.)

X/OPEN A hardware and software consortium involved in operating system, language and applications development tool standardization. It is building on existing de facto and official standards.

X3J11 The ANSI Standards Committee that established a standard for the C language. Each language standard committee has a numerical designation within the languages group X3J, which is, itself, part of the X3 Secretariat.

Index